ZEW Economic Studies

Publication Series of the Centre for
European Economic Research (ZEW),
Mannheim, Germany

ZEW Economic Studies

Further volumes of this series can be found at our homepage:
springeronline.com/series/4041

Thomas Hempell

Computers and Productivity

How Firms Make a General Purpose Technology Work

With 8 Figures
and 40 Tables

Physica-Verlag
A Springer Company

ZEW
Zentrum für Europäische
Wirtschaftsforschung GmbH
Centre for European
Economic Research

Series Editor
Prof. Dr. Dr. h.c. mult. Wolfgang Franz

Author
Dr. Thomas Hempell
Centre for European Economic Research (ZEW)
L 7, 1
68161 Mannheim
Germany
hempell@zew.de

ISBN-10   3-7908-1647-7 Physica-Verlag Heidelberg New York
ISBN-13   978-3-7908-1647-1 Physica-Verlag Heidelberg New York

Cataloging-in-Publication Data applied for
Library of Congress Control Number: 2005932300

Physica-Verlag is a part of Springer Science+Business Media

springeronline.com

© Physica-Verlag Heidelberg 2006
Printed in Germany

Cover design: Erich Dichiser, ZEW, Mannheim
Picture on the cover: BMW AG

SPIN 11548775   43/3153-5 4 3 2 1 0 – Printed on acid-free paper

To my parents

Preface

When it comes to personal experience with computers, everybody can tell stories of breakdowns, inaccessible software, viruses, and other little disasters. During the work on my dissertation, I was no exception in this respect; but I found out how lucky I was to work in an environment of engaged and cooperative colleagues who helped to keep these disasters very small. It thus should come at no surprise that one result of this book is that the benefits from computer use crucially depend on the people involved in joint work.

Most of the studies of this book originate from the research project "ICT as a General Purpose Technology" commissioned by the Landesstiftung Baden-Württemberg foundation, a project that was initiated to quantify the productivity effects resulting from computer use for firms in Germany. I am indebted to my supervisor Werner Smolny for his continuous advice and for supporting my academic work. Moreover, I am grateful to Bernd Fitzenberger and Rüdiger Kiesel for their critical and constructive comments. I also thank Manuel Arellano whose excellent lectures on panel econometrics at Pompeu Fabra University in Barcelona helped me a lot in acquiring the methodological tools necessary for my empirical work.

I would also like to thank my colleagues at the Centre for European Economic Research (ZEW) in Mannheim, in particular Irene Bertschek, who greatly encouraged and supported my research work, as well as François Laisney who patiently assisted me in various econometric questions. In addition, I owe much to the distinct commentaries resulting in fruitful discussions with Dirk Czarnitzki, Günther Ebling, Julia Häring, Ulrich Kaiser, Georg Licht, Martin Schüler, Alexandra Spitz, Elke Wolf and Thomas Zwick. I would also like to thank Meral Sahin for her excellent research assistance.

Without doubt, my wife Bärbel was by far the most important source of support during my work on the dissertation. I am very grateful to her for continuously encouraging me in my work and for bearing with me in times of mental absence. I am particularly happy that the finishing of the dissertation coincided with the beginning of a most wonderful and inspiring joint experience with her: the birth of our son Joschu.

Mannheim, July 2005   *Thomas Hempell*

Contents

1

Introduction

> *There is no reason for any individual to have a computer in his home.*
>
> Ken Olsen, founder of Digital Equipment Corporation (DEC), 1977

> *Conventional economics is dead. Deal with it!*
>
> Mark McElroy, IBM Global Knowledge Management Practice, in *Wall Street Journal*, 2000.

> *There are two things in particular that it [the computer industry] failed to foresee: one was the coming of the Internet (...); the other was the fact that the century would end.*
>
> Douglas Adams, *The Salmon of Doubt*, 2001

During the late 1990s, discussions about computers and the Internet frequently culminated in the proclamation of a *New Economy*, an economic paradise characterised by sustained productivity growth, soaring stock markets and a lot of fun at the job. Written four years after the end of the hype in 2000, this monograph is about what might be left about these dreams: the potentials and the difficulties that firms face in using information and communication technologies (ICTs) productively.

Entering 'new economy' as key words in the Internet search engine *Google* in 2004 yields an 'Encyclopedia of the New Economy' as the top result.[1] This web site provided by the technology magazine *Wired* holds the following view:

> "When we talk about the new economy, we're talking about a world in which people work with their brains instead of their hands. (...) A world in which innovation is more important than mass production. A

---

[1] The Internet address is http://hotwired.wired.com/special/ene/. Search results date from May 2004.

world in which investment buys new concepts or the means to create them, rather than new machines. A world in which rapid change is a constant. A world at least as different from what came before it as the industrial age was from its agricultural predecessor. A world so different its emergence can only be described as a revolution."

Contrasting these enthusiastic words, the *Google* result ranked second for the same key words is somewhat sobering. It is www.fuckedcompany.com, a homepage that defines itself as the "official lubricant of the new economy". This web site reveals news about numerous Internet companies whose success has been not all that revolutionary: they have gone out of business or are in serious trouble. Benefiting from this apparent demise of the *New Economy*, the site charges a monthly fee of $ 40 for full access to a database including rumours, comments, and internal memos forwarded by employees of troubled companies. It was even prized "site of the year" by *Yahoo!*, the *Rolling Stone*, and the *TIME* magazine.

These search results illustrate fairly well how close enthusiasm and disillusions still coexist in what was widely believed to become a *New Economy*. Experience during the last years has been quite mixed, with spectacular bankruptcies, frauds, and stagnating ICT markets on the one hand and ever more powerful electronic networks and a highly robust productivity growth in many countries (in particular in the U.S.) on the other. Against the background of these ambiguous facts, the occasionally fierce debate between apologists of a *New Economy* and its critics in the past has given way to a much more differentiated discussion of the topic.

ICTs comprise a large variety of items. These include not only products and services of information technologies (e.g. mainframes, personal computers, software, ICT maintenance services) but also telecommunication equipment and products, such as telephones, fax machines, telecommunication infrastructure and services as well as services by Internet providers. In the remainder, I sometimes refer to 'computers and the Internet' as the most popular applications of ICT. This alternation in denomination, however, is not meant as defining a subgroup of ICT but rather as an alternation in wording that is employed synonymously for the very broad notion of ICT.

There are no disagreements about the impressive technological advances that have been achieved in the worldwide production of ICTs. The computing power of microprocessors has been doubling about every 18 months since the 1950s (a development that is widely known as *Moore's Law*). And the more recent inventions from the past three decades like personal computers, notebooks, CD and DVD players, mobile phones, or the Internet are just a few examples of products and services that would have been unthinkable to be developed without the rapid technological progress in the ICT sector.

There is no doubt either that these developments have been largely beneficial for consumers of ICT goods and services. The technical advances and competition in the ICT sector have been strong enough to make prices for

ICT goods (and partly services as well) fall very rapidly over the last decades. In 1970, one megahertz of processing power cost \$ 7,600 and one megabyte of storage amounted to \$ 5,200. In 1999, both items were sold for only 17 cents (Woodall, 2000) and have continued to fall since then. This means that a large part of the productivity gains achieved in the ICT sector have been passed to downstream sectors and consumers.

What is more controversial and remains subject to debate in the economic literature is the question to what extent ICTs have initiated innovations and productivity gains also in other parts of the economy that may become a source of sustained overall economic growth. More recent contributions in the economic literature on 'endogenous' economic growth theories have highlighted the role of innovation and human capital formation as important drivers of economic growth in industrialised countries. These theories treat growth as an endogenous economic variable by considering technical advances as the outcome of economic decisions instead of treating them as exogenously given. To the extent that ICTs contribute to making innovation and human capital formation more productive (making 'rapid change a constant', in the above mentioned Encyclopedia's words), these theories predict the diffusion of ICT to raise the long-term growth potentials of industrialised economies.

Several economists have identified in ICT the characteristics of a *general purpose technology* (GPT) as being pervasive (i.e. employed in large parts of the economy), entailing a large potential for technical improvements, and facilitating or 'enabling' technological advances also in wide parts of the overall economy. With respect to these characteristics, the invention of the computer has frequently been compared to other important inventions in the past. The invention of the steam engine, for example, did not only allow to employ more powerful machines in mining and manufacturing. It also facilitated the invention and broad application of the railway which became an important source of increasing trade and productivity gains during the industrial revolution. Moreover, the invention of electricity towards the end of the 19th century not only substantially lowered the costs of artificial light, but also allowed enterprises to extend their operating hours and to reorganise production processes. Similarly, the largest benefits from ICT may accrue not from computers simply substituting typewriters and other types of equipments, but from firms using it as a tool for own innovational activities and adjustments, such as the improvement of products and services, changes in work organisation and processes, or new task compositions of workplaces.

These *general purpose* characteristics of ICT are the main topic of this monograph. Provided that ICT is primarily an *enabling* technology, the essential part of its contributions to productivity will be contingent upon certain firm strategies and complementary efforts. This contingency will be reflected both in firms' behaviour regarding input or strategy choices and in productivity differences between firms. The theoretical and empirical analyses of this monograph thus refer to various aspects of one central question: *to what extent and favoured by which complementary strategies has the use of ICT been contributing to firm productivity?* Answering the question what must be done to make ICT investments work productively is of interest for businesses, economists and policy-makers alike. Addressing this question both theoretically and empirically, the subsequent chapters devote special attention not only to the measurement of ICT productivity but also to the role of innovation activities and investment in employee training as prominent examples of complementary strategies to ICT use.

The empirical parts of the monograph are based on two large-scale surveys among German firms conducted by the Centre for European Economic Research (ZEW). The first source, the *ZEW survey on ICT*, contains data from nearly 4,500 firms in manufacturing and services on the use and diffusion of ICT in 2002. The second source, the Mannheim Innovation Panel in Services (*MIP-S*), consists of annual data from about 2,000 firms over the period 1994-1999. Jointly, these two data sets form a capacious basis to explore the productivity effects of ICT use and its consequences on firm behaviour from two complementary points of view: How does ICT use affect firms' choice of strategies? And how does the combination of ICT use and these strategies affect firm productivity?

Based on these data sets, this monograph contributes to the existing empirical literature on the productivity effects of ICT in five main respects: it stresses firm-level differences; focusses on the case of a European country; accounts for the importance of small and medium-sized enterprises; highlights the consequences of ICT use in services; and addresses important methodological issues in productivity measurement.

First, employing two large-scale sets of data from firms in Germany, this work complements existing macroeconomic studies on the topic. These aggregate analyses have documented substantial aggregate productivity gains in industrialised countries that can be attributed to the production and use of ICT. However, they are not suited to map any differences in how firms adopt ICT. These differences may form a key in understanding the impacts of ICT as a GPT but are wiped out in the process of data aggregation. Firm-level data, in contrast, allow to identify strategies associated to ICT use, like particular innovation activities, organisational changes or training efforts. Moreover, they facilitate to scrutinise whether additional complementary strategies (e.g. own innovation efforts) help to raise the productivity of ICT. These complementary aspects are particularly important since they are supposed to characterise ICT as an *enabling* input that distinguishes itself from other types of investments in equipment or structures.

Second, existing empirical efforts on the topic have primarily focussed on the United States, probably for two main reasons. First, the U.S. economy has been at the frontier of productivity and living standards for several decades and is strongly engaged both in the production and adoption of ICT. And second, the availability of relevant data (at firm, industry and aggregate level) is particularly well developed in the U.S., facilitating a variety of analyses that are simply impossible to conduct for other countries. However, economic conditions in Europe — and Germany in particular — are fairly different, with most countries in continental Europe being subject to stronger regulations of product and labour markets. Moreover, during the last decade, the U.S. economy has been much more dynamic in terms of GDP and productivity growth. U.S. results can thus not necessarily be generalised to other countries. The analyses in this monograph avoid U.S.-centricity and resort to data from representative surveys among firms in Germany as the largest European economy.

Third, most firm-level studies on ICT have focussed on large firms or corporations listed at the stock markets. Consequently, little is known about the impacts of ICT on small and medium-sized firms which form a particularly important part of the German economy and account for roughly 70% of employment. Both data sets employed in this monograph contain information on firms with five and more employees. The analyses from this monograph thus provide results that also apply to smaller companies that have been widely neglected by firm-level studies to date. To highlight this issue, the empirical parts of this monograph provide detailed information on the size distribution of the firms in the samples employed.

Fourth, while the productivity effects on manufacturing is fairly well documented, only few studies have explored the impacts of ICT on services. A stronger focus on services, however, seems worthwhile for at least three reasons. First, ICT investment is most pronounced and most dynamic in the service sector. Second, business-related services have been important drivers of economic growth over the last decades in industrialised countries and account for about two thirds of gross domestic product (GDP) in Germany (as in most other industrialised economies). Finally, quality changes are particularly difficult to measure in services and are frequently understated in official price statistics. ICT, in turn, is frequently used for raising productivity by enhancing the quality of products and services. This work (in particular chapter 3) highlights that firm-level studies may be better suited than aggregate analyses to account for productivity effects that result from improved output quality.

Fifth, measurement of productivities is a tricky issue even if large-scale samples are available. The major concern is reverse or spurious causality: instead of ICT being productive, it may be that well-managed firms are both more productive and more disposed to ICT applications. Similarly, firms tend to invest (in both ICT and other assets) during boom periods when demand, factor utilisation and productivity are high. In the empirical analysis I will employ suited panel-data approaches to address these (and other) methodological issues econometrically.

In essence, the analysis in this monograph proceeds as follows. Chapter 2 motivates the view on ICT as a GPT based on a fairly general theoretical framework and some empirical facts. The subsequent chapters then focus on assessing the productivity gains from ICT. Chapter 3 scrutinises various methodological issues in productivity measurement and derives a preferred econometric approach that captures the average impacts of ICT on firm productivity. Extending this approach, chapters 4 and 5 then investigate to what degree the productivity contributions of ICT are contingent on firms' innovative activities and on human capital investment. Heterogeneous efforts with respect to these complementary strategies are found to be important sources of varying capabilities of firms to use ICT productively.

In order to facilitate selective reading of individual parts of the monograph, the individual chapters are conclusive enough to be read likewise as independent studies on various aspects of ICT as a general purpose input to production. In addition, the autonomy of the chapters is reflected by the fact that each of them contains an extensive review of the literature concerned with the correspondingly relevant topics.

The content and main results of the individual chapters are as follows. Chapter 2 discusses *general purpose* characteristics of ICT and explores first theoretical, then empirical issues. The former part discusses economically relevant theoretical aspects of GPTs (pervasiveness, potential for technical improvements, innovational complementarities) and illustrates that ICTs broadly satisfy these properties on the basis of some examples. I then present theoretical approaches that are commonly used in the economic literature for assessing the economic consequences of these properties on productivity growth and on the choice of complementary strategies in firms. For this purpose, I review approaches in the tradition of growth accounting analyses and discuss a model of complementarities based on the fairly general mathematical concept of supermodularity.

In the empirical part, results from the *ZEW survey on ICT* are used to provide several statistical facts on firms in Germany highlighting the GPT properties of ICT. Based on the same data, I then use correlation and econometric regression analysis to identify strategies that are pursued by firms with high ICT use. The results indicate that various indicators of ICT use (including ICT expenditures and PC use in firms) are all strongly correlated with training measures. Moreover, the use of personal computers in firms is broadly adopted for innovating processes and distribution channels, such as e-commerce, supply chain management, outsourcing, and customer relationship management. Organisational changes that are targeted at increasing workers' autonomy are also correlated to ICT use. However, these correlations turn out to be mainly the result of product and process innovations facilitated by ICT use.

Chapter 3, which is drawing substantially on Hempell (2005b), focuses on assessing average productivity effects from ICT use at the firm level. In a theoretical part, I first show that quantitative analyses employing firm-level data are less affected by imperfectly measured changes in output quality and prices than analyses employing aggregate data. I derive a partial equilibrium model that interprets production function results at the firm level as the reduced-form outcome of a market equilibrium, where firms that increase output quality by ICT use are remunerated by gains in sales volume due to higher equilibrium prices. I then illustrate that measuring productivity contributions of ICT is subject to a variety of further biases. Interfering factors such as differing management abilities, qualification of employees, measurement errors, simultaneity of input and output decisions by firms as well as business cycles may lead to distortions in the quantitative results.

These effects are illustrated in the empirical part by applying different econometric techniques to panel data from the *MIP-S* survey covering, the years 1994 to 1999. Once all the mentioned interfering influences are controlled for, ICT is found to have, in fact, enhanced productivity in German services. These productivity contributions are increasing with the share of highly educated workers in firms. The overall productivity contributions as assessed are, however, substantially smaller than those obtained in various existing studies on the topic that do not consider the various methodological issues involved in the present econometric analysis. I find unobserved time-invariant characteristics to be the most important source of bias for estimated productivity of ICT. In order to control for these firm effects and other sources of bias, I employ instrumental approaches that exploit the panel structure of the data. The preferred econometric approach based on the Generalised Method of Moments (GMM) likewise forms the basis for the in-depth analysis of ICT productivity in the two subsequent chapters.

Chapter 4, which draws on Hempell (2005a), considers the role of product and process innovations for successful ICT use and highlights the role of innovative histories of firms. As illustrated in chapter 2, ICT investment is closely linked to complementary innovations. ICT use enables firms to restructure their internal organisation and to re-engineer business processes. The ability to innovate successfully, however, may well be determined by the learning effects compiled in the course of a firm's history. Innovation activities do not only create new knowledge but also help to accumulate expertise that eases exploitation of externally available knowledge. Moreover, they facilitate subsequent own innovation activities either in a specific technological field (e.g. ICT applications) or in terms of changes to organisational routines. I argue that due to the enabling character of ICT applications, the success of ICT use may thus depend on a firm's innovative history: given that ICT use is productive only with complementary innovations, firms that have introduced innovations in the past will be better prepared for using ICT than firms without such innovation experience. Consequently, productivity effects of ICT are predicted to be higher in firms with innovative experience.

In the empirical analysis, this hypothesis is broadly backed by econometric results. These results show that experience from past process innovations play a particularly important role, at least in the service sector to which the analysis is applied. The productivity contributions of ICT in firms that have introduced process innovations in the past are about five times as high as among other firms. Robustness checks show that this finding cannot be attributed to the fact that the skill level of the workers is positively correlated to both ICT use and innovation activities. Ignoring the historical dimension of innovation, however, yields smaller and statistically insignificant results. Jointly, these findings indicate that innovative trajectories are important determinants of the success of ICT applications in firms. The arrival of ICT as an increasingly better and cheaper GPT seems to favour firms that have already pursued innovation strategies in the past.

Chapter 5 investigates the consequences of ICT use for training requirements. Computers and networks increasingly allow workers to share access to databases, to connect their workplaces and to co-ordinate business processes with suppliers and clients. These changes in the composition of work tasks require a continuous updating of workers' skills. As illustrated in the first chapter, ICT applications may require firms to provide their workers increasingly with ICT-specific training. Beyond these technical aspects, ICT use may call for increased training efforts if firms complement ICT use by innovations and reorganisation of workplaces.

In the empirical analysis for German service firms, training expenditures are defined more broadly than in the analysis from chapter 2. The *MIP-S* data include not only ICT-specific training but also other types of training, e.g. in new tasks, processes, or communication and language skills. The econometric analysis shows that firms complement ICT investments by training programmes for their employees. Corroborating similar findings from chapter 2, training and ICT investments are highly correlated even if varying firm characteristics, such as e.g. industry and size, are taken into account. In addition, production function regressions also point to synergies between ICT use and training investments. I employ stocks of accumulated training expenditures to consider potential lags in the effects of training courses and to treat training as an investment instead of current expenses. The results from productivity analyses show that firms with investment in both training and ICT perform significantly better than those competitors engaged in more isolated investment strategies. An important prerequisite for this combined investment to work, however, is a high share of well-educated employees in the workforce. Obviously, the educational level of workers not only contributes directly to firm productivity but also forms a key factor for the effectiveness of training. Moreover, the chapter also assesses to what extent increases in wage costs reduce incentives of firms to invest in training measures. The results show that such disincentives exist, but are mitigated by ICT investments: the share of productivity gains that can be appropriated by the investing firm is higher in firms with sizeable ICT investment. These findings imply that falling prices of ICT entail both the requirement as well as an incentive for firms to provide training programmes for high-skilled workers.

In a final concluding chapter, I summarise the main results of the monograph and put them into a broader perspective. In particular, I assess the relevance of the results by comparing them to some more recent macroeconomic developments. Finally, I argue that innovative capabilities and skills of workers were not only relevant during the 1990s but are likely to stay so at least in the near future.

2

Impacts of ICT as a general purpose technology

> *I think there is a world market for maybe five computers.*
>
> Thomas Watson, chairman of IBM, 1943

> *Where a calculator on the ENIAC [the world's first digital computer] is equipped with 18,000 vacuum tubes and weighs 30 tons, computers in the future may have only 1,000 vacuum tubes and perhaps weigh 1.5 tons.*
>
> *Popular Mechanics*, March 1949

> *If it should ever turn out that the basic logics of a machine designed for the numerical solution of differential equations coincide with the logics of a machine intended to make bills for a department store, I would regard this as the most amazing coincidence that I have ever encountered.*
>
> Howard Aiken, pioneer of the computer industry, 1956

2.1 Introduction

Looking back some decades, the success story of the computer resembles a true miracle. As the quotes above illustrate, the potentials of computers have been widely underestimated even by ICT professionals with respect to at least three important dimensions. First, the world market for computers obviously exceeds the number five forecasted by Thomas Watson in 1943, reaching several hundred millions of mainframes, PCs and notebooks worldwide today. Second, the potential for technical improvements turned out to be large enough to ensure that employees today do not have to sit in front of 1.5 tons of vacuum tubes when using their computers. And third, the scope of use for computers has become so large that computers do not only solve differential equations and make bills for department stores but in fact today comprise a scope of highly elaborated purposes.

During the last decades, computers, the Internet and other applications of ICT have turned from helpful computational machines into indispensable tools in industrialised economies. Anticipating a number from section 2.4.1, about every second employee in Germany uses a computer at work and ICT (including software) accounted for nearly 42% of real investment expenditures of the German business sector in 2002, up from about only 8% in 1970 (Deutsche Bundesbank, 2004). The dominant role of computers in today's social and economic activities has been the result of rapid technical advances in computing potentials and manifold complementary inventions in related technological fields (such as laser technology or telecommunication) whose various mutually stimulating impacts could hardly be foreseen.

At the heart of ICT's success story is the ever increasing computing power of microprocessors and increases in memory components' storing capabilities. The boost of computing and storage power has continuously broadened the scope of use of ICT. A distinctive criterion for measuring the continuing progress is computing power per size of ICT equipment. Since the end of the 1950s, the number of transistors per square inch in a microprocessor has doubled about every eighteen months, a development that is widely known as *Moore's Law*.[1] In the course of this development, the introduction of the 1043 byte memory chip in 1969 and the silicon microprocessor by Intel one year later have been highlighted as important breakthrough events (David, 1990). At the same time, the technological advances in ICT production have gone along with a competitive pressure in the ICT-producing sector,[2] making prices of hardware drop at rates between 15 and 30% annually (OECD, 2003).

A particularly important innovation in the continued technical progress in the ICT sector was the invention of the personal computer (PC) and its mobile version, the notebook, that allowed to apply digital information processing and storage power to particular and personalised purposes (David and Wright, 1999). Simultaneously, the software industry developed more and more applications that allowed users to employ the computer in many more functions than just as a machine to solve mathematical problems. Increased computing power coupled with standardised software have led the computer to successively replace type writers, balance sheet books, audio tapes, cameras

---

[1] Barnett et al. (2003) provide a detailed discussion of Moore's Law, its forecasting power and its role as a self-fulfilling forecast. Jovanovic and Rousseau (2002) present a theoretical model of Moore's Law where efficiency of computer production rises as a by-product of experience.

[2] Aizcorbe (2002) reports evidence that Intel's markups from its microprocessor segment shrank substantially during the period from 1993-99, an observation that points to increased competition from other producers of microprocessors.

as well as television, making it resemble more and more a general purpose tool rather than a mere calculating machine.

Technical advances have thereby not been limited to the ICT sector. The increasing computing, storing and communication potentials of ICT have also facilitated a variety of innovations in products and services in other sectors of the economy. For example, cars are increasingly equipped with microcomputers that operate navigation systems and monitor operations of car components. Similarly, computers also facilitated new kinds of services. Cash machine tellers, online banking, e-commerce, and web-based after sales services are only some examples of how ICT has changed the character of services. Most importantly perhaps, ICT is used to improve the quality of existing products and services, in particular customer service, timeliness and convenience (Brynjolfsson and Hitt, 1995; Licht and Moch, 1999).

Finally, and maybe most importantly, ICT applications have great impacts also on processes and organisation inside firms and administrations (Bresnahan and Greenstein, 1996). Firms employ more flexible and more easily programmable manufacturing tools that incorporate ICT (Milgrom and Roberts, 1990); supply chain management tools increasingly link the production processes of suppliers and clients; and new tools for customer care, such as customer relationship management, help to recognise changes in demand more quickly (Hammer, 1990; Rigby et al., 2002). In various cases, these developments are associated with substantial organisational changes prompting prolonged implementation periods and often new skill requirements for workers (Brynjolfsson and Hitt, 2000).

These forces of ICT supply and demand are mutually reinforcing. Advances in ICT facilitate new economic activities which in turn demand more powerful computers to support their innovations (Milgrom et al., 1991). For example, ICT and the Internet have facilitated e-commerce, while the demand for digitalised products such as software, music and films was an important driver to foster the further development and diffusion of broadband access.

These developments have motivated researchers to designate ICT as a *general purpose technology* (GPT) and to compare it to other important inventions in the past such as electricity and the steam engine (David, 1990; Helpman, 1998; Rosenberg and Trajtenberg, 2001). A common feature of these inventions is that they have contributed significantly to overall productivity, economic growth and welfare.

However, GPTs have not favoured all firms and individuals equally. The invention of the steam engine, for example, has made firms more and more independent from the proximity of water power as a source of power supply for manufacturing. This has favoured cities as production sites due to agglomeration advantages while penalising rural locations (Rosenberg and Trajtenberg, 2001). These differences are important since the adjustment costs associated with a firm's change in production location are substantial. Analogously, firms are probably not equally well endowed to take advantage of ICT. The more difficult and more costly it is to adapt to the requirements of new technologies in firm organisation, for example, the more pronounced will be the differences in benefitting from ICT use.

In this chapter, I discuss main features of ICT that constitute its general purpose character and its economic relevance: pervasiveness, continued technological dynamics, and innovational complementarities. I then discuss the consequences of these properties for productivity and economic growth as well as for strategies and complementary investments inside firms. Finally, I expose some statistical findings from a recent survey on ICT diffusion and use of ICT in German firms. Supplementing these figures, I present econometric results that illustrate which firm characteristics and corporate strategies favour the use of ICT in the production process. The chapter concludes with a summary and an outlook on the subsequent chapters.

2.2 General-purpose properties of ICT

In their seminal article on the concept of GPTs, Bresnahan and Trajtenberg (1995) characterise GPTs by three key features: pervasiveness, potential for technical improvements and innovational complementarities. This definition is further refined by Lipsey et al. (1998b).[3] In the following, I briefly summarise a synthesis of these criteria and point out how they apply to ICT (with the microprocessor at its heart).

1. *Pervasiveness.* By pervasiveness, Bresnahan and Trajtenberg (1995) denote the characteristic that GPTs are used in a wide range of sectors throughout the economy. Lipsey et al. (1998b) call this characteristic "wide *range* of use". They point out that, in addition, GPTs are characterised by a "wide *variety* of use" in the sense that they can be used in a wide variety of products and processes. While most GPTs have a limited number of uses at the beginning, many further applications are discovered subsequently. This is not the same as *wide range of use* as the examples of the electric light bulb shows. Light bulbs are used in many different settings but have only one use, to produce light. Similarly, screwdrivers are widespread but have only a very limited scope of use. This is why they do not fall under the definition as a GPT.

---

[3] Lipsey et al. (1998b) identify a set of technological characteristics that define a GPT. For this purpose, they first review a broad set of historical examples of new technologies that caused changes that pervaded the entire economy, including diverse innovations like the invention of symbols, printing, the steam engine, electricity and the railway, among various others. To define a GPT, they then derive four main criteria that are wide enough to capture all these historical examples and that are narrow enough to exclude other less important technologies. Lipsey et al. (1998b) emphasise that their definition is nominalist not essentialist: "definitions are not judged as being right or wrong but only as being helpful or unhelpful in delineating useful categories" (p. 32).

ICTs are pervasive in both meanings. ICTs have a *wide range of use* since they are employed in all sectors of the economy. For example, at the end of 2002, more than every second employee in manufacturing and selected service industries in Germany worked mainly with the help of computers (see section 2.4.1). With the Internet continuing to gain in importance, firms increasingly have to resort to computers and the Internet to communicate with clients and suppliers. ICTs are also characterised by a *wide variety of use* since apart from calculation tasks they are used in diverse applications, such as communication, measurement devices, and control units in all their variants in companies as well as households.

2. *Potential for technical improvements.* GPTs are characterised by the property that they carry a large potential for further technical improvements. Lipsey et al. (1998b) emphasise that any GPT must go through a process of evolution. "Over time the technology is improved, the costs of operation in existing uses falls, its value is improved by the invention of technologies that support it, and its range of use widens while the variety of its uses increases." (p. 39)

   The use of microprocessors was fairly limited initially, but in a process of learning-by-doing, the computing power of microprocessors has grown over the past decades to its vast capacity of today. Increasing computing power jointly with improved storing facilities has enabled the invention of mainframes, personal computers and its variants such as notebooks and personal digital assistants (PDAs), to mention only some prominent examples.

3. *Innovational complementarities.* Bresnahan and Trajtenberg (1995) point out that "most GPTs play the role of 'enabling technologies', opening up new opportunities rather than offering complete, final solutions" (p. 84). These new opportunities involve innovational complementarities by raising the productivity of research and development (R&D) in downstream sectors. An important aspect of this link is that the innovation processes inside and outside the GPT-producing sector are mutually reinforcing: the increasing demand for the GPT in the downstream sectors raises the incentives for further innovations in the GPT-producing sector, and the advances of the GPT are conversely stimulating further innovation efforts in the downstream sector.[4]

   However, the notion of innovational complementarities may well extend far beyond narrowly defined R&D activities. Innovation efforts in firms often resort to formalised R&D activities, but include a variety of other aspects.

---

[4] This self-sustaining momentum of GPTs due to complementarities is also analysed by Milgrom et al. (1991) who show that complementarities among a group of core activities and processes can account for the emergence of a persistent pattern of change and price declines as observed, for example, in the ICT-producing industries.

For example, Milgrom et al. (1991) point out that these complementarities involve not only hardware but also changes in methods and organisation. Similarly, Lipsey et al. (1998a) specify a large variety of economic factors a GPT interacts with. These factors include product and process technologies, the 'facilitating structure' (e.g., physical capital, human capital, organisation of production facilities, managerial and financial organisations, location, infrastructure) as well as public policy (legislation, rules, regulations, etc.) and policy structure. ICTs are obviously involved in a large variety of such innovational complementarities. Not only are there numerous complementarities within the ICT sector (with the Internet being probably the most important innovational complement to computers), but also numerous interactions with innovations in downstream sectors. ICTs are used to re-engineer and coordinate production processes, work practices as well as to explore completely new economic fields, such as biotechnology where the observed dynamics would have been impossible without the large computing and storing facilities provided by ICT.

GPTs are of great interest for economists because of all three of its properties. *Pervasiveness* means that a GPT has economic repercussions in virtually all sectors and activities of an economy. The inherent *potential for technical improvements* implies that a GPT continuously evolves and thus impacts an economy for a considerable period in time. Finally, *innovational complementarities* — jointly with the extensive sectoral and temporal impact — create innovational dynamics reaching beyond the GPT-producing sector.

Underlying all these aspects is the question to what extent a GPT may help to increase productivity, economic growth and overall wealth. More recent macroeconomic theories on 'endogenous growth' point to innovations and R&D as one key to understanding the sources of economic growth.[5] In particular, Romer (1990a) emphasises the role of R&D as a source of economic growth, whereas Aghion and Howitt (1998) extend this framework to model the consequences of complementarities between education and R&D for economic growth. Exploring a theoretical model that takes repercussions of innovations on market structure into account, Smolny (2000) finds broad evidence for knowledge spillovers and productivity effects from innovation both at the micro and sectoral level. Bresnahan and Trajtenberg (1995) model the implications for growth if technical progress is localised mainly in one particular GPT. All these models coincide in pointing to the key role of innovation dynamics for the long-term growth prospects of industrialised economies.

---

[5] Neoclassical growth models in the tradition of Solow (1957) tried to explain economic growth as a result of capital accumulation while treating technical progress as exogenously given. In contrast, endogenous growth theories explicitly model technical progress as being a result of knowledge accumulation and spillovers. They are mainly inspired by seminal contributions by Romer (1990b) and Lucas (1988) who point to increasing returns and spillovers in the course of aggregate knowledge accumulation.

Two important inventions in the past, the steam engine and the electrification of industries after World War I, had led to substantial overall productivity gains. Similarly, the economic discussion of the role of ICT during the 1990s was very much focused on beliefs about a *New Economy* that was supposedly characterised by strong and self-sustaining economic growth. In the next section, I discuss some most common macroeconomic considerations and empirical evidence concerning the productivity impacts of ICT in industrialised countries. Moreover, I portray a microeconomic model of complementarities by Milgrom and Roberts (1990) that allows to focus on the implications of falling ICT prices for corporate strategies, such as human resource management, innovation, and investments in organisational capital.

2.3 ICT productivity and complementarities

Information and communication technologies are by far not the first great invention in economic history which deserves the labelling as a GPT. The cases of earlier GPTs such as the steam engine, the railway, or electricity, illustrate how GPTs have reshaped production techniques and organisational forms in downstream sectors. Moreover, these historical examples show that there may be considerable delays between key inventions and their productivity impacts to materialise. Due to its character as an enabling technology, some of the most important benefits from ICT may not accrue from simple cost savings by substituting the new technology for older machines but from using ICT for fundamentally revising production processes and organisation.

Highlighting these properties of computers by historical evidence, David (1990) and David and Wright (1999) consider various similarities between ICT and electrification at the beginning of the 20th century, in particular the fact that experimenting and reorganising with new GPT takes quite some time. In the case of electricity, the first carbon filament incandescent lamp by Edison and Swann was presented as early as in 1879. However, the diffusion of electricity did not acquire real momentum in the United States until the early 1920s when the so-called "second Industrial Revolution" began. Apart from drastically reducing the price of a lumen of light (Nordhaus, 1997), electricity was particularly beneficial in production by allowing to replace old systems of shafting and belts in firms by so-called "unit drive" systems where individual electric motors were used to run machines of all sizes.

> "The advantages of the unit drive for factory design turned out to extend well beyond the savings in inputs of fuel derived from eliminating the need to keep all the line shafts turning, and the greater energy efficiency achieved by reducing friction losses in transmission. Factory structures could be radically redesigned once the need for bracing (to support the heavy shafting and belt-housings for the transmission apparatus that typically was mounted overhead) has been dispensed with." (David, 1990, p. 358)

Electricity thus contributed to productivity in firms by allowing for lighter factory construction, a shift to building single-storey factories, closer attention to optimising material handling and flexible reconfiguration of machine placement as well as lower production losses during maintenance and rearrangement of production lines.

In a similar fashion, the direct cost savings due to ICT use, i.e. the lower costs of information processing, storing and exchange, may be relatively small when compared to the substantial productivity gains that can be achieved by process re-engineering, new workplace organisation, and more flexible and customer-oriented production. Similarly to the innovations that complemented the diffusion of electricity, these innovational complementarities take time and involve substantial adjustment costs. The historical analogies between ICT and earlier GPTs seem two suggest two things. First, ICT will have substantial impacts on aggregate productivity, even though these will take time to materialise. Second, there will be differences in the ways in which firms are using ICT, and corporate strategies with respect to innovation, organisation and human capital investments may be essential determinants of these differences between firms.

2.3.1 Contributions to productivity

For discussing the potentials of ICT for productivity effects it is helpful to differentiate between two concepts of productivity which in the economic literature are not always clearly distinguished. On the one hand, many (maybe most) studies refer to *labour productivity*. This may be measured either as output per worker or, more precisely, as output per working hour. A main virtue of this concept consists in its simplicity, which facilitates international comparisons of productivity and makes its use particularly frequent in macroeconomic studies. Moreover, labour productivity is closely related to the level of average wages and can therefore be considered a good indicator for the welfare of (working) population.

Alternatively, one may consider *multi-factor productivity* (MFP), which is sometimes (somewhat misleadingly) also denoted as *total factor productivity*. Refining the notion of labour productivity, this concept takes into account that producing output requires not only labour but also capital inputs, like equipment, structures, etc. Some even more elaborate approaches additionally include various sorts of intangible capital as production inputs, such as human capital, R&D efforts, organisational capital, etc. The more tangible inputs are considered, the broader is the productivity concept. All these additional inputs have in common that they contribute to output and may serve as substitutes for workers. Differences in labour productivity may thus differ merely to the fact that capital intensity (i.e. capital per worker) varies between firms, industries, or economies, which makes labour productivity an imperfect measure of how productively all these inputs are used in combination. The concept of MFP aims at taking this shortcoming into account. It is a measure of how productive firms are after the output contributions of the various individual factors have been subtracted. However, it is far more difficult to calculate and requires specific assumptions about the underlying production technology in order to determine the contribution of the individual inputs to output.

The most frequently used functional form of the production function is inspired by Solow (1957) and is based on a Cobb-Douglas technology (see also Berndt, 1991). Firms are assumed to produce output Y by combining labour L and capita as inputs. For taking explicitly into account the role of computers, networks etc., it has become well established in the literature to decompose total capital into ICT capital ICT and non-ICT capital K. Imposing constant returns to scale to these inputs, and considering A as a parameter capturing MFP (as disembodied or Hicks neutral technical change), the production function is:

$$Y_t = A_t \cdot F(L_t, ICT_t, K_t) = A_t \cdot ICT_t^{\gamma_1} \cdot K_t^{\gamma_2} \cdot L_t^{1-\gamma_1-\gamma_2} \qquad (2.1)$$

In this setup, A reflects multi-factor productivity, i.e. the part of output contributions that are not explained by the inputs L, ICT, and K. It is neutral insofar as changes in A leave marginal rates of substitution untouched. The coefficients γ_1 and γ_2, reflect the input elasticities of the two capital inputs. Dividing both sides by L and letting bars denote the corresponding variables per worker ($\bar{Y} = Y/L$, $\bar{ICT} = ICT/L$, and $\bar{K} = K/L$) then leads to expressing labour productivity $\bar{Y}$ in the following way:

$$\bar{Y}_t = A_t \cdot \bar{ICT}_t^{\gamma_1} \cdot \bar{K}_t^{\gamma_2}. \qquad (2.2)$$

Equation (2.2) illustrates that labour productivity $\bar{Y}_t$ rises as a consequence of increases in ICT or non-ICT capital stocks per worker $\bar{ICT}$ and $\bar{K}$ (capital deepening) or due to an increased level of productivity of all these factors A (multi-factor productivity).

There are mainly two approaches used in the economic literature in order to determine γ_1 and γ_2. One is to directly estimate the production function, by regressing the log of output on the logs of inputs.[6] This is done most frequently in the log-log form resulting from equation (2.2):

$$\log \bar{Y}_t = \log A_t + \gamma_1 \log \bar{ICT}_t + \gamma_2 \log \bar{K}_t. \qquad (2.3)$$

An alternative approach uses the property of constant returns to scale and the further assumption of perfect competition among firms. In this case, profits of firms are zero and the elasticities γ_1 and γ_2 equal the corresponding shares of total output that are paid for capital services to ICT and K. This approach is most commonly used in studies analysing aggregate data to decompose economic growth.[7] In this 'growth accounting' technique, equation (2.3) is

---

[6] A recent application to firm-level data can be found in Black and Lynch (2001).

[7] For a recent application of both approaches to firm-level data with capital inputs separated according to ICT and non-ICT capital, see Brynjolfsson and Hitt (2003).

considered in growth rates (after differentiating with respect to time t) with change in MFP reflecting the part of output growth that cannot be attributed to the growth in inputs and that is denoted as the *Solow residual* (Romer, 1996). After taking derivatives with respect to time t, equation (2.3) becomes:

$$\frac{\dot{\bar{Y}}_t}{\bar{Y}_t} = \frac{\dot{A}_t}{A_t} + \gamma_1 \frac{I\dot{\bar{C}}T_t}{I\bar{C}T_t} + \gamma_2 \frac{\dot{\bar{K}}_t}{\bar{K}_t} \tag{2.4}$$

where dots ($\dot{\bar{Y}}_t \equiv d\log \bar{Y}_t / dt$ etc.) denote the derivatives with respect to time, and the fractions $\dot{\bar{Y}}_t / \bar{Y}_t$ etc. are the corresponding growth rates. Equation (2.4) clarifies that aggregate growth in labour productivity may be achieved either by capital deepening (i.e. an increase in ICT or non-ICT capital per head, $I\dot{\bar{C}}T_t / I\bar{C}T_t > 0$ or $\dot{\bar{K}}_t / \bar{K}_t > 0$) or by an increase in multi-factor productivity $\dot{A}_t / A_t$.

It is the impressive productivity growth in the U.S. in the first place that seems to have convinced most economists of the leading role of ICT as a new GPT that fed into a *New Economy* (e.g., Jorgenson and Stiroh, 2000; Oliner and Sichel, 2000). The most prominent critic of this enthusiastic view was Robert Gordon who carried out own decompositions of productivity growth in the U.S. and who found that nearly all of the productivity revival in the U.S. in the second half of the 1990s occurred in the ICT-producing sector and some very limited parts of the durable goods manufacturing (Gordon, 2000). These findings imply that the productivity revival observed in the U.S. and some other countries could last only as long as innovations and price declines in the ICT sector persisted. This would not mean that ICT is rendered irrelevant, but it could no longer be considered as a GPT that compares to the invention of electricity or the steam engine.

This critique has made economists pay more attention not only to the distinction between capital deepening and MFP growth as sources of productivity growth, but also to the question in which parts of the economy MFP growth was most pronounced. Various studies carried out after Gordon's critique have thus carefully distinguished three ways in which ICT may contribute to aggregate labour productivity: capital deepening, MFP growth in the ICT sector, and MFP growth in other sectors of the economy.

1. *Capital deepening.* Quality and capabilities of ICTs have improved considerably over the last decades, while nominal prices for most ICTs have decreased. Jointly, these developments involve large price declines in real (quality-adjusted) terms. For example, one megahertz of processing power used to cost about $ 7600 in 1970 and one megabyte of storage capacity amounted to more than $ 5200. Both prices have fallen to only $ 0.17 until the end of the 1990s (Woodall, 2000).

   Encouraged by the large declines of prices for ICT, downstream sectors have increased their capital spending in real (quality-adjusted) terms. The resulting increases in endowment of workplaces with capital (capital deepening) tends to increase labour productivity. Jorgenson (2003) calculates that capital deepening due to ICT contributed 0.41 percentage points to annual labour productivity growth, which amounted to 1.81% in Germany during the period 1995-2000. In the U.S., ICT capital deepening accounted even for 0.97 percentage points or nearly half of of annual labour productivity growth.

This development implies that a substantial part of the productivity gains generated in the ICT sector are transferred to downstream sectors, a phenomenon that Griliches (1992) denotes as "pecuniary externalities": The higher the competitive pressure in the ICT-producing sector, the lower is the part of the productivity gains that can be appropriated by the producing firms and the higher are the benefits for ICT-using firms (as well as consumers). An important implication is that falling ICT prices and the resulting capital deepening contribute to overall labour productivity growth, but not to MFP growth (Jorgenson and Stiroh, 2000; Stiroh, 2002a). As highlighted by Baily and Gordon (1988) "there is no shift in the user firm's production function" (p. 378) due to these mechanics, and thus no increases in MFP among users.

2. *Technical progress in the ICT sector.* For several decades, there have been remarkable technological advances in industries that produce ICT goods and services (ICT sector). In particular, the quality of ICT goods and services have considerably improved (see section 2.1). Quality-adjusted output has excelled whereas labour and capital inputs employed in the ICT sector have increased at far lower rates, leading to substantial productivity gains in the ICT sector. In a recent contribution, Jorgenson (2003) finds that the productivity advances in the ICT sector have contributed substantially to GDP growth in the G7 countries.[8] He finds that the productivity gains in the German ICT sector have contributed 0.57 percentage points to average annual labour productivity growth of 1.83% (and thus also to 1.78% annual GDP growth) in Germany during the second half of the 1990s.[9] This implies that about a third of labour productivity growth during this period can be directly attributed to MFP growth in the ICT sector. In the U.S., the relative importance of the ICT

---

[8] These are the U.S., Canada, France, Germany, Italy, Japan, and the U.K.

[9] Jorgenson's figures differ from official statistics in two important ways. First, he counts firms' spending on software as investments rather than current business expenses such that they contribute to output. Second, he employs internationally harmonised price deflators based on hedonic techniques as calculated by Schreyer (2000). This latter procedure may lead to an overestimation of true productivity contributions of the ICT sector in countries outside the U.S., however. The ICT price index in the U.S. is strongly influenced by products characterised by rapid price declines, such as electronic computers. Applying this index to ICT sectors in other countries with a different pattern of specialisation may thus lead to an overestimation of the decline of ICT prices in these countries (Pilat et al., 2002).

sector for economic growth was slightly smaller. Labour productivity grew by 2.11% per year over the same period, from which 0.44 percentage points can be ascribed to the productivity gains in the ICT sector.

Analysing the U.S. productivity revival during the late 1990s, Stiroh (2002b) reports evidence that corroborates the leading role both of the ICT sector and of the capital deepening effects. Using data for 61 industries, he finds that the ICT sector and industries that intensively use ICT capital accounted for all of the direct industry contributions to the U.S. productivity acceleration towards the end of the 1990s.

3. *Spillover effects.* Apart from the direct productivity contributions of ICT through productivity increases in the ICT sector and capital deepening, ICT may contribute to overall economic growth through non-pecuniary spillover effects in other (non-ICT) sectors of the economy (for a broad discussion of the implications of spillover effects from ICT, see Stiroh, 2002a). As emphasised earlier (and discussed more broadly in section 2.3.2), ICT can be used for innovating organisations, processes and products in other sectors of the economy, and these co-inventions may contribute to MFP in these sectors. Moreover, users of software may benefit from network externalities, as suggested on empirical grounds by Neil Gandal (1994) and Brynjolfsson and Kemerer (1996). Apart from the capital deepening effects due to pecuniary spillovers, complementary innovations and network effects in downstream sectors may thus also increase MFP in the downstream sector.

At the aggregate level, however, there is only limited evidence for spillover effects from ICT. Using industry data for U.S. manufacturing, Stiroh (2002a) finds no statistically significant evidence that ICT-related spillovers or network effects drive MFP growth. Similarly, Schreyer (2000) reports no evidence indicating a correlation between ICT capital and MFP growth for the G7 countries in the first half of the 1990s.

Measuring the productivity effects from ICT and distinguishing between the three sources mentioned strictly depends on the correct measurement of quality-adjusted price changes of ICT goods and services. In many countries, official statistics tend to understate quality changes and thus real price declines of ICT goods (Hoffmann, 1998; Schreyer, 2002).[10] As a consequence, both the

---

[10] One way to take rapid quality changes in products into account is to use 'hedonic' methods. The central idea underlying this concept is to treat a heterogeneous good (e.g., a PC) as a bundle of individual product characteristics, such as computing power, memory capacity, etc. The implicit prices of these characteristics are then estimated econometrically. The quality of a complex good is then treated as being equal to the combination (usually the sum) of the values of its properties. For a discussion of hedonic methods, see Triplett (1990); for more recent applications, see Berndt and Rappaport (2001). In Germany, the Federal Statistical Office introduced hedonic techniques for calculating price indices for PCs in 2002 (Linz and Eckert, 2002; Moch et al., 2002).

productivity contributions of the ICT sector and the productivity gains from capital deepening are understated while the spillover effects are overstated. In contrast, the bias in measured overall productivity contributions of ICT is ambiguous, depending on whether a country is a net-exporter of ICT goods.[11]

Innovational complementarities between innovations in the ICT sector and in downstream sectors may imply that innovation activities are suboptimal in both sectors in a decentralised economy. In a theoretical model, Bresnahan and Trajtenberg (1995) point to the consequences for productivity and growth if technical progress is based on one specific GPT-producing sector that is characterised by monopoly power. They identify two types of spillovers. First, vertical externalities from GPT producers to downstream sectors arise if the GPT increases the productivity of innovations in downstream sectors and if GPT producers cannot appropriate these indirect returns resulting from the GPT. Second, horizontal externalities arise among users in downstream sectors. Simplifying this idea, an increase in demand for the GPT enhances innovation incentives in the GPT-producing sector, which will favour all other innovators in downstream sectors as well. Since both types of externalities cannot be internalised in a decentralised economy, innovation activities in both the GPT-producing and the GPT-using industries will be suboptimal and will imply suboptimal rates of overall productivity growth. One important caveat of the model applying to the dynamics in ICT is the fact that most parts of ICT (including software) can be traded easily. Worldwide competition may not only have cut monopoly power of ICT producers (Aizcorbe, 2002) but also have substantially extended the demand side. Jointly, these effects may make suboptimal innovation incentives a less severe problem in practical terms.

While productivity gains in the ICT-producing sector have been visible in the form of continuously improving computer power and falling ICT prices, the productivity gains from ICT use and spillover effects remained a subject of long debate. In the late 1980's, a variety of studies emerged that questioned the assumption that ICT really contributed to productivity (see e.g. the discussion provided by Baily and Gordon, 1988). Some studies even found ICT to be associated with decreases in productivity or subnormal investment returns.[12] The contradiction between the leading role of ICT as a GPT that dominates economic activities on the one hand, and the lack of evidence for its productivity effects on the other, became well established as the "computer paradox" which had been summarised by Robert Solow as soon as in 1987 by saying "we can see the computer age everywhere but in the productivity statistics" (Uchitelle, 2000).

---

[11] Schreyer (2002) and Vijselaar and Albers (2002) find that the overall contributions of ICT to productivity growth do not vary greatly with different price indices for ICT.

[12] See, e.g., Osterman (1986), Loveman (1994), Roach (1991) and Morrison and Berndt (1991). For surveys of early literature on the productivity effects of ICT, see Berndt and Malone (1995), Brynjolfsson and Hitt (1995) and Brynjolfsson and Yang (1996).

In the meanwhile, new empirical evidence found in studies in the late 1990s seems to have resolved this paradox and there has emerged a consensus among economists in acknowledging that ICT diffusion has broadly contributed to productivity in nearly all economic sectors. More recent evidence provided by Stiroh (2002b) illustrates that ICT-producing industries jointly with industries making intensive use thereof accounted for all of the productivity revival in the U.S. during the late 1990s. Even Robert J. Gordon, one of the most prominent sceptics about the productivity effects (see, e.g, Gordon, 2000) acknowledges in a study based on more recent data that ICT investments have exerted a sustained impact on U.S. productivity that cannot be ascribed to mere cyclical effects (Gordon, 2003).

Two important gaps in the literature remain, however. First, a predominant part of the empirical literature (in particular concerning studies using data at the industry and firm level) deals with U.S. data where the success of ICT is well documented. Evidence for other countries, in contrast, is still quite scarce. In particular, there is only a very limited number of empirical studies analysing the firm-level effects of ICT for non-U.S. data. Second, there is only very limited evidence explaining the vast and persisting *differences* between firms, industries and countries as regards their ability to exploit ever cheaper and more powerful ICTs for productivity improvements. These issues are important motivations for productivity analyses at the firm level that are presented in the subsequent chapters which are based on data from German firms.

2.3.2 Complements to ICT use

As illustrated above, it took a considerable period of time until the acceleration of ICT investment since the 1980s became perceivable in productivity statistics. The economic literature offers two main cases to explain these substantial time lags. Both are closely related and are based on the argument that the successful implementation of ICT as an enabling technology requires a large set of investments in intangible assets, such as organisation structures, processes and workers' skills. This has two implications for productivity effects.

First, the returns to these investments in ICT and complementary assets take time to materialise since organisation structures, processes, and skills can be adjusted only gradually. Just as in the case of electricity, where systems of shafts and belts were substituted by unit drive systems, investments in ICT have been complemented gradually by internal restructuring and new work contents (Autor et al., 2003; Spitz, 2003) as well as closer interaction between firms which require agreements on a variety of standards, elaboration of contracts, etc. (Chesbrough and Teece, 1996). Second, these investments in complementary intangibles cost money and resources. However, it is extremely difficult to measure these investments. This is particularly true for investments in organisational structures or 'organisational capital' that seems to play an important role in the context of computerisation of firms. "Unlike physical capital, its value does not appear in the balance sheet of a firm and when firms undertake substantial organisational change or re-engineering this is typically treated as 'consumption' rather than an increase in the assets of a firm. There is no 'market' for organisational capital that we could use to generate a book value for it and unlike general human capital it is not portable." (Black and Lynch, 2002, p. 2). If investments in intangibles are counted as mere expenses instead of investments, measured productivity is understated in the transition period and overstated in the period when ICTs are established (Gordon, 2003).

More recent empirical explorations indicate that intangible investment is economically substantial indeed. Atkeson and Kehoe (2002) estimate that roughly 4% of output in U.S. manufacturing can be accounted for as payments to organisation capital and that this capital has roughly two thirds of the value of the stock of physical capital.[13] Black and Lynch (2002) report evidence indicating that changes in organisational capital may have accounted for approximately 89 percent of multi-factor productivity growth over the period 1993 to 1996 in U.S. manufacturing, or 30% of output growth.

The eminent role of unmeasured intangible investment that is necessary to make productive use of ICT also illustrates why the direct productivity contributions of ICT from capital deepening are so difficult to disentangle from spillovers. Suppose the use of ICT facilitates a firm's re-engineering its processes, for example by introducing automatical processing of client orders. Establishing these process innovations costs money and other resources, costs that may by far exceed the direct ICT investment costs (Brynjolfsson and Hitt, 2000). If these costs are treated as increases in expenses, productivity of ICT investment is underestimated initially when intangibles start to be created, but is overestimated once the intangibles have been established.[14]

In contrast, if these adjustment costs are suitably accounted for as investments in intangible assets, productivity may also increase in the long run due to the coaction of ICT and new processes, which takes time to materialise. Since both types of investment are complementary, however, it is subject to debate which part of these joint productivity effects is due to mere ICT capital deepening and which part is due to the complementary innovation (spillovers). The main difficulty here is to value intangible assets that are firm-specific

---

[13] Atkeson and Kehoe (2002) model the acquisition of organisational capital as resulting from endogenous learning-by-doing. It is thus embodied in the firm and increases with measured output. Their empirical calculations of organisational capital are thus not based on any measures of workplace practices but on plant-specific productivity and age.

[14] This aspect is emphasised by Gordon (2003) as an important reason why there was little evidence for productivity acceleration in the first half of the 1990s where ICT investments soared, but strong evidence for productivity increases after 2000. In this latter period, the benefits of created intangible assets boosted output while much of the labour input that created it was laid off.

and cannot be traded.[15] Against this background, Cummins (2003) proposes to determine the value of intangible assets as "whatever makes installed inputs more valuable than uninstalled inputs" (Cummins, 2003, p. 6). Based on firm-level data on market value of common equity and analysts' forecasts, he estimates organisational capital indirectly via the adjustment costs associated with ICT investments.

Intangible assets and corporate strategies that are complementary to ICT use can not only help explain the substantial time lags of ICT documented by productivity statistics. They may also be important in explaining differences between firms in their success of adopting ICT. A prominent example is the computer producer Dell whose business success depends on a unique organisational design that sells built-to-order computers directly to consumers. This business model is strongly based on the use of ICT for accepting orders via the Internet as well as ICT-coordinated assembling and distribution of products. On the contrary, Hewlett Packard also produces computers with a comparable tangible capital stock but with a much lower valuation at the stock markets (Cummins, 2003). Similarly, an important part of Wal-Mart's international success in retailing is based on its innovative way of making use of ICT (Schrage, 2002). For example, department managers are given great autonomy in running their departments. They have continuous access to real-time information on how well products are selling such as sales as compared with last year, mark-ups, and products in stock or transit. This allows department heads to run their sections like an independent store and to move stock faster. Moreover, Wal-Mart uses proprietary ICT systems to give suppliers full and free access to real-time data on how their products are selling in different stores (The Economist, 2001). Similar patterns of decentralisation also prevail outside the stores in the logistics departments. Because of these organisational forms Wal-Mart can make more effective use of ICT than most of its competitors. Even though these innovative practices inspired by ICT use are individually quite easily replicable, the joint adaption and coordination of such innovations is obviously not easy and makes them hard to replicate for competitors.

Intangible assets associated to organisational structures and processes are not the only complements that have been found to matter in the literature. Substantial efforts have been made to investigate the consequences of computerisation for increased demand with respect to human capital. Various studies have argued that ICT is a technology that favours the demand for high skilled workers, contributing to a skill-biased technological change (SBTC).[16] In more recent contributions, Falk and Seim (2001) find that firms with high ICT in-

---

[15] This problem is also related to the discussion in the management literature by Dierickx and Cool (1989) and Barney (1989) on the sustainability of competitive advantages and apparently above-normal returns to investments.

[16] Chennells and van Reenen (1999) provide an broad review of the literature on SBTC.

vestments employ a larger fraction of high-skilled workers at the expense of unskilled workers and plan to further increase this share in future periods. Autor (2001b), Autor et al. (2003) and Spitz (2003) report evidence that an important part of the demand shift towards more educated workers can be explained by computerisation and resulting changes in job content. Bresnahan et al. (2002) find that ICT use is correlated also to various human resource strategies such as training, pre-employment screen for education, and cross-training of workers. Moreover, they identify 'clusters' of innovation which, apart from ICT use and high skill levels, also include workplace reorganisations.

2.3.3 A theoretical model of complementarities

Milgrom and Roberts (1990; 1990) provide a theoretical framework for investigating the implications of complementarities based on the theory of supermodularity, which is summarised in the following. This very general mathematical approach allows to derive necessary conditions for activities to be complementary. The main results derived from this model are twofold. First, the demand for complementary inputs will be positively correlated. Second, firms that combine the complementary inputs will — other things equal — exhibit higher levels of productivity than firms that do not exploit these synergies. This theory has been applied empirically in varied contexts such as innovation strategies (Cassiman and Veugelers, 2002), organisational design (Athey and Stern, 1998), and ICT investment strategies (Kaiser, 2003; Hollenstein, 2004).

Two basic definitions are important in this theoretical framework. The first one is the definition of supermodularity which formalises the idea of synergies and complementarities or, broadly speaking, that 'the whole system is more than the sum of its parts':

Definition 2.1. *A function $f : \mathbf{R}^{\mathbf{N}} \to \mathbf{R}$ is supermodular if for all its arguments $\mathbf{x}, \mathbf{y} \in \mathbf{R}^{\mathbf{N}}$:*

$$f(\mathbf{x}) + f(\mathbf{y}) \leq f(min\{\mathbf{x}, \mathbf{y}\}) + f(max\{\mathbf{x}, \mathbf{y}\}) \qquad (2.5)$$

where $min\{\mathbf{x}, \mathbf{y}\} \equiv (min\{x_1, y_1\}, \ldots, min\{x_N, y_N\})$ and similarly $max(\mathbf{x}, \mathbf{y}) \equiv (max\{x_1, y_1\}, \ldots, max\{x_N, y_N\})$ denote the points in $\mathbf{R}^{\mathbf{N}}$ whose ith component are $min\{x_i, y_i\}$ and $max\{x_i, y_i\}$ correspondingly.

In words, supermodularity of $f(\cdot)$ means that the sum of the changes in the function that result from increasing several arguments separately is less than the change resulting from increasing all the arguments together. This can be seen most easily by subtracting $2 \cdot f(min\{\mathbf{x}, \mathbf{y}\})$ from both sides of (2.5) which gives the inequality:

$$\begin{aligned} f(\mathbf{x}) - f(min\{\mathbf{x}, \mathbf{y}\}) + f(\mathbf{y}) - f(min\{\mathbf{x}, \mathbf{y}\}) \\ \leq f(max\{\mathbf{x}, \mathbf{y}\}) - f(min\{\mathbf{x}, \mathbf{y}\}) \end{aligned} \qquad (2.6)$$

In production theory, two arguments (e.g. inputs in a production function) are defined as complements if an increase in one argument enhances the marginal contribution of the other argument to the function value (e.g. output).[17] Note that this definition deviates from the definition of complements (vs. substitutes) commonly used in the theory of factor demand where complementary inputs are defined by negative cross-price effects between inputs.[18]

Milgrom and Roberts show that, for continuous and twice continuously differentiable functions $f(\mathbf{x})$, supermodularity and complements are identical.[19] They state that f is supermodular if and only if its cross-derivatives $\partial f / \partial x_i \partial x_j$ are positive (Milgrom and Roberts, 1990, Theorem 2). A second definition introduces the notion of a *sublattice*.

Definition 2.2. *A set* $T \in \mathbf{R}^{\mathbf{N}}$ *is a sublattice of* $\mathbf{R}^{\mathbf{N}}$ *if* $\forall \mathbf{x}, \mathbf{y} \in \mathbf{R}^{\mathbf{N}}$: $min\{\mathbf{x}, \mathbf{y}\} \in T$ *and* $max\{\mathbf{x}, \mathbf{y}\} \in T$.[20]

With x_i reflecting activity i of a firm, a sublattice reflects the idea that if it is possible for the firm to engage in low (and, respectively, high) levels of each of the activities separately, then it is also possible to engage in low (high) levels of all of the activities simultaneously. This property of sublattices thus expounds that increasing one activity never prevents one from increasing the others as well, and that decreasing some variables never prevents one from decreasing others.

---

[17] This definition is broadly used in the economic literature, see e.g. Milgrom and Roberts (1990; 1995), Arora and Gambardella (1990), Athey and Stern (1998), Bresnahan et al. (2002).

[18] To illustrate this consider, for example, inputs x_1 and x_2 in a simple Cobb-Douglas production function $f(x_1, x_2) = x_1^{\alpha} x_2^{1-\alpha}$ with $0 < \alpha < 1$. According to the first definition x and y are complements since $\partial^2 f / \partial x_1 \partial x_2 = \frac{\alpha(1-\alpha)}{x_1 x_2} f(x_1, x_2) > 0$. According to the definition in factor demand theory, however, they are substitutes. To see this, define w_1 and w_2 as the corresponding input prices. The corresponding cost function is $c(w_1, w_2, y) = y w_1^{\alpha} w_2^{1-\alpha}$ and the demand for input x_1 (by Shephard's Lemma): $x_1(w_1, w_2, y) = \alpha y w_1^{\alpha-1} w_2^{\alpha}$. The cross-price effect is $\partial x_1(w_1, w_2, y) / \partial w_2 = \alpha(1-\alpha) y w_1^{\alpha-1} w_2^{\alpha}$ and is thus positive, indicating that both inputs are substitutes under this definition since an increase in one input increases the demand for the other input.

[19] More specifically, Milgrom and Roberts (1990) show that some weaker conditions suffices for this equivalence to hold, namely that f can be written as an indefinite double integral with a non-negative integrand.

[20] Amending this definition, a *lattice* $(X, \geq)$ is a set X with partial order $\geq$ with the property that $\forall \mathbf{x}, \mathbf{y} \in X$, X contains a smallest element under the order that is larger than both x and y and a largest element that is smaller than both (Milgrom and Roberts, 1995). For two sets $S, U \in \mathbf{R}^{\mathbf{N}}$, define the partial ordering $S \geq U$ as being equivalent to the condition that $\forall \mathbf{x} \in S$ and $\forall y \in U$: $max\{x, y\} \in S$ and $min\{x, y\} \in U$}. Then it follows that the Euclidean space $\mathbf{R}^{\mathbf{N}}$ and ordering $\geq$ form a lattice.

Milgrom and Roberts (1990; 1990) show that these assumptions contained in the definition of supermodularity and sublattices suffice to derive the following necessary conditions for complementarities:

Corollary 2.3. Supermodularity and correlated demand. *If the domain of a supermodular function $f(\mathbf{x}, \theta)$ is a sublattice consisting of I choice variables $\mathbf{x} = (x_1, \ldots, x_I)'$ and K parameters $\theta = (\theta_1, \ldots, \theta_K)'$, the optimal value for the choice variables $\mathbf{x}^*(\theta) = \arg\max_{\mathbf{x}} f(\mathbf{x}, \theta)$ is monotone nondecreasing in the parameters θ.[21] In cross-sectional statistical studies (with heterogeneity in θ across firms) any two endogenous variables $x_i(\theta)$ and $x_j(\theta)$ will be positively correlated.[22]*

This result states that for profit-maximising firms, complementary choice variables are correlated with each other since they tend to move up or down together in a systematic, coherent fashion in response to environmental changes. In particular, even though a change in parameter θ_k may only affect one choice variable directly (e.g. the demand for ICT goods), it will also raise the demand for the activities due to the indirect effects initiated by the complementarities.

It is important to note, however, that positive correlation of the choice variables forms a *necessary* but not *sufficient* condition for complementarities. This is because the correlation between two choice variables may be due to the fact that they are both complementary to a third activity (or to two distinct activities that are complementary). In order to exclude the part of the correlation that is due to other variables, in empirical applications it is thus important to consider the correlation after conditioning on a broad set of control variables that may drive the results. For example, computer use (x_1) and training programmes (x_2) may be correlated only because both are complementary to the skill level of workers (z). In order to consider whether there is a direct complementarity between training and computers, it is thus important to consider the correlation conditional on z. More generally, the empirical implementation should include as conditioning parameters z_i all activities or variables that may drive the correlation between x_1 and x_2. If not all of these activities can be observed, the empirical analysis may give misleading results with respect to the hypothesis of complementarity.

For a related but less general model of complementarities, Arora and Gambardella (1990) derive sufficient (though not necessary) conditions under which complementarities can be inferred from correlation for a continuous and twice continuously differentiable payoff function. The main conditions are that the set of control variables $\mathbf{z}$ must be comprehensive enough such that the (remaining) unobserved firm-specific differences in costs and benefits from implementing strategies x_i are uncorrelated with the control variables $\mathbf{z}$; and that the correlations between these unobserved differences are zero once the

---

[21] For multidimensional parameters θ it is enough that $f(\cdot)$ is supermodular in $\mathbf{x}$ and each of the components of θ individually (Milgrom and Roberts, 1995).

[22] See Milgrom and Roberts (1995), p. 185.

effects of $\mathbf{z}$ are controlled for. The formal derivation of these conditions is summarised in Appendix 2.6.1 to this chapter.

Beyond correlations in the demand for choice variables, complementarities imply a second result: the complementarities should also be observable directly in the production outcomes. If two activities are complements such that $\partial f / \partial x_i \partial x_j > 0$ (equation (2.5) holds with strict inequality), the productivity gains that are due to complementarities can be captured by including an interaction term between the hypothesised complements $x_i \cdot x_j$ in the econometric specification of the production function.

To illustrate this, consider the case where two complementary activities are measured by dummy variables x_1, x_2, with $x_i = 1$ if the corresponding activity is carried out by the corresponding firm and zero otherwise. Moreover, define an indicator function $I(x_1, x_2)$ that is unity whenever x_1, x_2 take the values in parentheses, and zero otherwise. Then the vector $\mathbf{D} = \{I(0,0), I(0,1), I(1,0), I(1,1)\}$ with exclusive dummy variables indicates how a firm organises the two activities. Assuming linearity in the control variables $\mathbf{Z}$ for simplicity, let the production function for output Y have the functional form:

$$Y = f(\mathbf{D}, \mathbf{Z}; \theta, \beta) = \mathbf{D}\theta + \mathbf{Z}\beta \qquad (2.7)$$
$$= \theta_{00} I(0,0) + \theta_{01} I(0,1) + \theta_{10} I(1,0) + \theta_{11} I(1,1) + \mathbf{Z}\beta$$

Then the test for complementarity between activities x_1 and x_2 is:

$$\theta_{11} - \theta_{10} > \theta_{01} - \theta_{00} \qquad (2.8)$$

In words, this hypothesis means that introducing activity x_i will yield higher output contributions when the complementary activity is introduced, too, $(x_j = 1, j \neq i)$ than when x_i would be introduced without the corresponding other activity.[23]

An alternative specification to (2.7) is to specify non-inclusive indicators for activities $\tilde{I}(\cdot)$, which are one if the condition specified in parentheses is true, and zero otherwise. Including a constant in the extended set of regressors $\tilde{\mathbf{Z}}$ then yields:

$$Y = \tilde{\theta}_1 \tilde{I}(x_1 = 1) + \tilde{\theta}_2 \tilde{I}(x_2 = 1) + \tilde{\theta}_{12} \tilde{I}(x_1 = 1) \tilde{I}(x_2 = 1) + \tilde{\mathbf{Z}}\beta \qquad (2.7a)$$

The first two coefficients $\tilde{\theta}_1$ and $\tilde{\theta}_2$ measure the output contributions from each activity in isolation, and the parameter $\tilde{\theta}_{12}$ of the interaction term corresponds to the 'extra' output effects due to complementarities. In this specification, the relevant test for complementarity is simply:

---

[23] The econometric issues involved with estimating this test of complementarity are reviewed in Athey and Stern (1998). An empirical application to innovation activities can be found in Cassiman and Veugelers (2002).

$$\tilde{\theta}_{12} > 0 \qquad\qquad (2.8a)$$

Specification (2.7a) with test (2.8a) can be extended to applications with continuous variables x_i and are frequently used in the literature. Examples are Caroli and van Reenen (2001) and Bresnahan et al. (2002) who test for complementarities between new technologies, ICT and worker skills, and Brynjolfsson et al. (2002) who investigate complementarities between ICT use and organisational capital.

To sum up the arguments of this section, complementary strategies and activities may be important for firms to reap benefits from ICT as a GPT. These complementary strategies may also be interpreted as investments in intangible assets that take time to be accumulated and that may contribute to explaining the time lags in the productivity effects from ICT to materialise in the productivity statistics. Complementarities may be investigated empirically in two essential ways: first, indirectly through correlated factor demand by optimising firms; and second, directly through 'extra' gains observed in production function estimations from simultaneity of complementary activities.

The following section presents some first evidence illustrating the properties of ICT as a GPT in Germany, i.e. its pervasiveness, its scope of use and its innovational complementarities. Evidence concerning complementarities is exclusively based on the indirect approach focussing on firm behaviour. The production function approach will play a major role in the subsequent chapters where several methodological issues will be discussed to estimate these effects econometrically.

2.4 Empirical evidence for Germany

The vast majority of existing empirical studies analysing the consequences of ICT as a GPT during the late 1980s and 1990s are based on U.S. data. There seem to be at least two major reasons for this. First, the U.S. have been the technology leader both in the production and in the uptake of ICT. As a natural consequence, interest in analysing the conditions and implications of a 'New Economy' have been particularly pronounced in the U.S. leading to particularly strong efforts in empirical research.

Second, the U.S. were particularly fast in responding to the data needs for investigating the computer age. The Bureau of Economic Analysis (BEA) started collecting detailed data on investments in ICT as early as in 1972.[24] This work of data collection was complemented by substantial research efforts in constructing suitable price deflators as well as capital stocks and capital

---

[24] However, data prior to 1982 are not published by the BEA. For a discussion of collection and quality issues of ICT data by the BEA, see the discussion in the Appendix to Oliner and Sichel (1994).

services from ICT.[25] Moreover, private companies like the Computer Intelligence InfoCorp (CII) and International Data Group (IDG) contributed firm-level data on stocks and investments in computer capital, facilitating early firm-level studies on ICT, e.g. by Brynjolfsson and Hitt (1995) or Lichtenberg (1995).

In Germany like in most other European countries, in contrast, data collection on ICT was practically absent for many years. These deficits were highlighted very clearly by the German Council of Economic Experts in their report 2000/2001: "Difficulties emerge if one wants to analyse the driving forces of the New Economy for Germany in a similar fashion as has been done for the United States. The database is simply poor." (German Council of Economic Experts, 2001, p. 133)[26]. Taking account of the rising importance of ICT investments in particular in services, the Mannheim Innovation Panel in Services (MIP-S) conducted by the Centre for European Economic Research (ZEW) was one of the first broad-scale surveys in Germany to collect information on firm-level expenditures on ICT starting in 1994.[27] It took until 2003 for the German Statistical Office (*destatis*) to publish statistics on ICT use by firms and households for the very first time.[28]

In order to address the lack of data, the ZEW conducted specific surveys on the use and diffusion of ICT among firms in Germany in the years 2000 and 2002 (referred to as 'ZEW survey on ICT' in the remainder).[29] These data were collected in computer-assisted telephone interviews (CATI) with 4450 representatively chosen firms in the manufacturing sector and selected services industries with 5 and more employees.

Based on these data, the subsequent two subsections confront some of the previously discussed GPT properties of ICT with empirical evidence on ICT use and strategies of firms in Germany. In the first part, I discuss the overall importance of ICT in Germany as compared to other industrialised countries and provide figures on the diffusion of ICT as well as on the underlying aims and hampering factors as perceived by firms in Germany. These figures are

---

[25] Acknowledging the rapid quality improvements of computers and peripherals, the BEA introduced a hedonic price index for computers in the U.S. national income and product accounts (Baily and Gordon, 1988). The first systematic approaches to calculate capital stocks and capital services from ICT investment data were conducted by Oliner and Sichel (1994) and Jorgenson and Stiroh (1995).

[26] Quotation translated from German into English by the author.

[27] See Janz et al. (2001) for a summarising description of the survey design and Licht and Moch (1999) for empirical results based on this data set.

[28] See Destatis (2003a; 2003b). One year earlier, in 2002, the German Statistical Offices started using hedonic methods to calculate price indices for personal computers, i.e. 14 years after the BEA in the U.S. had started to apply these techniques (Linz and Eckert, 2002).

[29] The ZEW survey on ICT 2000 had a special focus on ICT skill shortages (Licht et al., 2002), and the wave conducted in 2002 put a particular emphasis on e-commerce and organisational changes associated to ICT use.

based on the results from the ZEW survey on ICT and are extrapolated to the corresponding population of firms in Germany to yield a valid picture of the overall importance of ICT in the German economy. In the second part, I employ the same data to explore some of the consequences that ICT adoption brings about in firms. Using correlation and regression analysis, I discuss evidence on how ICT use in firms is related to firm activities in diverse business areas such as innovation activities, human resource practices, or export propensity. Jointly, these explorations form the basis for a more in-depth analysis of the productivity effects of ICT in the subsequent chapters.

2.4.1 ICT diffusion

Over the last decades, the overall importance of ICT has increased in all industrialised countries. As highlighted in the introduction to this chapter, the main force behind these dynamics were the impressive technical advances in the ICT sector coupled with competitive pressure that made quality-adjusted prices for ICT goods and services fall extremely fast. In addition, the invention and rapid diffusion of the Internet was an important driver for increasing ICT expenditures both by firms as well as private users. The case of the Internet illustrates how the combination of technical advances and network effects have been mutually stimulating. Ever more powerful computers and infrastructure allowed to transfer data at increasing speeds while the utility of the network increased with the rising number of participants. As Fig. 2.1 illustrates, the diffusion, as measured by the share of population with access to the Internet, has accelerated particularly at the end of the 1990s. Beyond this, the figure illustrates that Germany as well as other European countries have been lagging the U.S. Simple horizontal comparison indicates that the temporal lag between the U.S. and Germany is about three years.

These international differences in ICT diffusion also apply to other indicators. In 2002, the share of total ICT expenditures (including ICT investment as well as expenses on ICT services) in GDP has varied between 5.5% in Italy and more than 9% in Sweden (see Fig. 2.2). In Germany, this share amounts to 6.4%, ranging slightly below the European average. This intermediate position of Germany in international comparisons is corroborated by a variety of other indicators on ICT diffusion. For example, Germany ranks slightly above EU average in terms of Internet access and slightly below European average concerning the diffusion of mobile phones (see Hempell, 2003a, for more details).

An important question left open by most international statistics is the question about the reasons for the substantial differences in speed and extent of ICT adoption. Even though this monograph cannot provide answers to this question in an international context either, some results from the *ZEW survey*

Fig. 2.1. Internet diffusion 1990-2002

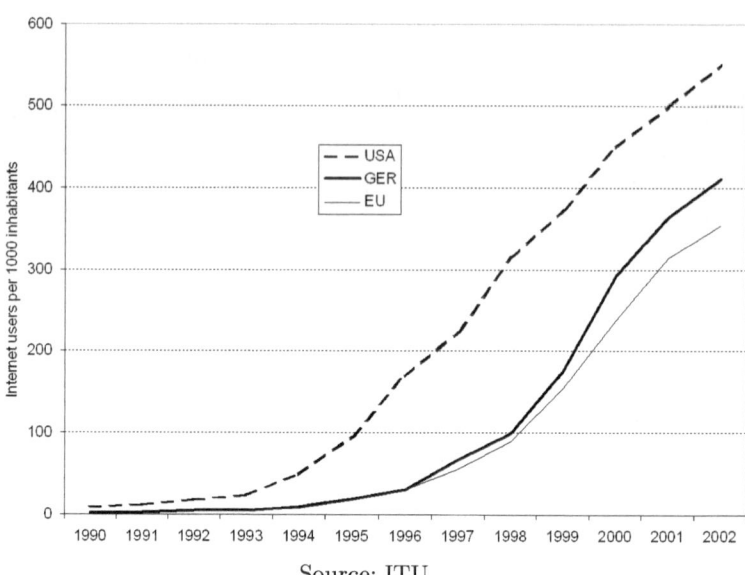

Source: ITU

on ICT help to shed some light on sectoral and firm-specific differences that are important in the case of Germany.[30]

As a starting point, Figure 2.3 summarises the overall spread of ICT applications with different degrees of sophistication. All firms with 5 and more employees resort to computers and about 94% have access to the internet. A large share of firms uses the Internet also for advanced purposes with 75% maintaining an own homepage or web presence and more than 60% using the Internet for procurements, and for ordering intermediate goods and materials from other firms. In contrast, highly advanced ICT applications, such as using the Internet as a distribution channel, are used only by a minority of firms. The secure provision of goods and services via the Internet, for example, requires the employment of secure socket layer (SSL) servers whose maintenance costs are substantially higher than those for regular servers. In addition, the setup of a corresponding web site for receiving orders is associated to substantial setup costs. Consequently, the share of firms using the Internet for e-commerce is far lower than the share of firms that use it for procurement. Only about every third firm receives orders from other firms via the Internet (business-to-business e-commerce), and less than every fourth firm is engaged in business-to-consumers e-commerce. Modern management methods based on electronic networks, such as customer relationship management (CRM) and supply chain management (SCM), are used only by 18 and 9% of the

---

[30] In the subsequent part of this chapter, the same data are also used to investigate some correlations between ICT use and corporate strategies.

Fig. 2.2. International comparison of ICT expenditures 1998-2002

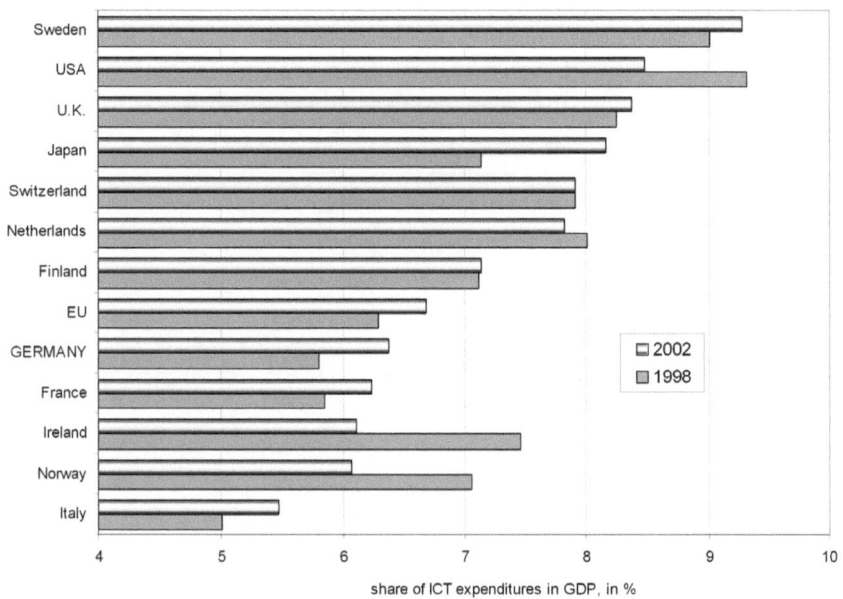

share of ICT expenditures in GDP, in %

Source: EITO, own calculations

firms, respectively. At the same time, firm size is important for the attractiveness of ICT applications. For example, in manufacturing 58% of large firms with 500 and more employees use e-commerce as a channel of distribution as compared to only 36.6% of small firms with less than 50 employees.

The adoption of ICT also varies substantially between sectors. Figure 2.4 depicts industry differences with respect to two indicators: first, the share of workers who do their work primarily with the help of a computer; and second, the share of workers that have access to the Internet during their work. Both indicators yield a very similar pattern. The most intensive users of ICT are firms from the service sector: banking and insurances, electronic data processing and telecommunication, technical services as well as other business-related services and wholesale trade. In manufacturing, only electrical engineering and production of medical, precision, and optical instruments are above the overall average of about 50% of workers with computer work and 43% with access to the Internet. This pattern of ICT diffusion by industries, in particular the leading role of the service sector, corresponds very well to similar findings on ICT intensity for other countries, notably the U.S. (Stiroh, 2001; Pilat et al., 2002; OECD, 2003).

ICTs are used for a broad range of purposes. The most important aim for firms in Germany who invest in ICTs is to accelerate processes, which applies to 90% of the firms in Germany (Figure 2.5). Customisation of products and

Fig. 2.3. ICT applications in firms in Germany 2002

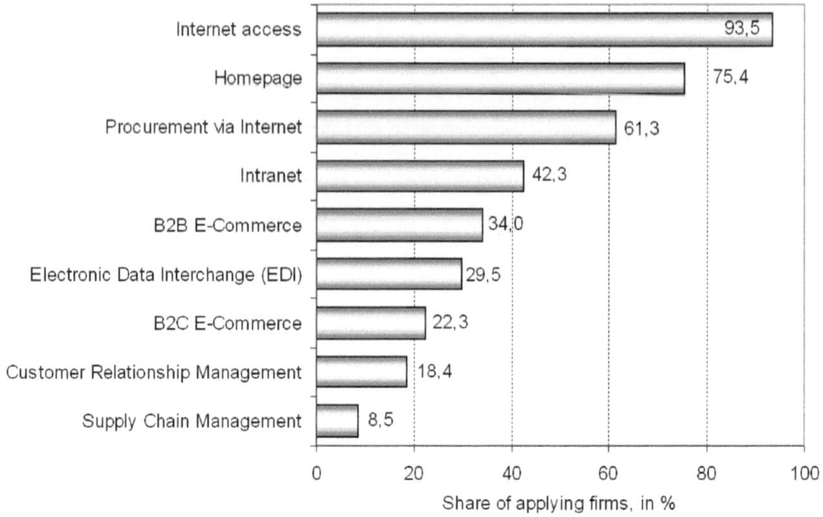

Source: ZEW ICT survey 2002

services and quality improvements are mentioned by about 72 and 63% of all firms correspondingly. Cost savings, in contrast, rank substantially lower as motives for ICT investments. Reductions of personnel and material costs are relevant for 55% and 45%. And only 41% use ICT for developing new products or services. These figures suggest that incremental innovation of existing products and services (acceleration of production, customisation, quality improvements) are major motives for ICT use, whereas cost savings and more fundamental product innovations are less important. These results confirm findings from other surveys and show that ICTs tend to have an important impact on the quality aspects of products and services (Brynjolfsson, 1994; Licht and Moch, 1999). These quality improvements, in particular in services, are often hard to measure. Moreover, unmeasured quality improvements have been highlighted as an important source for the difficulties in finding productivity effects from ICT in aggregate statistics (Griliches, 1994). As will be discussed more broadly in the next chapter, productivity analyses at the firm level may be less susceptible to imperfectly measured quality and may thus serve as an important complementary approach to productivity calculations using aggregate data.

Apart from the scope and the benefits from using ICT, also its user costs are important for a firm's decision to invest in ICT. While the direct costs of ICT, i.e. the prices for hardware, software, and ICT services, do not vary by too much between firms or industries, the indirect costs may be extremely different. Among a large variety of aspects, these indirect costs comprise the

Fig. 2.4. Computerisation of workplaces in firms in Germany 2002

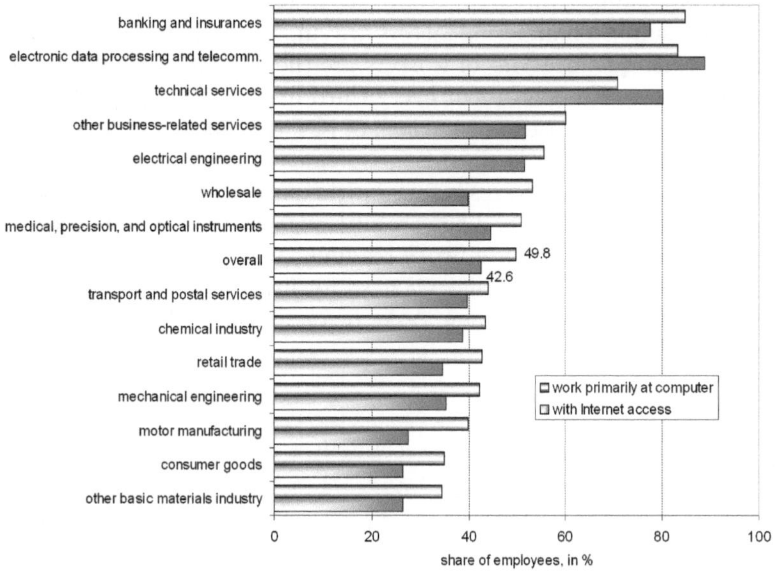

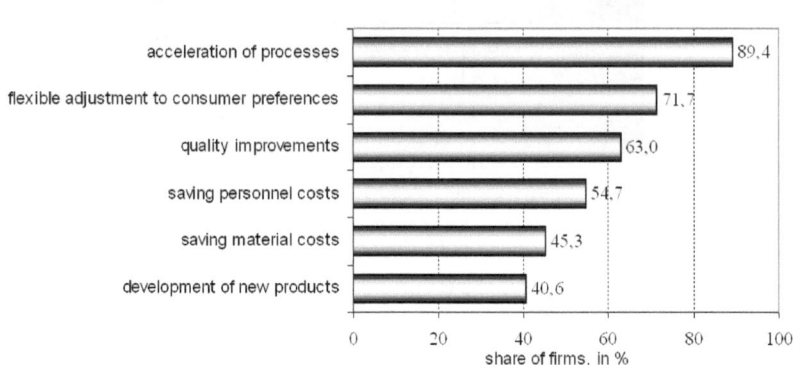

Source: ZEW ICT survey 2002

Fig. 2.5. Aims of ICT use in firms in Germany 2002

Source: ZEW ICT survey 2002

costs to finance the investments, to implement them in the firm, to change processes and work organisation, and to recruit or train workers for the requirements of ICT applications. These indirect costs of ICT investments may by far exceed the direct costs (Bresnahan et al., 2002) but are particularly difficult to measure. As an auxiliary approach to explore the importance of these costs, however, the ZEW survey contains firms' assessment on various factors that may hamper further investments in ICT.

The main results on hampering factors are summarised in Figure 2.6. Most strikingly, missing qualifications of workers are the most important barrier to ICT investments, applying to about every third firm. A slightly smaller share of firms perceives direct costs and the lack of ICT specialists as barriers. Lack of skills in a broader sense is thus as important as the direct costs of ICT applications. On the contrary, resistance on the part of employees of the firm played a relatively minor role. These results suggest that the knowledge of employees is highly relevant for a firm's readiness for implementing ICT. The lack of qualified personnel may make it hard for firms to apply ICT solutions if employees cannot be trained new tasks or organisational procedures or if the costs of doing so are very high.

Fig. 2.6. Factors hampering ICT use 2002

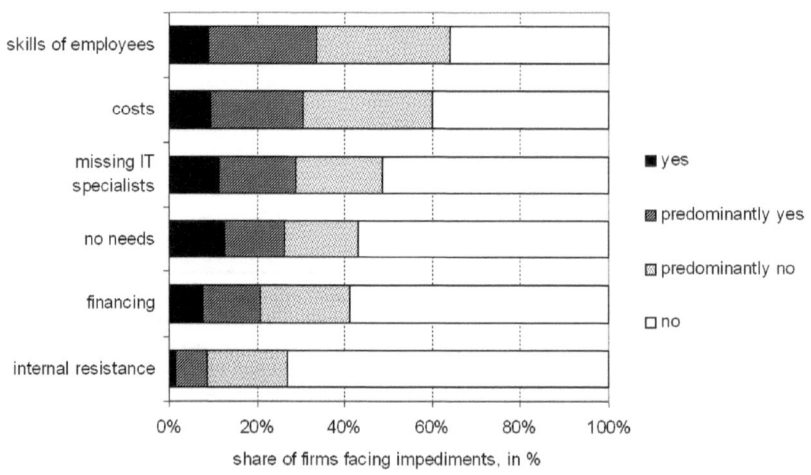

Source: ZEW ICT survey 2002

The figures on hampering factors also reveal some insights in the perceived benefits from ICT. 'No need' for further ICT applications is mentioned by about 26% of the firms. This item largely differs with respect to firm size. In manufacturing, 35% of small firms, but only 3% of large firms with 500 and more employees do not see any useful application areas for further ICT investments. Similarly, in services 28% of small firms (less than 50 employees) compared to 10% of large firms (with 200 and more employees) refrain from

ICT investments due to lack of need. This dependence on firm size cannot be found for the other hampering factors. Obviously, large firms can benefit far more from ICT. This is not surprising given that ICTs are mainly used to improve information flows, an issue that is of strategic importance to large firms.

Summarising these findings from the ZEW survey on ICT, three issues are particularly important for the subsequent productivity analysis. First, ICT use is most pronounced in services and is very frequently used for incremental quality improvements. Quality improvements (in services in particular) are very hard to measure and may lead to an underestimation of the productivity contributions of output. Second, while simple ICT applications such as access to the Internet have become a commodity, the degree to which ICTs are used for innovations in processes varies greatly between firms. This raises the question to what extent innovations are important for making ICT work productively in firms. Finally, apart from the direct costs, the benefits from ICT applications are constrained by the availability of sufficiently qualified employees. Training and education are thus reasonable channels along which differences in productivity contributions between firms can be explained. These are not only relevant for the ICT-related behaviour of firms explored in the following part, but are also important motivations for the in-depth productivity analyses in the subsequent chapters.

2.4.2 Corporate strategies associated with ICT use

The data collected in the ZEW survey on ICT do not only contain information on various aspects of ICT use of the interviewed firms, but also on a variety of other variables that have been hypothesised as complements to ICT use in the economic literature. For example, Milgrom and Roberts (1995) discuss a model that predicts a decline in the costs of flexible manufacturing equipment and computer-aided design equipment to lead to a systematic increase in output, more frequent product and process innovations, higher levels of training, greater autonomy for workers, more cross-training, and use of teams among a variety of other consequences.

While the empirical analysis provided in this chapter aims at illustrating some first straightforward evidence on complements to ICT use, the subsequent chapters 4 and 5 will consider in much more detail the extent to which innovations on the one hand and firm-sponsored training programmes on the other help to make the use of ICT in firms more productive. These analyses will be based on a different data set, the Mannheim innovation panel, in order to apply econometric techniques that require a longitudinal structure of the data to yield consistent results for measuring the direct productivity contributions of inputs.

In the following, I explore to what extent evidence may be brought up to substantiate the view that several strategic choice variables serve as complements for ICT use in firms. As suggested by the theoretical model in section

2.3.3, complementarities imply that in a cross section of firms the candidate choice variables are positively correlated with ICT use conditional on a set of control variables. Subjecting this implication to a straightforward test, I consider their correlations with ICT intensity. I distinguish three different types of variables: indicators of intensity of ICT use in firms, corporate strategies that are expected to be complementary to ICT use, and a set of control variables that are fixed or quasi-fixed in the short term. The variables and their economic relevance as a measure of ICT use are briefly discussed subsequently.

For measuring the *intensity of ICT use* in firms, I employ four different indicators from the ZEW survey, all of them referring to the year 2001. As shortly discussed in the following, these indicators have differing strengths and weaknesses in reflecting ICT uptake in firms. Jointly, they may by means of subsequent correlation analysis provide a comprehensive picture as to which aspects of computerisation are complemented by other strategic choices at the firm level.

- *ICT expenses.* The most comprehensive indicator for ICT use in firms is total expenses on ICT per employee (measured in logarithms, $LNICT$). This variable includes not only investment in software and hardware but also expenses for ICT personnel and external ICT services. The main virtue of this indicator is the fact that it covers all kinds of ICT engagement. Its main drawback consists in the fact that it is a flow variable that depends not only on real capital services of ICT, but is also strongly driven by other determinants, such as expected sales, cash flow, firm performance, liquidity, etc.
- *Computers.* A second ICT indicator is (the log of) the number of computers per employee $LNPC$ (comprising mainframes, PCs and notebooks). Computers are the most frequent application of ICT and the invention of the PC has been identified as one of the most important innovations based on the microprocessor (David and Wright, 1999). Moreover, notebooks and microcomputers facilitate mobile computing power that is no longer restricted to the inside of the firm. A main virtue of this measure is that it is a stock variable and compared to investment expenses is thus less dependent on transitory shocks . However, the quality of PCs may vary substantially, and their quality may be contingent upon existing complementary ICT infrastructure in firms, such as networks, servers, and kind of Internet access.
- *Computer use.* ICT expenses and the mere number of computers are not very informative about how intensively computers are actually used by employees. This aspect is captured by a third variable $PCWORK$. It measures the share of workers that predominantly use a computer at their workplace. It is thus a good indicator of the impacts of computerisation on job content of employees. However, the quality or difficulty of tasks executed at a computer may vary substantially since the variable equally includes involved management tasks (such as computer-based controlling

that may require substantial computing power) as well as cash operations using bar scanners in retail shops. Similarly, the quality of the computers used may vary strongly and may also depend on how intensively they are linked with servers and other computers via electronic networks.

- *Internet use.* A fourth measure is the share of workers that have access to the Internet $(INTER)$. It informs about the importance of electronic networks in firms. To continue the earlier examples, stand-alone bar scanners in retail shops are relatively cheap whereas cash systems connected to servers to deliver real-time information for storage and orders (like in the case of Wal-Mart) require substantial additional expenses and may have much stronger impacts on organisation, work content and type of collaboration between workers. Access to electronic networks may thus improve coordination of activities inside a firm and may also contribute to closer relations to suppliers and clients. On the downside, one Internet access in firms may be shared by various workers and some employees may use the Internet access only irregularly. Moreover, even though it informs about connectivity, it does not provide information about the importance of firm-specific networks.

In the empirical application, I will analyse to what extent the four measures of ICT intensity are linked to a set of firm-specific *strategy variables*. These comprise a variety of strategic choices in diverse business areas that from a theoretical point of view may be affected by the use of ICT. These variables and their potential relevance for ICT use are briefly discussed in the following.

- *Introduction of new products or services.* As the survey results summarised in the previous section show, ICTs are frequently implemented in order to improve the quality of products and services or to develop new ones (see also Licht and Moch, 1999; Brynjolfsson, 1994). The underlying dummy variable $(PRODINNO)$ in the questionnaire takes the value one if the corresponding firm introduced any new or significantly improved products or services during the period 1999 to 2001.
- *ICT-based process innovations.* Firms may use ICT in order to innovate both their internal and external processes (Bresnahan and Greenstein, 1996; Brynjolfsson and Hitt, 2000). Two prominent applications are e-commerce, i.e. the use of Internet for accepting and processing orders, and supply chain management (SCM), which generally involves automated acceptance and sending of orders to suppliers and clients. The dummy variables $ECOMM$ is one if the corresponding firm was engaged in e-commerce (either B2B or B2C or both) and the variable SCM is one if the firm applied some form of supply chain management in 2001.
- *ICT-related training programmes.* In order to make computers work productively, workers must learn how to use them and exploit their productivity potentials. In many instances, this requires firms to provide formal ICT-related training courses to their employees. Consistent with this hypothesis, Brynjolfsson and Hitt (1998) report that firms that invest in

ICT intensively train a higher fraction of their workers and screen new employees more intensively for education than less ICT-intensive firms do. Moreover, Black and Lynch (1996) report evidence that employer-provided computer training has a positive and significant effect on productivity for enterprises in the service sector (though not in manufacturing). In the current analysis, the variable $TRAIN$ measures the share of employees who took part in ICT-related training programmes during the year 2001.

- *New management methods based on ICT.* The largely increased possibilities of storing and computing data of clients have also encouraged firms to introduce new management methods (McKinsey Global Institute, 2001; Schrage, 2002). One example is customer relationship management (summarised by the dummy variable CRM), which is primarily aimed at aligning business processes with customer strategies to build customer loyalty and increase profitability. CRM programmes are a prominent example of management practices enabled by ICT. Even though CRM involves a variety of technical issues, its successful implementation requires the bundling of customer strategy and processes, which signifies a considerable managerial challenge (Rigby et al., 2002).

- *Organisation of firms.* The productivity of ICT may be improved by giving a higher degree of autonomy to workers (Brynjolfsson and Hitt, 2000; Bertschek and Kaiser, 2004). Higher autonomy helps firms to react more rapidly and flexibly to changes in demand and competition, but typically involves higher complexity of information flows inside the firm (Malone, 1987; Radner, 1993). With the costs of ICT falling, the advantages of decentralised decision making may more than compensate for the higher costs associated with information processing and transmission (see, e.g., Bresnahan et al., 2002). Similarly, Lindbeck and Snower (1996) provide a theoretical model that considers advances of ICT as one factor that promotes the transformation of firms from 'Tayloristic organisations', with standardised inputs and output and centrally coordinated departments, towards 'holistic organisations', characterised by greater production flexibility, multi-tasking for employees, as well as decentralised decision making. The variables $TEAM$ and $UNIT$ measure the share of employees that work in autonomous teams and in units with profit responsibility, respectively, in 2001. A further dummy variable $OUTSOURCE$ indicates whether a firm outsourced any of its activities to other firms during the period 1999 to 2001. The use of ICT helps to coordinate activities between firms and enables firms to involve suppliers in complex and creative tasks such as joint design and engineering. Moreover, ICTs reduce the costs of finding appropriate suppliers, to monitor subcontractors and to co-ordinate ordering, scheduling, and payment systems (Bensaou, 1997; Innocenti and Labory, 2002).

All of these variables can thus be expected to relate positively to ICT intensity in firms. Table 2.1 shows that indeed all four measures of computerisation

Table 2.1. Correlations between ICT use and corporate strategies

	LNICT	LNPC	PCWORK	INTER
LNICT	1.000			
LNPC	0.568	1.000		
PCWORK	0.430	0.640	1.000	
INTER	0.374	0.574	0.631	1.000
PRODINNO	0.175	0.131	0.102	0.063
ECOMM	0.095	0.093	0.125	0.071
SCM	0.147	0.061	0.040	0.015
TRAIN	0.313	0.328	0.341	0.318
CRM	0.259	0.214	0.193	0.163
TEAM	0.179	0.138	0.153	0.132
UNIT	0.186	0.111	0.143	0.115
OUTSOURCE	0.133	0.062	0.058	0.049

The correlation coefficients are based on a common sample of 1691 firms. For the definition of variables, see Table 2.7 and the more comprehensive discussion in the text.

are highly correlated to the strategic choice variables considered above. Moreover, the correlations with the strategy variables are all significantly positive (with the correlation between *INTER* and *SCM* being the only exception). This positive link between computerisation and the strategic variables, however, may well be due to a variety of other unobserved factors. For example, firm size may determine both the propensity of introducing innovative organisational structures and the intensity of ICT use. As pointed out in part 2.3.3, it is thus important to control for a variety of other firm characteristics as control variables to obtain more reliable results on whether these correlations in fact reflect complementarities. These further controls and their potential relevance are discussed in the following.

- *Firm size.* The size of a firm may be an important determinant affecting ICT use and complementary strategies simultaneously. The setup of networks and shared databases may be more beneficial in large firms than in small ones due to network effects (Motohashi, 2001). Moreover, these investments may help to facilitate knowledge transfer and information access inside firms. Knowledge and information are non-rival goods and are characterised by scale economies, which is a further reason for why large firms may invest more in ICT. Finally, there is evidence that larger firms are more likely to employ newer technologies than smaller ones (see, e.g., Dunne, 1994).

  In addition, large firms are known to have a higher propensity to innovate (Cohen and Klepper 1996a; 1996b; Cohen and Levin 1989) and to train their workers (Nestler and Kailis, 2003). Moreover, organisational changes are more relevant for large firms since organisational interactions increase more than proportionally with firm size and coordination costs crucially depend on the way work is organised (see, e.g., Malone, 1987). To control for firm size in a flexible functional way, I include both the log of the number of employees ($LNEMPL$) and the log of employees squared ($LNEMPLSQ$) as control variables. Moreover, I include a dummy variable $GROUP$ that is one if the firm belongs to a group of firms.

- *Industry affiliation.* As illustrated in the previous section, the scope of applying ICT varies substantially between industries. For example, most service industries tend to have larger technological opportunities for introducing ICT than industries in manufacturing do. Similarly, the opportunities for innovation, work organisation, as well as human resource management may differ substantially between industries. I include 14 industry dummies to control for the correlation that is due to industry-specific variation. The underlying classification with the corresponding NACE codes are summarised in Table 2.3.

- *Formal qualification.* Skills of the workforce may have a simultaneous impact on ICT intensity and complementary efforts as well. Chun (2003) finds that both ICT adoption and use are complementary to worker education. Similarly, educated workers receive more training (OECD, 2002) and may facilitate innovations and organisational changes in firms (Bresnahan et al., 2002). In order to control for these effects, I include the shares of a firm's employees with university degree ($UNIV$) and vocational training (VOC) as control variables for education.

- *Capital intensity.* Firms may invest in ICT simply because they are generally more capital intensive or employ new vintages of capital also in the case of non-ICT equipment. Moreover, ICT intensity may be determined by financing constraints that are very similar for non-ICT equipment. ICT and non-ICT investments are thus expected to be highly correlated. At the same time, a high general investment intensity may also induce a higher training propensity. Moreover, high non-ICT investments may be necessary for innovating products and processes. The log of non-ICT investments ($INVOTHER$) is thus considered as an additional control.

- *Firm age.* To the extent that investments are irreversible, young firms may spend more money on new vintages of capital in general and ICT in particular.[31] Similarly, young firms may start with innovative products and business models. The inclusion of the log of firm age in 2001 ($LNAGE$) is included to account for these correlations.

- *Exports.* The use of ICT may facilitate international trade relations. Exporting firms (characterised by the dummy variable EXP taking the value one) are thus expected to be more intensive ICT users than non-exporters. Similarly, exporting firms may be more innovative than their competitors. The causal link may be in either direction. Innovations may be higher due

---

[31] Dunne (1994), however, finds little evidence for correlations between plant age and technology use.

to stronger competitive pressure in global markets; alternatively, exports may be higher due to innovative products that sell in global markets.[32]

For the empirical explorations, I use a sample of 1691 firms for which information on all these variables are available. Table 2.4 provides a comparison of the composition of the sample by industry with the corresponding population of firms in Germany. Since the sample of the ZEW survey is stratified by industry (with each industry given roughly equal weight), industries with a very large number of small firms (like 'other business related services' or 'retail trade') are substantially undersampled whereas industries with a comparatively small number of larger firms (e.g., chemical industry, electrical engineering, motor manufacturing) are oversampled. As reported in Table 2.5, more than three quarters of the firms in the sample are small and medium-sized firms with less than 200 employees. Table 2.7 summarises some descriptive statistics for the sample jointly with a brief description of the variables.

Analysing the correlation between ICT use and strategy choices while including the various controls, I run regressions of the four ICT measures on the choice variables using the above firm characteristics as controls. For $LNICT$ and PCL as dependent variables, I use simple OLS regressions. In contrast, the variables $PCWORK$ and $INTER$ are restricted to the interval $[0, 1]$ and the corresponding regressions are thus based on Tobit estimations (see e.g. Wooldridge, 2002) with corresponding upper and lower threshold. The results are summarised in Table 2.2.

For interpreting these results it is important to keep in mind that investigating complementarities in the indirect or demand approach is not about causality. For complementarities, it is in principle not important whether, for example, 'ICT use causes training' or 'training causes ICT use'. If ICT use and training programmes are complements, the demand for both will increase simultaneously when the price for one of the inputs decreases.[33]

Considering the relevance of the control variables first, the results in Table 2.2 show that nearly all of them are relevant for the intensity of ICT use in firms. The relationship between ICT use and firm size is non-linear and follows a U-shape for all measures of ICT use considered. That is, ICT use is most intensive among very small and very large firms. The coefficients for $LNEMP$ and $LNEMPSQ$ in the first specification (with $LNICT$ as the dependent) imply that total ICT expenditures per employee reach a minimum at a firm size of 462.[34] The high ICT intensity among large firms may be explained by network effects inside firms; however, partially contradicting this explanation, there is no statistically significant link between ICT intensity and the fact that a firm may belong to a group of firms. The intense ICT use among small

---

[32] Ebling and Janz (1999) analyse the causal relationship between innovation and exports for German firms in the service sector.

[33] See also the related discussion provided by Bresnahan et al. (2002).

[34] This minimum firm size results from $size_{min} = \exp\{0.5989/(2 \cdot 0.0488)\}$.

Table 2.2. ICT use and corporate strategies

dependent variable:	(1) OLS LNICT	(2) OLS LNPC	(3) Tobit PCWORK	(4) Tobit INTER
PRODINNO	0.073	0.071**	0.020	0.008
	(0.068)	(0.035)	(0.016)	(0.020)
ECOMM	0.167*	0.085**	0.057**	0.037
	(0.089)	(0.043)	(0.021)	(0.026)
SCM	0.097	0.111**	0.038**	0.012
	(0.076)	(0.035)	(0.019)	(0.024)
CRM	0.343***	0.182***	0.057**	0.038*
	(0.066)	(0.032)	(0.017)	(0.021)
TRAIN	0.841***	0.424***	0.308***	0.343***
	(0.181)	(0.082)	(0.042)	(0.053)
TEAM	0.035	0.002	0.024	0.085**
	(0.087)	(80.044)	(0.022)	(0.027)
UNIT	0.066	0.108**	-0.002	0.026
	(0.083)	(0.042)	(0.022)	(0.027)
OUTSOURCE	0.204**	0.100**	0.038**	0.044**
	(0.063)	(0.031)	(0.016)	(0.020)
LNEMPL	-0.599***	-0.443***	-0.046**	-0.147***
	(0.094)	(0.050)	(0.022)	(0.028)
LNEMPLSQ	0.049***	0.029***	0.003	0.010**
	(0.011)	(0.006)	(0.002)	(0.003)
GROUP	0.001	0.036	0.020	0.022
	(0.068)	(0.036)	(0.017)	(0.021)
LNINVOTHER	0.182***	0.040***	-0.006	-0.001
	(0.022)	(0.012)	(0.005)	(0.007)
LNAGE	0.060**	0.016	0.010	0.005
	(0.025)	(0.013)	(0.006)	(0.008)
UNIV	1.099***	1.250***	0.578***	0.661***
	(0.184)	(0.092)	(0.045)	(0.057)
VOC	0.551***	0.486***	0.145***	0.097**
	(0.126)	(0.069)	(0.031)	(0.038)
EXP	0.309***	0.181***	0.026	0.064**
	(0.070)	(0.037)	(0.017)	(0.021)
				. . .

(continued on next page)

Table 2.2. ICT use and corporate strategies (continued)

dependent variable:	(1) OLS LNICT	(2) OLS LNPC	(3) Tobit PCWORK	(4) Tobit INTER
INDUSTRY DUMMIES:[§]				
CONS	-0.200	-0.325***	-0.048	-0.025
	(0.129)	(0.076)	(0.034)	(0.042)
CHEM	0.041	-0.065	-0.029	-0.010
	(0.140)	(0.067)	(0.038)	(0.047)
BASIC	-0.410**	-0.340***	-0.013	-0.049
	(0.129)	(0.063)	(0.034)	(0.043)
MECH	-0.289**	-0.223***	-0.018	-0.050
	(0.117)	(0.060)	(0.031)	(0.038)
MED	-0.010	-0.067	-0.026	0.025
	(0.123)	(0.068)	(0.035)	(0.043)
MOTOR	-0.445**	-0.434***	-0.047	-0.104**
	(0.156)	(0.071)	(0.039)	(0.049)
WHOLES	0.157	0.084	0.158***	0.153**
	(0.172)	(0.090)	(0.043)	(0.054)
RETAIL	-0.427**	-0.140*	0.011	-0.033
	(0.145)	(0.082)	(0.038)	(0.047)
TRANS	-0.429**	-0.380***	0.071*	0.119**
	(0.156)	(0.081)	(0.037)	(0.046)
FIN	1.046***	0.606***	0.516***	0.356***
	(0.186)	(0.076)	(0.047)	(0.057)
COMP	0.710***	0.392***	0.488***	0.478***
	(0.179)	(0.077)	(0.045)	(0.056)
TECHS	0.414**	0.231**	0.157***	0.208***
	(0.147)	(0.077)	(0.042)	(0.053)
BSERV	0.272*	0.078	0.219***	0.176***
	(0.163)	(0.091)	(0.040)	(0.050)
R^2	0.312	0.507		
Pseudo-R^2			0.560	0.378

[§] Electrical engineering (*ELEC*) is employed as reference for industry dummies.
*,** and *** denote significance at the 10%, 5% and 1% level, respectively. Standard errors reported in parentheses (heteroscedasticity-consistent for OLS). All regression contain a constant. Regressions are based on a common cross-section sample of 1691 firms. For definitions of the variables, see Tables 2.3 and 2.7 in the Appendix to this chapter.

firms is difficult to be interpreted from a theoretical perspective. In particular, this finding cannot be attributed to the fact that firms in services tend to be small and ICT intensive since industry-specific effects are controlled for by the inclusion of corresponding industry dummy variables.

The results for these industry dummies indicate that indeed ICT intensity varies strongly between different sectors of the economy. In the regressions, electrical engineering ($ELEC$) is taken as the reference group. The results corroborate findings from the previous section (in particular from Figure 2.4, p. 35) and highlight that also when controlling for a variety of other determinants, ICT intensity is particularly high in financial services (FIN), computer and telecommunication services ($COMP$), technical services $TECHS$, and other business-related services ($BSERV$). In contrast, industry-specific effects in other service sectors, in particular retail trade ($RETAIL$) and transport and postal services ($TRANS$), are very low and are comparable in size to the least ICT intensive manufacturing industries, i.e. basic goods industry ($BASIC$) and motor manufacturing ($MOTOR$).

Moreover, the results are consistent with findings from a variety of studies that find that ICT use is particularly productive with highly educated workers (see e.g. Bresnahan et al., 2002; Autor et al., 2003). Both the share of employees with university degree ($UNIV$) and the share of workers with vocational training (VOC) have significantly positive coefficients in the regressions. Similarly, as expected, exporting firms spend significantly more money on ICT and have a higher fraction of workers with access to the Internet than non-exporters do.

Young firms, however, are *not* more ICT-intensive than old firms are. On the contrary, older firms spend significantly more on ICT overall than younger firms do, as the coefficient of $LNAGE$ in the first specification shows. One explanation for this somewhat unexpected result is perhaps that older firms find it easier to attract sources for financing (uncertain) ICT projects than young firms do. Further robustness checks reveal that the somewhat surprising result with respect to the role of firm age is not due to the specific functional form. In additional (unreported) regressions, I classify firms with respect to three age categories (younger than 4 years, 4 to 7 years and older than 7 years) and replace $LNAGE$ by two dummy variables for firms belonging to the latter two categories.[35] However, the results remain broadly unchanged with only the dummy for 'older than 7 years' being significant in the regression with $LNICT$ as the dependent variable.

The conjecture that financing may play a role is further corroborated by the positive coefficients of non-ICT investments $LNINVOTHER$. This vari-

---

[35] This classification, which has been used in earlier empirical studies (e.g. Bertschek and Fryges, 2002), is based on a study by Prantl (2001) who shows that hazard functions of firms reach two local maxima approximately three years and seven years after formation correspondingly. After seven years, the hazard rates stay on a comparably low level such that these firms can be regarded as 'mature' firms.

able is significantly and positively linked to the first two indicators $ICTALL$ and PCL (that mainly reflect expenses and stock of ICT) but not to the shares of workers that primarily work at PCs or have access to the Internet (which focus more on the relevance of ICT for work tasks). This finding indicates that firms with a generally low capital intensity are not necessarily more reluctant with respect to the use of ICT at workplaces but rather spend less money on ICT equipment and services.

Coming to the strategy variables, the results yield very robust findings supporting the hypothesised complementarities with ICT use. Most strikingly, the share of workers receiving ICT-related training is correlated positively to all four measures of ICT intensity. Note that this correlation is not due to the educational level of workers since this aspect is controlled for by the share of workers with university degree $(UNIV)$ and vocational training (VOC). These results indicate that training employees forms an essential part of implementing ICT and highlight the importance of adjusting worker skills for the use of ICT.

Similarly, customer relationship management (CRM) and outsourcing $(OUTSOURCE)$ are positively related to all four measures of ICT intensity as well. This indicates that these innovative business practices are not only related to substantial expenditures on ICT but also foster a more intensive use of computers and the Internet by workers. Supply chain management (SCM) and e-commerce $(ECOMM)$ are significantly and positively correlated to $LNPC$ and $PCWORK$ but not to $INTER$. This result is somewhat surprising since both SCM and e-commerce are Internet-based. It may point to the fact that both strategies require an intensive use of PCs by the majority of workers while the direct contact to suppliers and customers via the Internet may be limited to a few employees only.

The results are more mixed when it comes to product innovations and organisational changes. Both product innovations (PD) and the share of employees working in units with profit responsibility $(UNIT)$ are significantly and positively correlated to the number of computers per worker $(LNPC)$, but not to the other ICT measures (even though the sign is also positive in most cases). The interpretation of these findings are anything but straightforward. One possible resolution of this puzzle is that in the case of these innovations, it may not be so important how many employees in a firm work with computers, but how well individual groups of workers are equipped. Endowment with PCs (and notebooks in particular) may be one way to simultaneously reward and motivate selected employees that are crucial for the performance of business units as well as product innovations, for example employees with management tasks or in R&D departments. These explanations, however, must remain speculative since their validation would require more detailed information on the ways ICTs are assigned to different groups of workers.

Finally, with the exception of the ICT indicator $INTER$, there is no significant correlation between ICT use and work in autonomous teams $(TEAM)$.

This finding is at odds with findings from a related study by Bresnahan et al. (2002) who report a positive link between decentralised workplace organisation (proxied by a condensed measure of the importance of self-managing team work[36]) and ICT use. One way to reconciliate the divergent findings is that the variable *TEAM* is correlated with innovation variables which are included in the specifications of Table 2.2, but not in the specifications of Bresnahan et al. (2002, Table VI).

For analysing the source of differences, I repeated the regressions from columns 1 and 2 of Table 2.2, but excluded the variables *PD*, *ECOMM*, *SCM*, *CRM*, and *TRAIN* to make the specification more comparable to the one in the cited study. The results of this more parsimonious specification are reported in Table 2.6 in the Appendix to this chapter (p. 54). In these modified regressions, all three variables *TEAM*, *UNIT*, and *OUTSOURCE*, which reflect the degree of decentralisation, do enter with significantly positive coefficients for some of the ICT measures. While the coefficient of *OUTSOURCE* is significantly positive in all four columns (as it was in the extended specifications from Table 2.2), the results for *TEAM* and *UNIT* are less clear-cut. The variable *UNIT* enters positively in all four columns but fails statistical significance in the case of *PCWORK*. This implies that establishing units with profit responsibility is associated with higher ICT expenditures and Internet access but not necessarily with an intensive use of computers by a higher share of workers. In contrast, the coefficient of *TEAM* is significantly positive only in the regressions with *PCWORK* and *INTER*. This may indicate that work in autonomous teams is associated with a particularly strong use of computers and the Internet by workers, but not necessarily with higher ICT expenditures.[37]

These additional findings suggest that ICT use is indeed associated with a stronger decentralisation of workplaces. However, as the insignificant coefficients in the richer specifications in Table 2.2 show, this correlation is much weaker (in particular for the measure of team-work) once changes in ICT-related management methods and training efforts are controlled for. This indicates that the impact of ICT use on organisational structures may be a more indirect consequence of ICT use: cheaper ICT favours innovation of processes and management techniques (e-commerce, SCM, CRM) which on their part go along with more decentralised organisational structures.

---

[36] This measure includes information from measures of team use, team-building activities, teamwork as a promotion criterion, quality circles or involvement groups, and two further measures concerning the allocation of decision authority between workers and managers.

[37] In some further regressions, I also omitted the variables *UNIT* and *OUTSOURCE* from the specification. After omitting these indicators of decentralisation, the variable *TEAM* enters significantly positive for all four measures of ICT use.

2.5 Conclusions

This chapter depicts and empirically explores important characteristics and implications of the major role that ICTs have achieved to play in industrialised economies. ICT looms large because it is a pervasive technology that carries large potentials for technical improvements and acts as an 'enabling technology' that facilitates a variety of innovations in application sectors. While for a long time economists had failed to find evidence for productivity gains from the diffusion of ICT, things have changed more recently. Backed by first evidence for productivity gains from ICT at the firm level, economists today widely agree that both ICT production and its application have contributed significantly to productivity and output growth in industrialised countries.

It is the character as an enabling technology that may help explain not only the substantial productivity gains from ICT but also the long delay for these benefits to become evident. Viewing ICT predominantly as a GPT implies assuming that it primarily acts as a catalyst for innovative activities in application sectors. This hypothesis means that the largest benefits from ICT can be obtained by using its potentials for innovation activities such as innovating processes, improving the quality of products and services, reorganising workplaces, applying new management techniques and training workers for dealing with the new technologies efficiently. These changes and adjustments need time to be implemented: corporate structures cannot be changed immediately and may even lower productivity during the phase of transition due to increased expenses or foregone output. These features make the delayed impacts of ICT on productivity far less paradoxical than they may seem if ICT is regarded as a ready-to-use technology that can be implemented easily to save costs and replace other, more expensive inputs in production.

Moreover, based on a theoretical model of supermodularity, the chapter has illustrated that the complementarities between ICT use and innovational efforts have two kinds of implications that can be checked on empirical grounds. First, complementarities should be mirrored by coordinated choices: profit-maximising firms with high ICT intensity will also engage more in innovative practices such as renewed processes, a focus on quality improvement, new management methods, and more efforts in training their workers. Second, firms that achieve to complement ICT use by these measures should be able to use ICT more productively than firms that refrain from such complementary efforts.

Based on representative data from a firm survey on ICT use among German firms in 2002, the empirical part of this chapter has provided evidence both on the pervasiveness of ICT and some results on the first of these implications following from the enabling character of ICT. The pervasiveness of ICT is reflected both by the quantitative importance of the ICT market and the impact of computers on workplace practices. Industrialised countries spend between 5.5 and 9% of their GDP on the new technologies (with Germany ranking at close to average with a share of 6.4%), and about every second employee in Germany is working primarily with computers.

Moreover, both statistical and econometric evidence has provided broad support for the characteristics of ICT as an enabling technology. Firms use ICT for accelerating processes and improving the quality of products and services in the first place. In contrast, direct cost savings are only of secondary importance. Similarly, in a cross-section analysis of firms, various measures of intensity of ICT turned out to be strongly correlated to innovations in processes, products, management techniques, and to some forms of organisational changes. These correlations are robust with respect to controlling for a broad variety of other dimensions such as firm size, industry affiliation, or skill structure.

One important caveat remains. Measuring complementarities via correlations in factor demand requires to assume that firms behave rationally and optimise production processes with respect to efficiency. However, this assumption is not self-evident. The successful use of new technologies is a risky enterprise and often requires substantial experimentation to find effective ways to use it. As the enormous stock-market bubbles have shown, economic behaviour of managers and other economic agents may be largely determined by trends. The fact that certain strategies are correlated may thus be an expression of following such trends rather than the consequence of optimising behaviour.

Moreover, the capability of firms to make use of ICT may vary substantially between firms due to differences in adjustment costs related to ICT. To the extent that the adoption of new technologies requires technical knowledge and experience, the ability to use ICT must be acquired over time. These trajectories may vary between firms and may make the correlation between ICT use and its complements less obvious. Early adopters of electronic data interchange (EDI), for example, may find it easier to engage in e-commerce or supply chain management while firms with a high share of well-educated workers may find training their workers for new tasks easier. Moreover, as shown by Jovanovic and Stolyarov (2000), if adjustment costs are non-convex (i.e. by involving high fixed costs), profit-maximising firms may adopt complementary inputs asynchronously, i.e. at different points in time. This may be particularly relevant for innovations and organisational changes which often involve large and irreversible investments.

Both these aspects — bounded rationality and varying adjustment costs — may make correlation of observed factor demand and strategies an incomplete approach to measuring complementarities. The indirect (correlation-based) approach to complementarities should thus be amended by assessing the second implication mentioned above. This approach necessitates a production function framework to assess whether the productivity of firms that combine ICT use with additional innovational efforts are more productive than other firms that do not account for such complementarities.

Estimating productivity effects with production functions, however, involves a variety of methodological issues that may have substantial consequences on the empirical results. These methodological issues are particularly severe in attempts to measure the productivity contributions of ICT. I will discuss these aspects in detail in the next chapter 3 and present a preferred econometric approach that allows to suitably address these issues. The subsequent chapters 4 and 5 will use this preferred approach for analysing more elaborately the role of innovations and innovative experience on the one hand and worker skills and training on the other as two particular cases of complementarities in ICT use.

2.6 Appendix

2.6.1 Inferring complementarity from correlation

This part summarises formal contributions by Arora and Gambardella (1990) who derive sufficient conditions under which complementarities between two strategies x_i and x_j can be inferred from a positive correlation between both strategies in profit-maximising firms, conditional on a set of firm characteristics.[38]

Let $V(\mathbf{x}; \mathbf{z})$ denote the payoff function for each firm that is concave in $\mathbf{x}$. The vector of choice variables is $\mathbf{x} = (x_1, \ldots, x_s)'$ (with, e.g., x_1 denoting ICT capital), and $\mathbf{z} = (z_1, \ldots, z_k)'$ denotes firm characteristics as control variables. The firm maximises over $\mathbf{x}$:

$$V(\mathbf{x}; \mathbf{z}) - (\mathbf{p} + \omega)' \cdot \mathbf{x} \tag{2.9}$$

where $(\mathbf{p} + \omega)$ represents the cost of a unit of $\mathbf{x}$, where $\mathbf{p} = (p_1, \ldots, p_k)'$ is the average unit cost of x and $\omega = (\omega_1, \ldots, \omega_k)'$ is a vector of firm-specific cost variations as deviations from average costs $\mathbf{p}$. In this setting, complementarity between ICT and strategy x_i implies that $\partial^2 V(\cdot)/\partial x_1 \partial x_i$ is positive. Defining $\mathbf{V_x} \equiv \partial V(\cdot)/\partial \mathbf{x}$, the first-order conditions for an interior solution (2.9) are:

$$\mathbf{V_x^*} \equiv V_x(\mathbf{x^*}; \mathbf{z}) = \mathbf{p} + \omega \tag{2.10}$$

where $\mathbf{x^*}$ denotes the optimal choice of $\mathbf{x}$ in (2.10). Defining $\hat{\mathbf{x}} = \hat{\mathbf{x}}(\mathbf{z})$ such that $\hat{V}_x \equiv V_x(\hat{\mathbf{x}}; z) = V_x(z) = \mathbf{p}$, first-order Taylor approximation around $\hat{\mathbf{x}}$ yields:

$$\mathbf{V_x^*} \approx \hat{\mathbf{V}}_\mathbf{x} + \hat{\mathbf{V}}_\mathbf{xx}(\mathbf{x^*} - \hat{\mathbf{x}}) \tag{2.11}$$

with $\hat{\mathbf{V}}_\mathbf{xx} = \partial \hat{\mathbf{V}}_\mathbf{x}/\partial \mathbf{x}$.[39] Rewriting, one gets:

---

[38] For a further extension of this framework, see also Arora (1996).

[39] Note that $\hat{\mathbf{x}}$ does not depend on ω, and that thus, by construction, also $\hat{\mathbf{V}}_\mathbf{x}$ and $\hat{\mathbf{V}}_\mathbf{xx}$ do not depend on ω.

$$\hat{\mathbf{V}}_{\mathbf{xx}}(\mathbf{x}^* - \hat{\mathbf{x}}) \approx \omega \tag{2.12}$$

Equation (2.12) can be extended by multiplying both sides by $(\mathbf{x}^* - \hat{\mathbf{x}})$. Substituting and rearranging yield:

$$(\mathbf{x}^* - \hat{\mathbf{x}})(\mathbf{x}^* - \hat{\mathbf{x}})' = \hat{\mathbf{V}}_{\mathbf{xx}}^{-1}\omega\omega'\hat{\mathbf{V}}_{\mathbf{xx}}^{-1} \tag{2.13}$$

Based on this specification, Arora and Gambardella (1990) make the following two assumptions and show that they are sufficient for inferring complementarities from positive correlation of the choice variables.

1. $E\{\omega|\mathbf{z}\} = 0$. Taking expectations conditional on $\mathbf{z}$ of both sides of (2.12), this assumption implies that $E(\mathbf{x}^*|\ \mathbf{z}) = E(\hat{\mathbf{x}}|\ \mathbf{z}) = \hat{\mathbf{x}}$.[40]
2. $E\{\omega_i\omega_j|\mathbf{z}\} = 0$ for $i \neq j$. This is equivalent to assuming $\Sigma \equiv E(\omega\omega'|\mathbf{z})$ to be diagonal.

Using both these assumptions, taking the expectation conditional on $\mathbf{z}$ on both sides of (2.13) and replacing $\hat{\mathbf{x}}$ by $E(\mathbf{x}^*|\mathbf{z})$ gives:

$$E\{(\mathbf{x}^* - E(\mathbf{x}^*|\ \mathbf{z}))(\mathbf{x}^* - E(\mathbf{x}^*|\ \mathbf{z}))'|\ \mathbf{z}\} = \hat{\mathbf{V}}_{\mathbf{xx}}^{-1}\ \Sigma\ \hat{\mathbf{V}}_{\mathbf{xx}}^{-1} \tag{2.14}$$

Finally, Arora and Gambardella (1990) show that if all considered strategies are complementary (such that $V(\cdot)$ is supermodular), the matrix on the right-hand side of (2.14) is a non-negative matrix, i.e. all its elements are non-negative. From this, it follows that the covariance between any strategies x_i and x_j, $i \neq j$, conditional on $\mathbf{z}$ is non-negative.

---

[40] Since $\hat{\mathbf{V}}_{\mathbf{xx}}$ is a function of $\mathbf{z}$ only, (2.12) can be written as $\hat{\mathbf{V}}_{\mathbf{xx}}E\{\mathbf{x}^* - \hat{\mathbf{x}}|\mathbf{z}\} = E\{\omega|\mathbf{z}\}$. With concavity of $V(\cdot)$ and $E\{\omega|\mathbf{z}\} = 0$ it follows that $E(\mathbf{x}^*|\ \mathbf{z}) = E(\hat{\mathbf{x}}|\ \mathbf{z}) = \hat{\mathbf{x}}$, where the last equality follows from the fact that $\hat{\mathbf{x}}$ is a function of $\mathbf{z}$ only.

2.6.2 Tables

Table 2.3. Industry classification

Code	Industry	NACE-Code
CONS	Consumer goods industry	15-22, 36, 37
CHEM	Chemical industry	23, 24
BASIC	Other basis goods industry	25, 26
MECH	Mechanical engineering	28, 29
ELEC	Electrical engineering	30-32
MED	Medical, precision and optical instruments	33
MOTOR	Motor manufacturing industry	34, 35
WHOLES	Wholesale trade	51
RETAIL	Retail trade	50, 52
TRANS	Transport and postal services	60-63, 64.1
FIN	Financial intermediation	65-67
COMP	Computer and telecommunication services	64.2, 72
TECHS	Technical services	73, 74.2, 74.3
BSERV	Other business services	70, 71, 74.1, 74.4-.8, 90

Own classification.

Table 2.4. Composition of sample and population by industry

Industry	sample	population*	
	% firms	% firms	% employees
CONS	9.3	5.3	11.1
CHEM	6.1	0.5	3.4
BASIC	8.8	2.2	6.8
MECH	14.1	4.2	10.5
ELEC	7.5	0.9	4.8
MED	8.1	0.7	1.7
MOTOR	5.1	0.3	6.5
WHOLES	3.9	8.6	8.4
RETAIL	6.7	28.3	14.8
TRANS	7.5	9.7	8.2
FIN	4.2	1.4	6.8
COMP	6.6	2.9	3.2
TECHS	6.2	8.6	3.1
BSERV	6.0	26.3	10.8
total	100.0	100.0	100.0

All values in %.
*firms in Germany with 5 and more employees in the selected industries. Source: German Statistical Office, ZEW and own calculations

Table 2.5. Composition of sample by size class

Size class (employees)	# firms	% firms
5-9	196	11.59
10-19	220	13.01
20-49	365	21.58
50-99	313	18.51
100-199	213	12.60
200-499	210	12.42
500 and more	174	10.29
all size classes	1,691	100.00

Table 2.6. ICT use and corporate strategies

	(1) OLS	(2) OLS	(3) Tobit	(4) Tobit
dependent variable:	LNICT	LNPC	PCWORK	INTER
TEAM	0.138	0.065	0.049**	0.106***
	(0.088)	(0.045)	(0.022)	(0.027)
UNIT	0.189**	0.179***	0.028	0.052*
	(0.083)	(0.043)	(0.022)	(0.027)
OUTSOURCE	0.237***	0.121***	0.046**	0.049**
	(0.064)	(0.032)	(0.017)	(0.020)
LNEMPL	-0.640***	-0.463***	-0.061**	-0.162***
	(0.092)	(0.051)	(0.023)	(0.028)
LNEMPLSQ	0.055***	0.032***	0.005**	0.012***
	(0.010)	(0.006)	(0.003)	(0.003)
GROUP	0.015	0.043	0.025	0.026
	(0.069)	(0.037)	(0.017)	(0.021)
LNINVOTHER	0.203***	0.053***	0.000	0.005
	(0.022)	(0.012)	(0.005)	(0.007)
LNAGE	0.057**	0.014	0.008	0.005
	(0.026)	(0.013)	(0.006)	(0.008)
UNIV	1.325***	1.372***	0.644***	0.728***
	(0.187)	(0.093)	(0.046)	(0.057)
VOC	0.585***	0.500***	0.155***	0.110**
	(0.129)	(0.071)	(0.032)	(0.039)
EXP	0.384***	0.235***	0.047**	0.077***
	(0.070)	(0.037)	(0.017)	(0.021)
R^2	0.278	0.476		
Pseudo-R^2			0.511	0.356

*,** and *** denote significance at the 10%, 5%, and 1% level. Standard errors reported in parentheses (heteroscedasticity-consistent for OLS). All regressions contain a constant and industry dummies analogue to the specification of Table 2.2. Regressions are based on a common cross-section sample of 1691 firms. For definitions of variables, see Tables 2.3 and 2.7.

Table 2.7. Summary statistics of sample

Variable	Short Description	Mean	Std.	Min.	Max.
LNICT	log of ICT expenditures per worker (in € million)	-6.707	1.376	11.330	-2.148
LNPC	log of number of computers per worker	-0.794	0.826	-4.007	1.609
PCWORK	share of workers predominantly using computer	0.479	0.330	0	1
INTER	share of workers with Internet access	0.439	0.367	0	1
PRODINNO	product innovation in 1999-2001	0.646	0.478	0	1
ECOMM	selling via e-commerce	0.139	0.346	0	1
SCM	supply chain management	0.226	0.418	0	1
CRM	customer relationship management	0.312	0.467	0	1
TRAIN	share of workers receiving ICT-related training	0.127	0.203	0	1
TEAM	share of workers in autonomous teams	0.311	0.352	0	1
UNIT	share of workers in units with profit responsibility	0.229	0.368	0	1
OUTSOURCE	having outsourced activities 1999-2001	0.273	0.445	0	1
LNINVOTHER	log of investments in non-ICT (in € million)	-1.353	2.169	-8.517	5.244
LNEMPL	log of number of workers	4.076	1.532	0	8.987
LNEMPLSQ	square of LNEMP	18.960	13.614	0	80.770
UGROUP	part of group of firms	0.367	0.482	0	1
LNAGE	log of age of firm	2.708	1.131	0	5.303
UNIV	share of workers with university degree	0.186	0.233	0	1
VOC	share of workers with vocational training	0.561	0.273	0	1
EXP	exporting firm	0.551	0.498	0	1

3

Contributions of ICT to firm productivity*

> *Computers make it easier to do a lot of things, but most of the things they make it easier to do don't need to be done.*
> Andy Rooney, CBS NEWS correspondent

3.1 Introduction

Since the end of the 1990s, a broad variety of empirical studies have emerged exploring the productivity impacts of ICT at the firm level.[1] Most of the studies employ a production function framework to estimate the elasticity of output with respect to ICT capital, controlling for the amount of other inputs. The quantitative results from these studies, however, vary considerably. Apart from varying definitions of ICT stocks and sample-specific variations, a substantial part of these differences may be due to differing quantitative methods and model specifications. In particular, interferences from firm-specific effects, simultaneity of input and output decisions, measurement errors, the omission of worker skills, autocorrelated productivity shocks, or functional form restrictions in the underlying production function may induce biases in the empirical analysis. However, previous firm-level studies on ICT productivity address only some, if any, of these issues.[2]

---

* This chapter is largely based on Hempell (2005b).

[1] See for example studies by Bertschek and Kaiser (2004), Biscourp et al. (2002), Black and Lynch (2001), Bresnahan et al. (2002), Brynjolfsson and Hitt (1995, 1996, 1998, 2000, 2003), Brynjolfsson and Yang (1999), Greenan and Mairesse (1996), Greenan et al. (2001), Lehr and Lichtenberg (1999), Licht and Moch (1999), Lichtenberg (1995).

[2] Conducting a meta-analysis of results from 20 studies, Stiroh (2002c) shows that a substantial part of differing results in the literature can indeed be explained by differences in model specification, econometric techniques and underlying data

The main aim of this chapter is to explore the impacts of applying different quantitative approaches to firm-level data and to discuss econometric strategies that are suited to reveal the 'real' rather than 'spurious' productivity effects resulting from the use of ICT. The chapter discusses why using firm-level data (as compared to more aggregate data sources) may help to control for biases arising from quality changes in output which are not accounted for by official price statistics. Moreover, I derive calibration suggestions of how existing firm-level survey data can be transformed for the purpose of production function estimates.

An empirical application to a sample of more than 1100 firms in the German business-related and distribution service sector for the period 1994 to 1999 highlights the effects of applying different models and estimation techniques. The focus on services seems worthwhile for three main reasons. First, ICT investment has been most dynamic and most intensive in the service sector (e.g., OECD, 2000a). Second, business-related services have been important drivers of economic growth over the last decades in industrialised countries (OECD, 2000b). Finally, assessing service quality correctly forms a particularly difficult issue in determining the productivity impacts from ICT (Griliches, 1994). Firm-level results can be an insightful complement to findings from aggregate statistics. Beyond analysing the methodological issues, the study also aims at presenting evidence on the so far hardly explored productivity impacts of ICT use on German businesses.[3]

The results presented in this chapter are obtained from a preferred system GMM (SYS-GMM) approach and provide evidence of significant productivity effects from ICT usage in German services. According to these results, a 1% increase in ICT capital raises a firm's value added by 0.06%. This point estimate is substantially lower than values obtained from simple pooled OLS regressions and is overall robust with respect to varying parameters underlying the construction of capital stocks as well as to sample modifications. Among the various issues considered, unobserved heterogeneity between firms is found to be the most prominent interference in conventional estimates. Controlling for this interference by estimation in first differences, however, induces further problems that call for instrumental variable approaches.

The remainder of this chapter is organised as follows. Section 3.2 discusses the theoretical issues and introduces a basic production function framework with three extensions. Section 3.4 gives an overview of the employed data and describes calibrations for constructing separate stocks of ICT and conventional capital. These derived capital stocks will also be employed in the subsequent chapters 4 and 5. Section 3.5 discusses the econometric issues and presents empirical results. Section 3.6 summarises the main findings.

---

sets. Moreover, he finds similar variations for alternative specifications and quantitative methods in own estimations for a single set of U.S. industry-level data.

[3] To the best of my knowledge, the only related studies for Germany are cross-section analyses by Licht and Moch (1999) and Bertschek and Kaiser (2004).

3.2 Theoretical and methodological issues

In the empirical literature, the most frequently used framework for analysing the productivity impacts of ICT has been to use a production function setup with ICT capital entering as a production input.[4] Many studies based on aggregate data determine the corresponding elasticities rather indirectly by applying growth accounting approaches,[5] whereas firm-level (and sometimes industry-level) studies usually exploit a greater number of units of observations for directly estimating the elasticities in econometric approaches. In this section, I summarise several advantages of firm-level analyses. Employing a Cobb-Douglas production function framework as a reference model, I then discuss the relevance of several econometric issues and varying model specifications.

3.3 The scope of firm-level analyses

As pointed out by Brynjolfsson (1994), Licht and Moch (1999) and highlighted in the previous chapter,[6] quality improvements — in particular faster delivery and customisation — are a prominent goal of ICT investment decisions. Similarly, Griliches (1994) suggests that the problem of unmeasured quality changes in aggregate statistics is especially important in the case of 'unmeasurable' services like trade, finance, insurance and real estate where ICT investment has grown most rapidly. As a consequence, the contribution of ICT to real output growth inferred from aggregate data tends to be too small. Suitably specified firm-level studies, in contrast, may suffer less from measurement bias for mainly two reasons.

First, as subsequently set out in section 3.3.2, micro data allow to include time-specific industry dummy variables to make a firm's output directly comparable to the output of competitors. This helps to correct for potential

---

[4] The most frequently applied proxies for ICT capital are the value of computers installed, book values of office, computing and accounting machinery (OCAM) from balance sheets, or investment in ICT.

[5] The growth accounting approach aims to assign the contribution of the growth of different inputs to the overall growth of output. The residual in output growth that is not explained by the growth of the observed inputs is interpreted as a rise in multifactor productivity (MFP). The approach is based on the assumption of constant returns to scale and perfect competition, such that the elasticities of output with respect to the different inputs equal the income shares of the corresponding inputs. The direct growth contribution of ICT to output growth is calculated as the product of the share of ICT capital services in total income and the growth of the ICT capital stock. This approach and some empirical results from its application in the empirical literature are discussed in more detail in section 2.3.1.

[6] See subsection 2.4.1.

measurement errors in industry price deflators. Second, variations in output quality between firms of the same industry and in the same period can be accounted for, too. If a firm invests in ICT in order to improve the quality of products and services (faster delivery, customised product characteristics, extended shopping facilities or after sales support) while competitors continue to offer their old products and services, the innovating firm will be able to charge higher prices for better quality and to raise revenues. Brynjolfsson and Hitt (2000) argue that microeconomic studies will capture this effect and variations in output quality will contribute to measuring a higher output elasticity of ICT investment.[7] Supporting this view, the next section 3.3.1 shows that the production function estimates obtained from firm-level data can be interpreted as reduced-form estimates of coefficients for a model that implicitly takes into account productivity effects from quality improvements. A strong impact of ICT use on output quality will entail a higher estimate of the ICT coefficient in the production function.

However, there are also some limitations to estimating output elasticities using firm-level data. In particular, Klette and Griliches (1996) show that varying prices at the firm level due to imperfect competition may induce a downward bias on the estimated input elasticities. As illustrated in the next section, this type of bias affects the estimates of *all* inputs in a similar fashion such that this issue is not addressed in more detail in this study. Similarly, the firm-level approach fails to capture productivity effects from ICT use that are common across industries. The main idea behind this argument is that productivity gains achieved by an overall increase in ICT intensity across industry cannot be used by firms to distance themselves from their competitors.

Apart from these more technical arguments, the firm-level approach can offer various insights that are much more difficult to obtain from aggregate data. Most importantly, the productivity of ICT may vary between firms, if some firms are better enabled than others to use new technologies successfully and if complementary factors like skills, innovations and organisational assets are important.[8] In industry- or country-level data, a large part of firm-specific variation disappears in the process of aggregation. The issues discussed in this chapter aim at contributing to finding suitable methodological approaches to assess these questions. In the subsequent chapters 4 and 5, I analyse the role of innovation and training of employees using the preferred SYS-GMM approach explored in this chapter.

---

[7] This argument is backed by empirical support from a firm-level study by Brynjolfsson and Hitt (1995) who do not find any significant differences in ICT productivity between sectors with 'measurable' and 'unmeasurable' quality, indicating that appropriate quality measurement is mainly a problem at the aggregate level.

[8] See Bresnahan and Greenstein (1996), Brynjolfsson and Hitt (2000), and Yang and Brynjolfsson (2001).

3.3.1 A model of ICT-induced quality improvements

In the following, I derive a simple partial equilibrium model to show how ICT-enabled quality improvements are accounted for as productivity gains in production function estimations based on firm-level data. This model extends a model by Klette and Griliches (1996) — denoted by KG in the remainder — by quality aspects that affect consumers' marginal willingness to pay and thus by market equilibrium prices. The equilibrium outcome of the framework will not be used as a structural model in the empirical application due to data limitations. It is mainly designed to show that production function estimates based on firm-level data can be interpreted as reduced-form estimates that take quality improvements due to ICT input into account.

Consider a Cobb-Douglas technology with labour and two types of capital as inputs:

$$Y_{it} = F(A_{it}, L_{it}, ICT_{it}, K_{it}) = A_{it} L_{it}^{\gamma_1} ICT_{it}^{\gamma_2} K_{it}^{\gamma_3}, \qquad (3.1)$$

where Y_{it} is value added of firm i in period t, L_{it} represents labour input, ICT_{it}, and K_{it} are the corresponding amounts of ICT and conventional (non-ICT) capital, and A_{it} denotes multi-factor productivity. After taking logs on both sides, (3.1) can be rewritten as:

$$y_{it} = a_{it} + \gamma_1 l_{it} + \gamma_2 ict_{it} + \gamma_3 k_{it}, \qquad (3.2)$$

where small letters denote values in logarithms. Suppose that firm i is operating in an industry $j(i)$ for which output deflators $P_{j(i)t}$ are available and that y_{it} is real output calculated using industry deflators. (For notational simplicity, I designate industry specific variables such as $P_{j(i)t}$ by the simpler form P_{jt} in the remainder.) Suppose further that firms do not follow the same pricing strategies rendering aggregate industry deflators P_{jt} an imperfect measure of output prices at the firm level. The heterogeneity in pricing induces an aggregation error such that (imperfectly) measured (log of) output $\tilde{y}_{it}$ can be defined as a combination of true output and a measurement error:

$$\tilde{y}_{it} \equiv y_{it} + p_{it} - p_{jt}, \qquad (3.3)$$

where $p_{it} - p_{jt}$ is the measurement error due to aggregation. Inserting (3.2) into (3.3) and abstracting from a_{it} for simplicity (which will be considered explicitly in the next section) gives:

$$\tilde{y}_{it} = \gamma_1 l_{it} + \gamma_2 ict_{it} + \gamma_3 k_{it} + p_{it} - p_{jt}. \qquad (3.4)$$

Output, however, may differ not only in terms of prices but also in terms of quality. As argued in the previous section, the use of new technologies may be particularly suited to improve ancillary aspects of product quality. To focus on the role of ICT for product quality, consider the simplest case in which product quality Q is determined by the intensity of ICT used in the production process (defined as the fraction of ICT over non-ICT capital) such that for firms and industry average:[9]

$$Q_{it} = B \cdot \left(\frac{ICT_{it}}{K_{it}}\right)^{\omega} \quad \text{or} \quad q_{it} = b + \omega(ict_{it} - k_{it})$$

$$\text{and} \quad Q_{jt} = B \cdot \left(\frac{ICT_{jt}}{K_{jt}}\right)^{\omega} \quad \text{or} \quad q_{jt} = b + \omega(ict_{jt} - k_{jt}), \qquad (3.5)$$

where subscripts j denote the corresponding mean values at the industry level $j(i)$. All firms are assumed to be sufficiently small such that the impact of changes in one variable in one firm has an negligible effect on industry averages. The marginal contributions of ICT to output quality are proportional to ω and, if $0 \leq \omega \leq 1$, the marginal contributions of relative ICT input to product quality are positive and decreasing with ICT intensity.

For the demand side, I use a slightly extended version of the model proposed by KG. The demand for goods of firm i at time t is given by:

$$Y_{it}^{D} = Y_{jt}^{D} \cdot \left(\frac{P_{it} \, Q_{jt}}{P_{jt} \, Q_{it}}\right)^{\eta} \quad \text{or} \quad y_{it}^{D} = y_{jt}^{D} + \eta(p_{it} - p_{jt} - (q_{it} - q_{jt})). \quad (3.6)$$

That is, the demand for output produced by firm i in period t depends on total demand for output produced in the corresponding industry Y_{jt}^{D} and price P_{it} relative to the average industry price level P_{jt}. The extension of the KG-model consists in the correction of prices for differentials in output quality Q_{it}/Q_{jt}. This extension is based on the idea that utility-maximising consumers take heterogeneous output quality into account when comparing prices. The parameter $\eta < 0$ reflects the elasticity of demand with respect to relative prices. Strong competition is mirrored by high (absolute) values for η, such that a small price deviation from industry average causes a strong decrease in demand for goods from firm i.[10]

Note that in this partial equilibrium model where total demand for industry output Y_{jt}^{D} is considered to be given exogenously, quality improvements will be rewarded by increased demand only if these improvements are above industry average, such that $\dot{Q}_{it}/\dot{Q}_{jt} > 1$, where dots above the variables denote the derivatives with respect to time ($\dot{Q}_t \equiv d \log Q_t/dt$).

In equilibrium with $y_{it}^{D} = y_{it}$ and $y_{jt}^{D} = y_{jt}$, inserting (3.3) and (3.5) into (3.6) yields:

---

[9] The intensity of ICT could equivalently be defined as the share of ICT input in output produced. This makes the model more involved without changing the main results.

[10] Alternatively, firms may use ICT for reducing the absolute value of the price elasticity of demand. Also in this case, profit-maximising firms could charge higher prices due to increased market power. For a related discussion of the impacts of product innovations on price elasticity of demand in a structural model with profit-maximising firms, see Smolny (1998).

$$\tilde{y}_{it} = y_{jt} + (1+\eta)(p_{it} - p_{jt}) + \eta\omega(q_{it} - q_{jt})$$
$$= y_{jt} + (1+\eta)(p_{it} - p_{jt}) + \eta\omega(ict_{it} - ict_{jt}) - \eta\omega(k_{it} - k_{jt}). \quad (3.7)$$

Solving (3.7) for $p_{it} - p_{jt}$, inserting into (3.4) and rearranging gives:

$$\tilde{y}_{it} = \frac{1+\eta}{\eta}[\gamma_1 l_{it} + \gamma_2 ict_{it} + \gamma_3 k_{it}] - \frac{1}{\eta}y_{jt}$$
$$-\omega(1+\eta)(ict_{it} - k_{it}) + \omega(1+\eta)(ict_{jt} - k_{jt}). \quad (3.8)$$

Equation (3.8) summarises the main theoretical issues of estimating the productivity effects of ICT. The first part of the equation is basically identical to the KG-model. It shows that if prices vary between firms due to imperfectly competitive markets (with $-1 > \eta > -\infty$), the estimates of the input elasticities obtained from a production function estimation as of (3.2) must be interpreted as reduced-form estimates that underestimate the true input elasticities by the factor $\eta/(\eta+1)$.[11] The second line of (3.8) results from the extension of the KG-model and captures the impacts of quality improvements on the estimated reduced-form elasticities.

The reduced-form elasticities can be interpreted more easily by rearranging (3.8) to:

$$\tilde{y}_{it} = \left[\frac{1+\eta}{\eta}\gamma_1\right]l_{it} + \left[\frac{1+\eta}{\eta}\gamma_2 - \omega(1+\eta)\right]ict_{it} + \left[\frac{1+\eta}{\eta}\gamma_3 + \omega(1+\eta)\right]k_{it}$$
$$-\frac{1}{\eta}y_{jt} + [\omega(1+\eta)](ict_{jt} - k_{jt}) + \epsilon_{it}.$$

This equation shows that the higher the impact of ICT intensity on output quality, i.e. the higher ω, the higher will the reduced-form coefficient γ_2^{red} of ICT corresponding to $\gamma_2^{red} = (1+\eta)\gamma_2/\eta - \omega(1+\eta)$ be. Even though this term does not correspond to the output contributions of ICT in a narrow sense (measured by γ_2), this broader measure also takes into account welfare effects from improved output quality. Moreover, the impact of quality improvements is closely linked to the competition parameter η. The more competitive markets are (i.e. the more negative η), the stronger the impacts of quality improvements on the reduced-form estimate γ_2^{red}. Moreover, as pointed out by the GK-model, higher absolute values for η also imply a lower bias of the reduced-form elasticities induced by the term $(\eta+1)/\eta$.

An empirical strategy to obtain the parameters γ_1, γ_2, γ_3, η, and ω would be to regress measured firm-level output $\tilde{y}_{it}$ on firm-level inputs l_{it}, ict_{it}, and k_{it} and on industry-level data y_{jt}, ict_{jt}, and k_{jt}. The structural coefficient η could then be recovered from the coefficient of y_{jt}. In combination with the estimate for $ict_{jt} - k_{jt}$, this would also allow for obtaining ω. Finally, with η and ω known, the elasticities $\gamma_1, \gamma_2, \gamma_3$ as well can be deduced from the

---

[11] An empirical approach to assess the size of this bias is to include industry output y_{jt} in the regression to get an estimate of the coefficient η.

estimates. For the analyses of this study, however, the corresponding industry-level data for Germany are not available. In the empirical application, I will use interacted time and industry dummies to control for the industry-specific heterogeneity of y_{jt}, ict_{jt}, and k_{jt}.

3.3.2 Reference framework

In this section, I consider various empirical issues that may be relevant for the estimation of the production function and will therefore be taken into account in varying empirical specifications and econometric techniques in the empirical part of this chapter. In order to keep things tractable, I abstract from the equilibrium model derived in the previous section and only consider the following variant of the production function (3.2) as a reference specification:

$$y_{it} = \gamma_1 l_{it} + \gamma_2 ict_{it} + \gamma_3 k_{it} + \eta_i + \lambda_{j(i),t} + \epsilon_{it}, \qquad (3.9)$$

where multifactor productivity $a_{it} = \log(A_{it}) = \eta_i + \lambda_{j(i),t} + \epsilon_{it}$ is decomposed into a firm-specific fixed part η_i, a time-variant industry-specific part $\lambda_{j(i),t}$ (with $j(i)$ denoting the industry j that firm i is operating in), and a time-variant firm-specific residual ϵ_{it}. The firm-specific effect η_i captures fixed or quasi-fixed factors affecting productivity, like management ability, organisational capital, branding, or location. The residual ϵ_{it} comprises measurement errors (m_{it}) and firm-specific productivity shocks (ξ_{it}) such that $\epsilon_{it} = m_{it} + \xi_{it}$. In this reference framework, both m_{it} and ξ_{it} are assumed to be serially uncorrelated and only their sum ϵ_{it} is considered.

The industry time-variant part $\lambda_{j(i),t}$ captures variations in productivity that are specific to a particular industry and left unexplained by the input variables. In this sense, $\lambda_{j(i),t}$ helps to ensure that outputs of firms are more readily comparable across industries. In particular, demand fluctuations induced by industry-specific business cycles may lead to variations in factor utilisation that are similar across firms of one industry. The resulting industry-specific changes of productivity are then captured by $\lambda_{j(i),t}$.

In a similar manner, $\lambda_{j(i),t}$ helps to correct for mismeasurement of prices at the industry level. To illustrate this, measured prices $\hat{P}_{j(i),t}$ for industry $j(i)$ are defined as the product of true prices $P_{j(i),t}$ and an industry-specific measurement bias M_{jt} such that $\hat{P}_{j(i),t} = P_{j(i),t} M_{j(i),t}$ or $\hat{p}_{j(i),t} = p_{j(i),t} + m_{j(i),t}$ in logarithms.[12] With z_{it} denoting nominal output of firm i in period t, real output y_{it} of firm i operating in industry $j(i)$ is $y_{it} = z_{it} - p_{j(i),t} = z_{it} - \hat{p}_{j(i),t} + m_{j(i),t}$, and observed real output (i.e. output deflated with observed prices) is $\hat{y}_{it} = z_{it} - \hat{p}_{j(i),t} = y_{it} - m_{j(i),t}$. If, as argued above, ICT is most

---

[12] Note that $M_{j(i),t} > 1$ and $\log(M_{j(i),t}) \equiv m_{j(i),t} > 0$ if the quality of output in industry $j(i)$ is understated such that measured prices $\hat{P}_{j(i),t}$ are higher than the true ones.

heavily used in industries for which product quality tends to be understated (and official prices are overstated consequently), ict_{it} and $m_{j(i),t}$ are positively correlated. The omission of $m_{j(i),t}$ will then lead to underestimating the true productivity contributions of ICT. Since this mismeasurement affects *all* firms of industry j in period t in the same way, the projection of output on a common dummy variable $\lambda_{j(i),t}$ helps to control for this potential measurement bias.

While the industry-specific component $\lambda_{j(i),t}$ will be controlled for by including time-variant industry dummies,[13] distorting effects from unobserved η_i and ϵ_{it} will be addressed by econometric techniques. I will account for the fact that both η_i and ϵ_{it} may be correlated with the inputs in general and ICT capital in particular if, e.g., firms with good management (i.e. a high η_i) are both more productive and more inclined to make use of ICT (in the following referred to as *firm effects*), or if a demand shock (high ϵ_{it}) raises both productivity and investment (*simultaneity issues*).

3.3.3 Extensions

In the following, I extend the reference model (3.9) by further aspects, allowing for 1.) serial correlation of the errors ϵ_{it}, 2.) heterogeneous labour inputs and 3.) a more flexible functional specification. At best, these issues would be considered simultaneously. Unfortunately, data limitations render this impossible and the extensions are thus explored separately.

Extension 1: Serially correlated residuals. Potential biases in the econometric exploration of equation (3.9) may arise if the productivity shocks ξ_{it} are serially correlated such that $\xi_{it} = \rho\xi_{i,t-1} + e_{it}$, with $e_{it} \sim i.i.d.$[14] This serial correlation may occur if, e.g., the effects from demand shocks were only partially captured by the industry-specific control variables $\lambda_{j(i),t}$. Measurement errors m_{it}, in contrast, are assumed to be serially uncorrelated. In order to estimate equation (3.9) for this case, a dynamic or common factor representation can be obtained by subtracting $\rho y_{i,t-1}$ from both sides of (3.9). Inserting $e_{it} = \xi_{it} - \rho\xi_{i,t-1}$ and rearranging yields:

$$y_{it} = \rho y_{i,t-1} + \gamma_1 n_{it} + \gamma_2 ict_{it} + \gamma_3 k_{it} \qquad (3.9a)$$
$$-\rho\gamma_1 n_{i,t-1} - \rho\gamma_2 ict_{i,t-1} - \rho\gamma_3 k_{i,t-1}$$
$$+\eta_{it}(1-\rho) + \lambda_{j(i),t} - \rho\lambda_{j(i),t-1} + w_{it},$$

where $w_{it} = e_{it} + m_{it} - \rho m_{i,t-1}$ is MA(1). In order to obtain estimates of the structural coefficients γ_1, γ_2, γ_3, and ρ, a two-step procedure is applied. In the first step, I estimate the following reduced-form model:

---

[13] Alternatively, these dummies can be conceived as interactions between time and industry dummies.

[14] This extension is similar to the one in Blundell and Bond (2000).

$$y_{it} = \pi_1 y_{i,t-1} + \pi_2 n_{it} + \pi_3 ict_{it} + \pi_4 k_{it} \tag{3.10}$$
$$+ \pi_5 n_{i,t-1} + \pi_6 ict_{i,t-1} + \pi_7 k_{i,t-1}$$
$$+ \eta_{it}(1 - \rho) + \lambda_{j(i),t} - \rho\lambda_{j(i),t-1} + w_{it}.$$

In the second step, the factor restrictions $\pi_1 = \rho$, $\pi_2 = \gamma_1$, $\pi_3 = \gamma_2$, $\pi_4 = \gamma_3$, $\pi_5 = -\gamma_1\gamma_2$, $\pi_6 = -\gamma_1\gamma_3$, and $\pi_7 = -\gamma_1\gamma_4$ can be tested and imposed by a minimum-distance estimator (see Appendix 3.7.2 for mathematical details).

Extension 2: Heterogeneous labour. Heterogeneity in the quality of labour can be important if, e.g., the use of ICT is most intensive in firms with a high share of high-skilled workers. Omitting this heterogeneity may lead to overstating the productivity of ICT capital. To account for this bias, I decompose a firm's workforce into employees who are high-skilled N_h (with university degree or equivalent), medium-skilled N_m (vocational training), and low-skilled N_l (no formal qualification) with $N_{it} = N_{l,it} + N_{m,it} + N_{h,it}$ representing the total number of employees. Letting ϑ_h and ϑ_m denote the productivity differential of high and medium skilled workers compared to low-skilled workers, effective labour input L_{it} is:

$$L_{it} = N_{l,it} + (1 + \vartheta_m) \cdot N_{m,it} + (1 + \vartheta_h) \cdot N_{h,it} \tag{3.11}$$
$$= N_{it} - N_{m,it} - N_{h,it} + (1 + \vartheta_m) \cdot N_{m,it} + (1 + \vartheta_h) \cdot N_{h,it}$$
$$= N_{it} + \vartheta_m \cdot N_{m,it} + \vartheta_h \cdot N_{h,it}$$
$$= N_{it} + \vartheta_m \cdot \frac{N_{m,it}}{N_{it}} N_{it} + \vartheta_h \cdot \frac{N_{h,it}}{N_{it}} N_{it}$$
$$= N_{it} \cdot [1 + \vartheta_m s_{m,it} + \vartheta_h s_{h,it}]$$

with $s_{m,it} = N_{m,it}/N_{it}$ and $s_{h,it} = N_{h,it}/N_{it}$ denoting the shares of medium- and high-skilled employees in total workforce of the firms.

The main assumption underlying this approach is that qualification raises the productivity of workers by a fixed proportion. An alternative specification could let the three skill-groups enter the production function as separate inputs with each having its own elasticity. This is equivalent to assuming that effective labour can be decomposed into $L = N_l^{\lambda_l} N_m^{\lambda_m} N_h^{\lambda_h}$. This approach, however, has two main drawbacks. First, from a theoretical point of view, it implies that each of the three labour inputs forms an essential input for production with $Y = 0$ if $N_l = 0 \lor N_m = 0 \lor N_h = 0$. This is a very restrictive assumption given that many firms (in particular small ones) produce output employing workers of only one or two of the skill groups. In contrast, specification (3.11) assumes that the existence of one worker (independently of his/her qualification) is sufficient such that $Y = 0$ if $N_l = 0 \land N_m = 0 \land N_h = 0$. Second, from an empirical point of view, firms that do not employ workers from each of the three skill-groups would have to be excluded in the alternative approach (since the specification is in logs). For the given sample, more than half of the 578 firms would have to be dropped. This would not only lead to a much lower precision of the estimates but can also entail a serious selection bias.[15]

With small values for ϑ_m, ϑ_h, $s_{m,it}$, and $s_{h,it}$, the term controlling for the skill structure can be simplified to:

$$\log L_{it} = \log N_{it} + \log\left(1 + \vartheta_m s_{m,it} + \vartheta_h s_{h,it}\right) \tag{3.12}$$
$$\approx n_{it} + \vartheta_m s_{m,it} + \vartheta_h s_{h,it}.$$

Inserting (3.12) into (3.9) then yields the model:

$$y_{it} = \gamma_1 n_{it} + \gamma_2 ict_{it} + \gamma_3 k_{it} + \beta_1 s_{m,it} + \beta_2 s_{h,it} + \eta_i + \lambda_{j(i),t} + \epsilon_{it}. \tag{3.9b}$$

with $\beta_1 = \gamma_1 \vartheta_m$, and $\beta_2 = \gamma_1 \vartheta_h$.

The inclusion of skill-shares in the production function estimations as in (3.9) is a very common way in the literature in order to control for heterogeneous labour quality.[16] However, anticipating some of the results and inserting mean shares for s_m and s_h, the implicit products $\beta_1 s_{m,it} \cong 0.110$ and $\beta_2 s_{h,it} \cong 0.549$ are quite high and make the approximation inaccurate. This measurement error is positively correlated with the skill measures and may induce a bias also in other regressors. Therefore, I additionally consider a more precise second-order Taylor approximation:

$$\log L_{it} = n_{it} + \log(1 + \vartheta_m s_m + \vartheta_h s_h) \tag{3.12a}$$
$$\approx n_{it} + \vartheta_m s_m + \vartheta_h s_h - 0.5 \cdot (\vartheta_m s_m + \vartheta_h s_h)^2$$
$$= n_{it} + \vartheta_m s_m + \vartheta_h s_h - 0.5 \cdot \vartheta_m^2 s_m^2$$
$$-0.5 \cdot \vartheta_h^2 s_h^2 - \vartheta_m \vartheta_h s_m s_h.$$

The model resulting from inserting (3.12a) into (3.9) is:

$$y_{it} = \gamma_1 n_{it} + \gamma_2 ict_{it} + \gamma_3 k_{it} \tag{3.9b'}$$
$$+\beta_1 s_{m,it} + \beta_2 s_{h,it} + \beta_{11} s_{m,it}^2 + \beta_{22} s_{h,it}^2$$
$$+\beta_{12} s_{m,it} s_{h,it} + \eta_i + \lambda_{j(i),t} + \epsilon_{it},$$

where the additional parameters correspond to $\beta_{11} = -\frac{1}{2}\vartheta_m^2$, $\beta_{22} = -\frac{1}{2}\vartheta_h^2$, and $\beta_{12} = -\vartheta_m^2 \vartheta_h^2$. Apart from relying on a more accurate approximation of labour quality, (3.9b') can also be used to explore the appropriateness of the underlying model for skills from (3.11) by testing the validity of the imposed common factor restrictions for $\beta_1, \beta_2, \beta_{11}, \beta_{22}$ and β_{12}.[17]

---

[15] Alternatively, a CES production function could be employed to allow for elasticities of substitution to be greater than one without imposing the condition of inputs to be essential. The panel estimation of such a function would go far beyond the empirical scope envisaged in this study, however.

[16] See, e.g., Lehr and Lichtenberg (1999), Caroli and van Reenen (2001), or Bresnahan et al. (2002).

[17] The calculations are analogue to the minimum-distance procedure described in detail in Appendix 3.7.2.

Extension 3: Flexible functional form. As it is well-known, the coefficients γ_j in equation (3.9) correspond to the elasticities of output with respect to inputs j. One disadvantage of the Cobb-Douglas production function, however, consists in the properties that the elasticities of the individual inputs are assumed to be constant and that the elasticity of substitution between the individual inputs is restricted to be one. A more flexible specification is the translog function (Christensen and Jorgenson, 1969) which allows both the output elasticities and the elasticities of substitution to vary. The translog extension of (3.9) is:

$$y_{it} = \gamma_1 l_{it} + \gamma_{11} l_{it}^2 + \gamma_2 ict_{it} + \gamma_{22} ict_{it}^2 + \gamma_3 k_{it} + \gamma_{33} k_{it}^2 \tag{3.9c}$$
$$+ \gamma_{12} l_{it} ict_{it} + \gamma_{13} l_{it} k_{it} + \gamma_{23} ict_{it} k_{it} + \eta_i + \lambda_{j(i),t} + \epsilon_{it}.$$

To keep the model tractable for the empirical analysis, I abstract from the skill level in this specification. The elasticity of output with respect to input j (α_j) depends on the levels of all inputs. For comparability to the Cobb-Douglas framework, these elasticities may be evaluated at the means of the corresponding logarithmic values (denoted by a bar). These implicit mean elasticities are then given by:

$$\bar{\alpha}_L = \partial y_{it}/\partial l_{it} = \gamma_1 + 2\gamma_{11}\overline{l_{it}} + \gamma_{12}\overline{ict_{it}} + \gamma_{13}\overline{k_{it}} \tag{3.15}$$
$$\bar{\alpha}_{ICT} = \partial y_{it}/\partial ict_{it} = \gamma_2 + 2\gamma_{22}\overline{ict_{it}} + \gamma_{12}\overline{l_{it}} + \gamma_{23}\overline{k_{it}} \tag{3.16}$$
$$\bar{\alpha}_K = \partial y_{it}/\partial k_{it} = \gamma_3 + 2\gamma_{33}\overline{k_{it}} + \gamma_{13}\overline{l_{it}} + \gamma_{23}\overline{ict_{it}}. \tag{3.17}$$

3.4 Data

To implement the production framework empirically, I employ data from the *Mannheim Innovation Panel in Services (MIP-S)* covering the period 1994 to 1999. This survey has been conducted by the Centre for European Economic Research (ZEW) on behalf of the German Federal Ministry for Education and Research. The data have been collected annually from more than 2,000 firms since 1994 in a representative survey of innovation activities in the German business-related service and distribution sector (Janz et al. 2001). It has an (unbalanced) panel structure in important key variables. Among various other items, the *MIP-S* contains annual data on sales, number of employees (full-time equivalents), skill structures, expenditures on gross investment and on ICT capital (including hardware, software, and telecommunication technology). Since similar information has been collected in various other existing data sets, too, I discuss in the following how information from external sources can be used to transform the survey data to variables applicable in a production function framework.

For output Y_{it}, two different measures could basically be used: sales or value added. If sales were used as an output indicator, intermediate goods should be included as an additional input in the production function. Unfortunately, the data set lacks information on the latter. Simply omitting intermediate goods, however, is an unsatisfactory solution. This proceeding may induce an omitted variable bias in the regressions since industries that operate rather at the end of the value chain (like wholesale and trade) resort more strongly to intermediate goods in quantitative terms than other industries do.

I therefore construct a measure of the second alternative, i.e. value added. For this purpose, I calculate the shares of real value added in nominal gross output at the NACE two-digit industry level.[18] I then multiply deflated firm-level sales with these industry-specific shares to obtain a proxy for firm-level value added. Formally, this corresponds to the following calculations. Let Z_{it} and Y_{it} be sales and value added of firm i in period t, and let $Z_{j(i),t}$ and $Y_{j(i),t}$ be sales and value added aggregated over all firms of the same industry $j(i)$ that firm i is operating in. Then the unknown value added of firm i is approximated by $Y_{it} \simeq Z_{it} \cdot Y_{j(i),t}/Z_{j(i),t}$.

For labour input, the number of employees in full-time equivalents is used. In order to construct stocks for ICT capital and conventional (non-ICT) capital from investment data, I compute investment on conventional capital as total investment expenditures minus ICT expenditures and use official producer price deflators for investment goods to deflate non-ICT investments. For ICT investments, official price statistics in Germany tend to understate real price declines (Hoffmann, 1998). Therefore, I apply harmonised ICT price indices for Germany calculated by Schreyer (2000). He takes official ICT price indices in the U.S., which are based on hedonic techniques, as a reference and assumes the differences between price changes for ICT and non-ICT capital goods to be the same across OECD countries.

Given the deflated investments for both types of capital, I apply the perpetual inventory method with constant, geometric depreciation to construct the capital stocks for ICT and non-ICT. Accordingly, the capital stock K_{kt} of type k in period t results from investment $I_{k,t-1}$ in the following way:

$$K_{kt} = (1 - \delta_k)K_{k,t-1} + I_{k,t-1}, \tag{3.18}$$

with $k = 1$ for conventional (non-ICT) and $k = 2$ for ICT capital and investment and δ_k denoting the depreciation rates of the capital stocks. For conventional capital, I calculate the depreciation rates δ_1 by industry as the shares of capital consumption in net fixed assets evaluated at replacement prices (time series 7719 and 7735 of the German Statistical Office). The unweighted mean over all service industries amounts to 9% with a maximum in NACE 72 (data processing) of 21% and a minimum in NACE 70 (real estate) with 2.2%. For ICT capital, I assume a rate of $\delta_2 = 0.30$. Relying on available data from the U.S. (Fraumeni, 1997; Moulton et al., 1999), depreciation rates are 31.2% for IT-hardware, 55.0% for prepackaged software, 33.0% for custom and own-account software and 15.0% for telecommunication capital. Using data by EITO (2001) for 1999, total ICT investment expenditures in Germany consist of 47.0% hardware, 26.9% software and 26.1% end-user and network telecommunication equipment. Taking these market

---

[18] I use time series 7711 and 7716 from the German Statistical Office.

shares as weights, I derive an average depreciation rate of ICT capital of $\delta_1 = 0.312 \cdot 0.47 + (0.55 + 0.33)/2 \cdot 0.269 + 0.15 \cdot 0.261 = 0.304$.

Since no information is available on the level of capital stocks, I construct initial capital stocks employing the method proposed by Hall and Mairesse (1995).[19] Under the assumption that investment expenditures on capital good k have grown at a similar, constant average rate g_k in the past in all firms, equation (3.18) can be rewritten for period $t = 1$ (1994) by backward substitution in the following way:[20]

$$K_{k1} = I_{k0} + (1 - \delta_k)I_{k,-1} + (1 - \delta_k)^2 I_{k,-2} + \ldots \qquad (3.19)$$

$$= \sum_{s=0}^{\infty} I_{k,-s}(1 - \delta_k)^s = I_{k0} \sum_{s=0}^{\infty} \left[\frac{1 - \delta_k}{1 + g_k} \right]^s$$

$$= \frac{I_{k1}}{g_k + \delta_k}.$$

In order to derive the initial capital stocks, assumptions about pre-period growth rates g_k of both types of investments must be made. For non-ICT investment expenditures, I assume an annual growth rate of approximately 5% ($g_1 = 0.05$).[21] Since there are no time series available for ICT investment in Germany, I refer to well-documented U.S. data as a rough guideline. Jorgenson and Stiroh (1995) calculate an average annual growth rate of 44.3% in real computer investment and of 20.2% for OCAM (office, computing, and accounting machinery) investment between 1958 and 1992 for the U.S. Since the share of computers in OCAM has been rising continuously — reaching 94% in 1992 —, I assume an annual pre-period growth rate close to the growth rate of computer investment of $g_2 = 0.4$ for ICT investment. The empirical part of this chapter also considers the sensitivity of the empirical results with respect to the parameters chosen for g and δ. Since there are time lags between the installation and the productive contribution of capital goods, I employ the capital stock at each period's *beginning* (or at the end of the corresponding previous period) as a measure of capital input.

In order to apply suitable econometric techniques, I consider only firms with consistent information on at least three consecutive periods. The resulting unbalanced reference sample ("full sample") consists of 1,177 firms with a total of 4,939 observations. The statistics of the sample are summarised

---

[19] Hall and Mairesse (1995) refer to R&D stocks for which methodological problems are very similar.

[20] In fact, the initial value of investment for firm i $I_{ik,1}$ is replaced by the average of the observed values of investment such that $I_{ik,1} \simeq \frac{1}{T} \sum_{t=1}^{T} I_{ik,t}$. With this "smoothing" I aim at correcting for cyclical effects which might affect investments in different initial years in the unbalanced panel. Sensitivity analyses show that the results are hardly affected if true initial investments instead of 'smoothed' ones are used.

[21] Calculations provided by Müller (1998) show that gross capital stock in German services has grown on average by 4.8% annually between 1980 and 1991.

in Table 3.8 in Appendix 3.7.3. The majority of firms in the reference sample are small and medium-sized firms with a median of 42 employees. About 10% of the sample consists of large firms with more than 500 employees. Tables 3.6 and 3.7 in the Appendix show that the sample reflects industry and size structure of the German business-related and distribution services fairly well.[22] Finally, the last two columns of Table 3.8 report the (cross-sectional) means and medians of the firms' (longitudinal) averages of capital and output intensity (capital per employee) for the sample. At the median firm, a workplace is equipped with ICT capital worth € 1,392, and with non-ICT capital worth about € 24,979. The median value added per employee is € 60,307.[23]

Estimating the first two extensions of equation (3.9a) and (3.9b) puts substantially more requirements on the data, which reduces the corresponding sample sizes remarkably. For estimating the dynamic specification (3.9a), there are only 708 firms with at least four subsequent observations. The data needs for estimating equation (3.9b) are even more restrictive. For 578 firms (denoted as 'small sample'), consistent data on the skill structure are available: the fraction of employees with vocational training (Berufs- or Fachschulabschluss) for medium-skilled, and the fraction of employees with a university degree including universities of applied sciences (Hochschul- or Fachhochschulabschluss) for high-skilled workers.[24] As indicated in Table 3.8, the structure of the small sample differs from the full sample. In particular, the average firm size (183 employees) is only about a third of the firm size in the full sample. Therefore, estimates based on the small sample will be used mainly to explore the effects of including human capital variables into the specification.

Some firms reported a zero share of ICT in total investment expenditures for all surveyed periods. With the econometric specification being in logarithms, these firms are excluded from the full sample. However, it seems more reasonable to assume that ICT investment in these firms is not zero but very low and rounded to zero by the respondents.[25] Excluding these firms might lead to overstating the real output contributions of ICT. For exploring this issue, I construct a further sample ('extended sample'). Here, I assume the ICT stock per worker in firms that reported zero ICT investment to be equal

---

[22] Exceptions are the undersampling of retail trade and the oversampling of transport, postal services, software and telecommunication. In terms of firm size, large firms are oversampled by their mere number (see Table 3.6 in the Appendix).

[23] The corresponding mean values are substantially higher than the median since some firms — in particular in the real estate sector — display very high values for both inputs as well as output per employee.

[24] In one question, firms were asked to report the total number of employees and in another question to report the number of employees by skill-groups. In various cases, the sum of the latter was not equal to the former. Some 15 firms, for which the reported total number of employees deviated more than 50% from the sum of the skill groups, were excluded from the sample.

[25] The definition of ICT investment in the survey is very broad, including expenditures for IT hardware, software, and telecommunication equipment.

to the corresponding industry minimum and impute the corresponding values. The statistics for the extended sample (see Table 3.8) indicate that the endowment of workplaces with ICT is slightly smaller, and the endowment with conventional capital slightly higher than in the full sample.

Independently of the specific sample used, the summary statistics indicate that the share of ICT capital in total capital stock is very low. Comparing the medians of ICT per worker and conventional capital per worker for the full sample (Table 3.8), ICT endowment amounts to 5.1% in total capital. Taking the corresponding means, the share is even lower (1.8%). Similarly, aggregating firms' time averages of both types of capital over all firms in the sample yields a share of aggregate ICT capital in total aggregate capital of 5% (not reported in the tables). These values are slightly higher than the share of 3% calculated by Schreyer (2000) using aggregate data for Germany in 1996 (including the less ICT-intensive manufacturing sector). As argued in Griliches (1994), the overall small shares of ICT input together with measurement errors make it difficult to distinguish output contributions of ICT from stochastic events and may make the identification of productivity effects of ICT resemble the search for the "needle in the haystack". In the empirical application, controlling for measurement errors will therefore be an important issue.

3.5 Empirical results

This section discusses several econometric issues that need to be addressed for estimating equation (3.9) consistently. The best suited system GMM estimator will then be applied to explore the three extensions (3.9a-c). Apart from the constant and the input variables, the empirical specification includes a regional dummy for East German firms and 6 year dummies interacted with 7 industries. Table 3.6 summarises the underlying classification of industries. Since there is no output data available for banking and insurance (only the balance sheet total and insurance premiums are available), these industries are excluded from the analysis. All regressions are computed using the DPD98 programme developed by Arellano and Bond (1998) running in GAUSS. All reported standard errors are heteroscedasticity-consistent.

3.5.1 Reference framework

The reference production function (3.9) is estimated first in a simple pooled OLS regression (see first column of Table 3.1). From an econometric point of view, a pooled regression corresponds to a simple cross-section regression except that a larger number of observations can be obtained from the inclusion of several years. The coefficients of all three inputs are significantly different from zero at the 1% level. While the output elasticity with respect to labour

Table 3.1. Results for the ICT-augmented production function

dependent variable: log(value added)

inputs	(1) OLS pooled	(2) OLS 1st diff.	(3) GMM[-1] 1st diff.	(4) GMM[-2] 1st diff.	(5) SYS-GMM reference	(6) SYS-GMM not interact.	(7) SYS-GMM extended
log(labour)	0.607***	0.598***	0.555***	0.282*	0.699***	0.717***	0.686***
	(0.020)	(0.075)	(0.087)	(0.154)	(0.056)	(0.056)	(0.058)
log(ICT)	0.244***	-0.025	0.024	0.032	0.060*	0.022	0.049*
	(0.020)	(0.017)	(0.026)	(0.041)	(0.034)	(0.034)	(0.026)
log(non-ICT)	0.149***	-0.035	0.140	0.310**	0.201***	0.213***	0.189***
	(0.015)	(0.052)	(0.119)	(0.157)	(0.036)	(0.037)	(0.036)
East-German	-0.127***				-0.386***	-0.402***	-0.384***
	(0.043)				(0.045)	(0.047)	(0.045)
observations	4939	3762	3762	3762	4939	4939	5107
firms	1177	1177	1177	1177	1177	1177	1222
R^2	0.844	0.236	0.218	0.137	0.843	0.839	0.836
WALD STAT. [DF]:							
inputs	24160[4]	65.1[3]	52.2[3]	17.3[3]	560[4]	561[4]	609[4]
time & ind. dummies	702[41]	133[35]	149[35]	113[35]	651[41]	550[11]	685[41]
SARGAN ⟨P-VALUES⟩:			0.187	0.248	0.258	0.119	0.193
ERRORS ⟨P-VALUES⟩:							
AR(1)	0.000	0.005	0.007	0.006	0.004	0.004	0.003
AR(2)	0.000	0.131	0.135	0.085	0.049	0.042	0.039

*, **, and *** denote significance at the 10%, 5% and 1% level. Heteroscedasticity-consistent standard errors reported in parentheses. All regressions contain a constant and industry interacted dummies for 6 years (1994-99) and 7 industries (no interaction only in regression 6). GMM[-1] and GMM[-2] refer to estimations using all lagged levels of explanatory variables $t - s$ with lag $s \geq 1$ and ≥ 2 correspondingly. See text and Appendix 3.7.1 for details. For the one-step results from the GMM and SYS-GMM specifications, see Table 3.9 in Appendix 3.7.3.

amounts to some reasonable 61%,[26] the ICT coefficient (24.4%) clearly exceeds the coefficient of conventional capital (14.9%) even though ICT forms only a small part of the total capital stock. Similarly high ICT elasticities have been found in cross section regressions for Germany by Bertschek and Kaiser (2004) and Licht and Moch (1999).

The high elasticity of ICT capital found in pooled or cross section OLS regressions raises serious doubts about the correctness of the applied estimation specification. Given the average share of ICT capital in value added of 6.2%, the results imply a gross rate of return to ICT investment of nearly 400%. These marginal returns to ICT (MPI) are calculated as the product of the output elasticity of ICT and the inverse ratio of ICT capital in output: $MPI_{it} = \partial Y_{it}/\partial ICT_{it} = \gamma_2 \cdot Y_{it}/ICT_{it}$. Assuming user costs of ICT of around 42% as suggested by Jorgenson and Stiroh (1995), the implied net returns still amount to more than 300%. For conventional capital, for which the share in value added is 258%, the results imply gross returns of only 5.8% which are close to its generally assumed user costs.

The large excess returns to ICT can hardly be explained by higher user and adjustment costs of ICT capital alone which may be 'hidden' behind ICT investment. Rather, the results may be biased due to three main sources: firm effects, simultaneity issues, and omitted variables (e.g., skills). While the latter aspect is treated in extension (3.9b), the first two involve econometric issues and are discussed for the reference specification (3.9). Exploring these issues, I will also discuss the impacts of measurement errors and the sensitivity of the results with respect to varying parameterisations in the construction of the ICT capital stocks.

Unobserved firm characteristics ('firm effects') may bias the results if investment strategies of highly productive firms are systematically different from their less productive competitors within the same industry.[27] Highly productive firms with a skilled and flexible management are likely to be both more productive and more prone to invest in new technologies than other firms. This would induce an upward bias in the ICT coefficient. The highly significant autocorrelation in the errors of both first- and second-order in the pooled regression further supports this conjecture.

---

[26] Under the assumption of constant returns to scale and perfect competition, the income share of labour in an economy should equal its labour coefficient in the production function. For Germany, the average share of labour payments in national income between 1994 and 1999 amounted to 72.4% (Statistisches Bundesamt, 2001).

[27] Productivity differences between different industries are captured by the industry dummies.

Table 3.1 reports the results of the estimation in first differences.[28] The figures indicate that once unobserved heterogeneity is controlled for, the output contributions of both types of capital are no longer significantly different from zero whereas the labour coefficient remains virtually unchanged. Obviously, the high coefficients of both types of capital in the pooled regression accrue from unobserved heterogeneity. This finding coincides with very similar findings by Brynjolfsson and Hitt (1995) and Black and Lynch (2001). Moreover, the autocorrelation in the disturbance terms found in the pooled specification has vanished and was obviously due to the firm effects.[29]

The implausibly low estimates of the capital coefficients in first differences may be caused by measurement errors as a second source of bias. Measurement errors are likely to be substantial in both types of capital stock since both the depreciation and the pre-sample growth rates are assumed to be equal across firms. Deviations from this assumption will add noise — though presumably not a systematic one — in the construction of the firms' capital stocks. As pointed out by Griliches and Hausman (1986), measurement errors may induce a downward bias in the OLS estimates.

However, this distortion may be offset by a simultaneity bias. If firms determine input and output simultaneously, exogenous shocks — like demand shifts, for example — result in an increase of both input and output for the profit-maximising firm.[30] In econometric terms, the disturbance term ϵ_{it} will be positively correlated with the input variables in equation (3.9) causing an upward bias in the input coefficients. However, the simultaneity bias may apply in particular to factors that can be adjusted easily in the short term. This is not so much the case for capital stocks. Moreover, in the construction of the data capital stocks at the *beginning* of the corresponding years have been used. Therefore, the (upwards) simultaneity bias is expected to be rather small for the two capital coefficients.

In order to analyse the distortions due to measurement errors and simultaneity, I apply GMM estimates with internal instruments to the production function in first differences. This approach exploits the panel structure of the data by instrumenting inputs in first differences with their level values in the past (see Appendix 3.7.1). More specifically, the third specification of Table 3.1 uses the (log) levels of lagged inputs $x_{t-1}, x_{t-2}, ..., x_1$ as instruments for the inputs in differences $\Delta x_t = x_t - x_{t-1}$ (GMM[-1]), with x denoting inputs

---

[28] This means that the firms' corresponding fixed effects are eliminated by explaining output growth by the growth rates of the inputs. The results from the alternative within estimation where deviations from means are used (not reported) are very similar.

[29] Note that the observed first-order correlation of the errors is induced by the data transformation. If the errors ϵ_{it} are i.i.d. with variance σ^2 their corresponding first differences will be AR(1): $E(\Delta\epsilon_{it} \cdot \Delta\epsilon_{i,t-1}) = E((\epsilon_{it} - \epsilon_{i,t-1})(\epsilon_{i,t-1} - \epsilon_{i,t-2})) = -\sigma^2$. Therefore, the relevant test for equations in first differences is whether the corresponding errors are AR(2) or not.

[30] See Griliches and Mairesse (1998).

L, ICT, and K. Including x_{t-1} as an instrument is based on the assumption that taking capital stocks at the beginning of each period ensures that the inputs are predetermined, i.e. uncorrelated with the contemporaneous shock ϵ_{it} since $E(x_{t-1}\Delta\epsilon_t) = 0 \Leftrightarrow E(x_{t-1}\epsilon_t) - E(x_{t-1}\epsilon_{t-1}) = 0$. The validity of this assumption can be tested (see footnote 32). In column 4 of Table 3.1 (as in the subsequent specifications), the instruments x_{t-1} are dropped to allow for simultaneity of capital stocks at the beginning of each period t and shocks arising in t (GMM[-2]).

The corresponding results from the two-step estimation[31] show that in both specifications the point estimates for the capital coefficients increase whereas labour elasticity decreases. This tendency is much more pronounced in the GMM[-2] specification where the coefficient of conventional capital rises to 0.310 and the labour coefficient drops to a (quite low) value of 0.285.[32] However, the capital coefficients remain insignificant from zero in both these specifications when the one-step results are considered (see Table 3.9 in Appendix 3.7.3). Summarising the results, these findings indicate that the measurement error bias in the capital coefficients clearly exceeds the counteracting simultaneity bias.[33] In contrast, for the case of labour input the simultaneity bias exceeds the bias due to measurement-error as expected. For both specifications, the Sargan test[34] does not reject the validity of the instruments. Finally, as in the specification with OLS in first differences, no autocorrelation of the error term is detected.

One reason for obtaining insignificant capital coefficients from the GMM regressions may be the small power of the instruments. Since a firm's capital stock is highly persistent over time, the correlation of the first differences with the second lag in levels is close to zero.[35] Blundell and Bond (1998)

---

[31] The one-step results are reported in Table 3.9 in Appendix 3.7.3. Even though the two-step estimates reported in the main part are more efficient, their standard errors are less appropriate for tests of significance. As pointed out by Blundell and Bond (1998) on the basis of Monte Carlo simulations, "[i]nference based on one-step GMM estimators appears to be much more reliable when either non-normality or heteroscedasticity is suspected" (p. 142).

[32] The results from a Sargan difference test (see Appendix 3.7.1) suggest that the additional moments employed in the GMM[-1] compared to the GMM[-2] specification ($E(x_{t-1}\Delta\epsilon_t)=0$) cannot be rejected (p=0.186).

[33] These findings coincide with similar results in Black and Lynch (2001) for estimates of the production function with one type of capital only.

[34] See Appendix 3.7.1 for technical details.

[35] Formally, this can be illustrated by assuming K_{it} being AR(1): $K_{it} = \rho K_{i,t-1} + r_{it}$ with $r_{it} \sim i.i.d$ and $E(r_{it}) = 0$. If K_{it} is weakly autocorrelated ($|\rho| \ll 1$ and $\rho \neq 0$), past levels are correlated with contemporaneous levels. For the first available instrument $K_{i,t-2}$, this is: $E(\Delta K_{it} \cdot K_{i,t-2}) = E((K_{it} - K_{i,t-1}) \cdot K_{i,t-2}) = E(K_{it} \cdot K_{i,t-2}) - E(K_{i,t-1} \cdot K_{i,t-2}) = \rho^2 - \rho$. If the evolution of K_{it} resembles a random walk ($\rho \approx 1$), the correlation between the variable in differences and its past values in levels will disappear ($\rho^2 - \rho \approx 0$) and the instruments will therefore turn out to be weak.

show that this may induce finite-sample biases of the GMM estimator in first differences. Based on an application to production function estimation, Blundell and Bond (2000) argue that in the specification in first differences, the weak instruments will bias the GMM estimates in the direction of the within group estimation, that is towards zero. They suggest using a system GMM (SYS-GMM) estimator proposed by Arellano and Bover (1995). In this estimation strategy, the equation in differences is instrumented by suitably lagged differences (like in the simple GMM estimation) and the equation in levels is instrumented by suitably lagged differences in addition. These two specifications are then estimated simultaneously.

The main virtue of the SYS-GMM approach consists in the fact that — unlike within or first-difference approaches — it does use the estimation in levels for estimation and thus exploits not only the variation in data over time but also between firms. It thus allows to preserve more information to identify the parameters of interest. Arellano and Bover (1995) show on the basis of Monte-Carlo simulations that this additional information results indeed in a substantial gain in the precision of the estimations. Moreover, they set out that a sufficient additional condition (compared to the GMM estimator) for the validity of the SYS-GMM estimator is to assume that the correlations between unobserved fixed effects and the explanatory variables are constant over time. In the case considered here, this means that for example the particular propensity of 'good management' for new technologies does not change considerably over the time period of 5 years. This assumption does not seem daring, but it can (and will) also be tested empirically nevertheless. Moreover, it is noteworthy to emphasise that the additional assumptions for the SYS-GMM estimator do not affect the assumption of predeterminedness of the inputs. As a consequence, the SYS-GMM allows to control for simultaneity of input and output decisions in the same way as the GMM estimator does. For a more extensive overview of the technical details involved in the GMM and SYS-GMM approach, see Appendix 3.7.1.

Specification 5 of Table 3.1 adds the production function equation in levels (with lagged differences of period $t-1$ as instruments) to the GMM[-2] specification. Like conventional capital and labour, the coefficient of ICT capital turns out to be positive and highly significant ($p = 0.014$ in the one-step estimation).[36] Several features support the appropriateness of this econometric specification. The output elasticity of labour amounts to about 70% which is consistent with aggregate statistics (see footnote 26). The coefficients of ICT and non-ICT capital are 6% and 20%, respectively, and the null hypothesis of constant returns to scale cannot be rejected at the 1% level (not reported).[37]

A further robust result is that East-German firms in services are significantly less productive than their West-German counterparts. The coefficient of the dummy variable designating firms located in East Germany (-0.386)

---

[36] The less reliable p-value in the two-step estimation amounts to 0.078.

[37] This result holds for both the one-step and the two-step estimation results.

implies that multi-factor productivity in East-German firms is only about two-thirds of the West-German level. This finding coincides fairly well with aggregate statistics on productivity differentials in Germany.[38]

While the test for serial correlation of the errors is at the border of significance ($p = 0.049$), the Sargan statistic ($p = 0.258$) does not reject the validity of the instruments at the usual significance levels. Moreover, the difference Sargan statistic (44.3[12]) does not reject the validity of the additional instruments obtained from the equation in levels (p=0.299). The background of this test is summarised in Appendix 3.7.1.

Since these results stem from the preferred specification of this study, a glance at the implied rates of return appears worthwhile. Given an average share of ICT capital in output of 6.2% for the firms in the sample, the results imply that one Euro invested in ICT capital yields returns of €1.96. In contrast, the results for non-ICT capital imply that one Euro invested yields a much smaller return of €1.078.

The high returns to ICT found corroborate very similar findings in various related studies.[39] Assuming again user costs of ICT of around 42%, the remaining excess returns to ICT of 54% may well be due to complementary investment like training of the workforce, innovation efforts or costs due to the re-structuring of organisational forms which are not accounted for as inputs in the framework employed here.

In order to further investigate the sources of biases in estimating the productivity of ICT, the effect of ignoring business cycles and mismeasured output prices is analysed. To isolate the role of including interacted time and industry dummies, the SYS-GMM approach is estimated with simple (not-interacted) time and industry dummies. Specification 6 of Table 3.1 shows that the ICT coefficient is indeed affected by this change. The point estimate decreases to roughly 2.2% and is only marginally significant.[40] In contrast, the other coefficients do not exhibit any remarkable changes compared to the preferred specification. Moreover, a Wald test of significance of the 30 additional interaction dummies included in specification (5) clearly rejects the null hypothesis of no joint significance.[41] These results suggest that controlling for industry-specific effects is indeed important in order to assess the contributions of ICT correctly.

In the last column of Table 3.1, results for the SYS-GMM estimation *with* interacted dummies are replicated, but now for the extended sample in which also those firms are included that reported zero ICT investment for all the periods surveyed. As described in section 3.4, this sample is extended by 46 firms

---

[38] For an empirical assessment of the productivity differentials between East and West Germany and explanations for the slow speed of convergence, see Smolny (2003).

[39] See, e.g., Brynjolfsson and Hitt (2000).

[40] The results from the one-step estimation (see Table 3.9) yield a significance level of p=0.099.

[41] The χ^2-test statistic is 189.9 with 30 degrees of freedom.

Table 3.2. Sensitivity analyses with varying parameters for capital stocks

	varying parametrisation of δ_{ICT} (with $g_{ICT} = 0.4$)						
	0.05	0.1	0.2	**0.3**	0.4	0.5	1.0
est. coeff. of log(ICT)	0.074**	0.072**	0.067**	**0.060****	0.052**	0.046**	0.007**
mean of log(ICT)	-1.617	-1.736	-1.947	-2.131	-2.297	-2.451	-3.596

	varying parametrisation of g_{ICT} (with $\delta_{ICT} = 0.3$)					
	0.1	0.3	**0.4**	0.5	0.7	0.9
est. coeff. of log(ICT)	0.106***	0.070**	**0.060****	0.052**	0.041**	0.033**
mean of log(ICT)	-1.825	-2.052	-2.131	-2.197	-2.303	-2.385

Notes: ICT denotes ICT capital stock measured in € million. Estimated coefficients (est. coeff.) are obtained from the reference specification employed in the regressions (Table 3.1, column 5). δ_{ICT} denotes the annual depreciation rate assumed for ICT capital, g_{ICT} the assumed growth rate of ICT investments in the pre-1994 periods (see also equation 3.19). The parameter values of $\delta_{ICT} = 0.3$ and $g_{ICT} = 0.4$ (bold letters) correspond to the preferred parametrisation used in the regressions reported in the other tables of the book.
** and *** denote significance at the 5% and 1% level.

that have reported zero ICT investment for all years observed, imputing the industry minimum in terms of ICT per worker. The inclusion of these firms slightly lowers the point estimate for ICT (4.9%) as compared to the values reported for the reference sample. Moreover, the ICT coefficient is significantly positive only in the two-step estimation.[42] These results appear quite reasonable if one considers that firms may differ in their output elasticities. Those firms with a lower output elasticity of ICT will be maximising profits with a lower share of ICT capital in output; excluding these firms might overstate the ICT coefficient.

A last exploration based on the reference model (3.9) concerns the sensitivity of the results with respect to the way in which capital stocks are constructed. As is obvious from equation (3.18) and (3.19) on page 69, both the level and the evolution of the capital stocks of the firms depend on the parametrisation used for annual depreciation δ and pre-period growth rates of investment g. Exploring the sensitivity of the econometric results with respect to the parameters assumed for the construction of ICT capital stocks, I subject the reference regression underlying specification 5 of Table 3.1 to two kinds of robustness checks. In the first, I calculate alternative ICT capital stocks using different values for depreciation rates δ_{ICT} while holding the assumed growth rate g_{ICT} constant. In the second I do the reverse, holding δ_{ICT} constant while varying g_{ICT}.

---

[42] The one-step estimates imply a p-value for the ICT coefficient of 0.107.

The estimates for the elasticity of ICT capital for these variations are reported in Table 3.2. Most strikingly, the qualitative result of significant productivity contributions of ICT is robust to both kinds of variations. Unsurprisingly, however, the point estimate of the elasticity decreases in both parameters. For the extreme case of a complete depreciation of ICT capital within one year ($\delta_{ICT} = 100\%$) the point estimate is very small. This finding shows that employing investments instead of capital stocks is an unreliable proxy for assessing the productivity contributions. Moreover, lowering the assumed depreciation of ICT from an annual rate of 30% to 20% increases the estimated elasticity of ICT only modestly from 0.060 to 0.067. The effects of a similar variation of g_{ICT} are only slightly higher. The message from this exercise is thus that the empirical results reported in Table 3.1 do not depend critically on assuming certain values for δ_{ICT} and g_{ICT}.

3.5.2 Extensions

This subsection reports further evidence for the variations of model equation (3.9) discussed in the theoretical part.

Extension 1: Serially correlated residuals. In Table 3.3, the estimated elasticities for the dynamic extension of equation (3.9a) are reported. Since the employed sample differs from the one used in the previous regressions,[43] also the results for the static model are displayed in the first row. Comparing the two-step results from column 2 to the analogue specification for the full sample (column 5 of Table 3.1) shows that the change in the sample impacts the results only very little.

As indicated in the theoretical section and described in detail in Appendix 3.7.2, the results for the dynamic specification reported in columns 3 and 4 are obtained from first estimating the reduced-form model and then imposing the common factor restrictions.[44] The reduced-form estimates are summarised in Table 3.10 in Appendix 3.7.3. Unlike in the results for the previous regressions, Table 3.3 reports both the results for the one-step and the two-step SYS-GMM results because the point estimates from the minimum distance procedure depend on both the point estimates and the variances of the reduced-form estimates. For the reduced-form model, variances from the one-step SYS-GMM results are preferred whereas the point estimates from the two-step findings are more efficient.

A common finding from both the one- and the two-step specifications is that there is strong evidence for serial correlation in the residuals with ρ

---

[43] In the dynamic specification, also the coefficients of the once lagged inputs as well as the lagged dependent variable are included. The lagged difference of these variables (e.g. Δict_{t-1}) is then instrumented by the levels lagged 3 periods ($ict_{i,t-3}$). Thus, in this specification only firms can be included for which at least four subsequent periods ($t, t-1, t-2, t-3$) are available.

[44] The corresponding programme code written in GAUSS is available upon request from the author.

Table 3.3. Structural coefficients for the static and dynamic specification

	dependent variable: log(value added)			
	(1) static[a] (one-step)	(2) static[a] (two-step)	(3) dynamic[b] (one-step)	(4) dynamic[b] (two-step)
AR(1) of error			0.774*** (0.112)	0.771*** (0.066)
log(labour$_t$)	0.768*** (0.099)	0.722*** (0.079)	0.464*** (0.153)	0.487*** (0.112)
log(ICT$_t$)	0.090** (0.042)	0.057* (0.030)	0.158 (0.122)	0.074 (0.070)
log(non-ICT$_t$)	0.109*** (0.069)	0.166*** (0.051)	0.320** (0.138)	0.216*** (0.088)
Minimised distance[df]			3.923[3]	8.778[3]
Common factor restr. (p-values)			0.270	0.032

*, **, and *** denote significance at the 10%, 5% and 1% level. Results are SYS-GMM estimates (see Appendix 3.7.1) with heteroscedasticity-consistent standard errors reported in parentheses.
[a] The static model corresponds to the specification underlying column 5 in Table 3.1 for the full sample except for sample differences. [b] The results for the dynamic specification are obtained from applying a minimum distance procedure to the estimated coefficients reported in Table 3.10 in Appendix 3.7.3. The test of the validity of the common factor restrictions is based on the value of the minimised distance function (see Appendix 3.7.2). The underlying sample for all results consists of 3,532 observations for 708 firms.

being roughly 0.77. Similarly, the estimates of labour elasticity are considerably lower than for the static model. The estimates of the capital coefficients, however, differ substantially between one- and two-step estimates with the one-step results being remarkably higher.[45] In contrast, the two-step results for the capital coefficients are not too far from the values obtained for the static model. Both capital coefficients are estimated more imprecisely for the dynamic model, however, with the ICT coefficient not being significantly different from zero.

The test of validity of the imposed common factor restrictions are rejected for the two-step estimates but not for the one-step estimates. This difference in the test statistics may be a direct consequence of the estimated standard errors of the reduced-form parameters which tend to be biased towards zero in

---

[45] In the dynamic one-step estimation, the sum of the two capital coefficients (roughly 0.48) as well as the labour coefficient correspond fairly well to comparable results by Blundell and Bond (2000) who report estimates of 0.49 for total capital and 0.48 for labour input for U.S. manufacturing firms during 1982-89.

the two-step estimation. Since the test for the validity of the factor restrictions depends on these standard errors, this test is not too informative about the question whether the one-step point estimates are more reliable than the two-step results.

To sum up the evidence from the dynamic model, accounting for serial correlation yields ambiguous results compared to the static specification. On the one hand, the point estimates are higher in the dynamic model. On the other hand, the coefficients are estimated much less precisely and fail to reach statistical significance.

Extension 2: Heterogeneous labour. A further issue in estimating the productivity of ICT is the potential bias owing to omitted variables that may be complementary to the firms' use of ICT. In particular, recent studies have found that differences in the skills of the workforce are important (Bresnahan et al., 2002). Ignoring differences in workers' skills might lead to overstating the true impacts of ICT on production. However, there are also reasons to believe that this bias might be negligible. A firm's 'skill-mix' tends to be persistent over time. Thus its effect may not be distinguishable from other quasi-fixed factors, which are controlled for as unobserved heterogeneity between firms. In this case, no distortions are expected.

In order to assess the role of omitting differences in workers' skills, the model is extended by including educational level of workers as summarised in equations (3.9b) and (3.9b'). The first specification of Table 3.4 applies the SYS-GMM reference estimation strategy (column 5 in Table 3.1) to the resulting small sample. Compared to the full sample, the estimated coefficient of labour (0.758) is slightly higher whereas both capital coefficients are substantially smaller.[46] A possible reason for these changes is that average firm size as well as average endowment of workplaces with ICT capital are notably lower in the small sample.[47] Moreover, the loss of precision of the estimates may be due to the reduced sample size.

The second specification of Table 3.4 includes the shares of the employees with high and medium skills (represented by '% university' and '% vocational') which are treated as exogenous. Both the share of employees with university degree and the share of workers with vocational training are highly significant and positive.[48] As the comparison to the first column reveals, including the

---

[46] Moreover, only the non-ICT coefficient is significantly different from zero in the one-step estimation. Note that values reported in parentheses of Table 3.4 are — unlike in the previous tables — the t-values from the one-step estimates. This presentation substitutes for further tables with one-step results in the Appendix.

[47] See last columns of Tables 3.8 in Appendix 3.7.3.

[48] The implicit values for the productivity differentials for medium- and high-skilled workers are $\vartheta_m = \beta_m/\gamma_1 = 0.419/0.726 = 0.577$ and $\vartheta_h = \beta_h/\gamma_1 = 0.970$. With competitive salaries in the labour market, these values should roughly correspond to the wage spread over the corresponding skill levels. For the service sector, Kaiser (2000) calculates wage premiums of $\vartheta_m^w = 0.325$ for medium-skilled workers and of $\vartheta_h^w = 1.025$ for high-skilled workers. This comparison indicates

Table 3.4. The effects of heterogeneous labour

inputs	(1)	(2)	(3)	(4)	(5)
	dependent variable: log(value added)				
log(labour)	0.758***	0.726***	0.758***	0.680***	0.565***
	(4.601)	(4.872)	(6.375)	(4.633)	(3.841)
log(ICT capital)	0.016	0.027	0.006	0.017	-0.098
	(0.362)	(0.380)	(0.589)	(0.168)	(-0.969)
log(non-ICT capital)	0.146*	0.150	0.147*	0.181	0.110**
	(1.855)	(1.386)	(1.677)	(1.242)	(2.189)
%university		0.704***	-0.190	1.581	1.752***
		(2.626)	(-0.947)	(1.576)	(2.878)
%vocational		0.419**	0.099	1.373***	0.676*
		(2.534)	(-0.231)	(3.661)	(1.802)
$(\%\text{university})^2$				-0.913	
				(-1.200)	
$(\%\text{vocational})^2$				-0.923***	
				(-3.202)	
%univ. × %voc.				-0.873	
				(-1.281)	
log(ICT) × %univ.					0.557**
					(2.026)
log(ICT) × %voc.					0.140
					(1.524)
observations	1847	1847	1847	1847	1847
number of firms	578	578	578	578	578
R^2	0.821	0.826	0.814	0.826	0.814
WALD STATISTICS[DF]:					
inputs	142[3]	173[5]	339[6]	294[8]	210[7]
time & ind. dummies	335[34]	341[34]	419[34]	326[34]	353[34]
SARGAN (P-VALUES)	0.677	0.794	0.385	0.772	0.806
RESIDUALS (P-VALUES):					
AR(1)	0.014	0.020	0.002	0.008	0.043
AR(2)	0.183	0.084	0.097	0.061	0.198

*,**, and *** denote significance at the 10%, 5% and 1% level.
Results are two-step SYS-GMM estimates as detailed in Appendix 3.7.1 with t-values reported in parentheses obtained from heteroscedasticity-consistent first-step estimation results (see comments in text and footnote 31, p. 76, in particular.). The signs of coefficients and t-values may therefore vary in some cases. Specifications include a constant, a regional dummy for East-German firms as well as interacted time and industry dummies as further regressors. Labour and capital inputs are instrumented by past values as described in the text, while % vocational and % university are treated as exogenous except in specification 3 where also past values are used as instruments.

that the approximation in equation 3.12 may lead to an overestimation of the corresponding coefficient for medium-skilled employees. Alternatively, firms may pay less than competitive wage premiums to skills.

human capital variables slightly reduces the coefficients of labour but leaves the coefficient of non-ICT capital broadly unaffected.[49] The elasticity of ICT increases slightly from 0.016 to 0.027 even though in the one-step estimates both the coefficient and its standard error remain virtually unchanged.

Further regressions reported in Table 3.11 show that including skill groups as separate inputs (instead of adding skill shares) does not yield very different results. For a sample of 222 firms with a non-zero number of employees for all three skill groups, both ways of considering heterogeneity of labour quality yield very similar but insignificant ICT coefficients of slightly more than 0.05 which are slightly higher than in the specification without controlling for skill structure of the employees.

Treating the skill composition as exogenous may be justified if productivity shocks impact the *quantity* of labour but not its composition by skills and if, moreover, the skill composition is not affected by firm effects. However, these assumptions may be violated and may also impact the estimates for ICT capital. Specification (3) of Table 3.4 is the same as in column (2) except that the skill variables are now treated as endogenous by using their past values as instruments in an analogue manner to the other inputs. The skill coefficients are estimated very imprecisely with the coefficient for high-skilled workers becoming even (insignificantly) negative.[50] Independently of the way of instrumenting skills, the coefficients of the other inputs remain broadly unaffected.

A further issue consists in the fact that the approximation of equation (3.12) is very imprecise. Specification 4 reports additional results for the more accurate model (3.9b'), with skills being instrumented by themselves again. The (insignificant) ICT coefficient is very close to the one obtained for the specification without controlling for labour heterogeneity while the coefficient of labour is notably lower and the one for non-ICT capital higher than in column 1. Again, there is no indication from the results that the omission of labour quality may exert any important bias on the estimated coefficient of ICT capital. A test of the validity of the common factor restrictions for the skill coefficients from equation (3.12a) does not reject the model at the 5% level (p-value 0.074).

Instrumenting skill shares and their interactions as in specification (3) yields even higher p-values for the test of the imposed common factor restric-

---

[49] Lehr and Lichtenberg (1999) report similar qualitative results.

[50] It is extremely difficult to trace the sources of these counterintuitive results. Finite sample biases due to poor instruments are unlikely to be the reason since further explorations show that the power of the instruments for the skill shares is even slightly higher than for the capital variables. There is neither evidence for outliers to be driving the results. Excluding firms with exceptionally high changes in the skill shares as potential outliers have no noteworthy effects on the results. Instrumenting present skill shares with lagged shares, however, yields results that are very similar to treating skill shares as exogenous.

tions. However, the structural parameters obtained from a minimum distance procedure imply implausibly high values for coefficients ϑ_m and ϑ_h.[51]

In order to obtain more evidence on the link between skills and ICT, specifications (4) and (5) additionally consider interaction terms between ICT and the skills variables. The interaction between ICT and human capital is significant, which indicates the productivity of ICT is increasing with the share of highly educated employees. The coefficient of ICT capital alone becomes even negative, which implies that in order to make productive use of ICT, skilled workers are even an essential prerequisite.[52]

In sum, there is no evidence that omitted heterogeneity in labour quality leads to an overestimation of the *average* productivity impacts of ICT. This may be due to the fact that the share of high-skilled workers tends to be highly persistent over time. Human capital might thus be treated as a firm's quasi-fixed asset that is controlled for by first differencing. However, the findings suggest that ICT must be complemented by highly educated employees in order to result in positive productivity effects — a result that is in line with similar findings in Bresnahan et al. (2002).

Extension 3: Flexible functional form. A final issue concerns the functional form of the production technology. In particular, the Cobb-Douglas specification may be too restrictive if scale effects and complementarities between the inputs affect the results. To assess this question, both the simplest (pooled OLS) and the best suited (SYS-GMM) estimations are applied to the translog production function of equation (3.9c). Unfortunately, the scope for empirical investigation of these issues is limited by data constraints. In particular, the data basis is too small to obtain meaningful estimates for a human-capital augmented translog function.[53]

The results and implicit average elasticities for equation (3.15-3.17) are reported in Table (3.5). Like in the Cobb-Douglas estimations, pooled OLS

---

[51] The corresponding coefficients are: $\vartheta_m = 1.413\,(0.155)$ and $\vartheta_h = 1.201\,(0.181)$ with standard errors in parentheses. A peculiarity of these results is that the coefficient for medium skills is higher than the one for high skills. A closer look at the results of Table 3.4 shows that this is mainly due to the very small precision of the estimates for high skills combined with a low absolute value for the interaction term %university × %vocational. Jointly, these two results push the structural parameter ϑ_h towards zero in the minimum distance approach.

[52] With skills being instrumented, the interaction of ICT and skills is positive, too, but smaller in both economic and statistical significance. The estimates of the direct productivity contributions of skills, however, are very low, which points to the same problems in the specification as discussed for the corresponding specification 3 without interaction.

[53] Including human capital into the translog specification would require to treat each skill group as a separate input in the production function. For this case, all the problems discussed in section 3.3.3 apply. Moreover, the number of regressors rises exponentially with the number of inputs considered in the translog function, which leads to a further decrease in the degrees of freedom of the regressions.

Table 3.5. Results for the translog production function

inputs (log)	dependent variable: log(value added)		
	OLS full	SYS-GMM full	SYS-GMM extended
labour	1.100***	1.178***	1.077***
	(0.104)	(0.137)	(0.144)
ICT capital	0.050	-0.045	0.006
	(0.068)	(0.085)	(0.070)
non-ICT capital	0.065	0.156***	0.169***
	(0.048)	(0.055)	(0.059)
labour²	-0.040***	-0.049***	-0.045***
	(0.011)	(0.013)	(0.015)
ICT capital²	0.006	0.001	0.008***
	(0.005)	(0.006)	(0.003)
non-ICT capital²	0.031***	0.013*	0.008
	(0.005)	(0.007)	(0.007)
labour × ICT	0.059***	0.049***	0.043***
	(0.012)	(0.016)	(0.013)
labour × non-ICT	-0.020*	-0.008	-0.004
	(0.010)	(0.012)	0.0144
ICT × non-ICT	-0.042***	-0.009	-0.009
	(0.008)	(0.008)	(0.007)
IMPLICIT AVERAGE ELASTICITIES OF INPUTS:			
labour	0.707	0.677	0.619
ICT capital	0.215	0.148	0.124
non-ICT capital	0.140	0.168	0.193
observations	4939	4939	5107
firms	1177	1177	1222
R^2	0.859	0.850	0.846
WALD-STATISTICS[DF]:			
all inputs	6,801[10]	7,479[10]	6,556[10]
additional inputs[†]	77.15[6]	22.88[6]	89.82[6]
time and ind. dummies	721.6[41]	767.1[41]	804[41]
SARGAN (P-VALUES)		0.144	0.080
ERRORS (P-VALUES):			
AR(1)	0.000	0.003	0.004
AR(2)	0.000	0.043	0.047

*,**, and *** denote significance at the 10%, 5% and 1% level. Heteroscedasticity consistent standard errors reported in parentheses. The results of columns 2 and 3 are based on a two-step SYS-GMM estimation and contain a constant and industry dummies interacted with year dummy variables and a dummy variable for location in East Germany. The corresponding one-step results are reported in Table 3.12 in Appendix 3.7.3. [†] refers to additional inputs *not* included in Cobb-Douglas specification. Implicit average elasticities are calculated according to equations (3.15–3.17).

and SYS-GMM estimates differ substantially in both the individual coefficients and the implicit average elasticities. Again, OLS estimates overstate the mean output contributions. A striking feature of the translog function is that even for the SYS-GMM estimation, the implicit average elasticity of ICT (0.148) is much higher than in the Cobb-Douglas specification.[54]

There are two features of the results, however, that raise doubts about the reliability of the translog specification. First, the Wald statistic for the joint significance of the additional translog inputs[55] from the one-step estimation rejects the relevance of these variables (4.96[6], p=0.549). Second, the translog estimates are highly sensitive to small changes in the sample. To illustrate this, the SYS-GMM estimator is applied to the extended instead of the full sample. This extension of the sample by 45 firms (3.8% of the sample) causes substantial changes in the ICT-related coefficients (see column 3). Moreover, the average elasticities for all three inputs change remarkably. In contrast, the sensitivity to sample changes was much smaller for the Cobb-Douglas specification (see columns 5 and 7 of Table 3.1). The underlying reason may be that in particular the quadratic terms are very sensitive to potential outliers in the sample.

3.6 Conclusions

The use of firm-level data is gaining importance for the analysis of productivity effects of ICT. In contrast to aggregate data, firm-level information is less dependent on the accuracy of price deflators and entails a higher variation in the factors that may determine the performance of businesses. Moreover, unlike growth accounting approaches, estimating production functions based on firm-level data does not necessitate assuming constant returns to scale and perfect competition.

This chapter has shown on both theoretical and empirical grounds that estimates of ICT productivity obtained from a production function framework are highly contingent upon the specific econometric methods applied. The empirical analysis based on firm-level panel data from the German service sector yields evidence of various interfering influences that call for an econometric treatment. First, and most prominently, well-managed firms are likely to be intensive users of ICT. If these unobservable firm effects are not taken into account by using a first-differences or a within estimator, the productivity impacts of ICT will be drastically overstated. Second, counteracting this effect, measurement errors in the explanatory variables may lead to an underestimation of the corresponding elasticities. This problem is particular severe in specifications using first differences or within estimation and is particularly important for the case of ICT capital. Even though ICT investments have increased substantially over the last years, the share of ICT equipment and

---

[54] In a similar comparison between the Cobb-Douglas and the translog specification, Brynjolfsson and Hitt (1995) find an only slightly higher average elasticity of ICT for the translog version.

[55] These are the regressors l^2, ict^2, k^2, $l \times ict$, $l \times k$, $ict \times k$ which are not included in the Cobb-Douglas specification.

software in total capital is still very small. This makes it difficult to distinguish the output contributions of ICT from statistical noise. In contrast, the third point to make is that simultaneity of input and output decisions by firms, which may induce an upward bias in estimated ICT productivity, is found to be less important. If panel data are available, both the measurement error and the simultaneity bias may be addressed by applying a GMM estimator that uses information from suitably distant previous periods as instruments for inputs. However, when unobserved firm effects are taken into account, too, this estimation strategy may suffer from small sample biases due to weak instruments. Therefore, a system GMM (SYS-GMM) strategy proposed by Arellano and Bover (1995) is identified as the most suited approach. It applies the GMM estimator to the production function equation both in levels and first differences simultaneously and employs more powerful instruments.

Fourth, potential mismeasurement of output prices and the omission of industry-specific business cycles may understate the productivity impacts of ICT also at the firm level. This bias may partially be addressed by including interacted time and industry dummies in the regression. Fifth, the explicit consideration of serial correlation of exogenous shocks at the firm level in a dynamic specification of the production function yields slightly higher but also less precise estimates for the coefficient of ICT capital. Sixth, the shares of high- and medium-skilled workers have a large and significant effect on productivity. However, the omission of these variables does not lead to an overestimation of the productivity contributions of ICT once firm-specific fixed effects are taken into account. Obviously, most of the variation in the skill structure is *between* rather than *within* firms. Finally, estimates based on the more flexible translog production function yield higher ICT elasticities than those based on the Cobb-Douglas specification. However, they are much more sensitive with respect to small sample changes and yield little improvements in the explanatory power compared to the more parsimonious Cobb-Douglas specification.

What about the implications for empirical work on the economics of ICT? From an econometric point of view, the data needs for addressing the methodological issues raised in this chapter are indeed quite demanding. In particular, a longitudinal structure of at least three observations per firm is required to apply the suited SYS-GMM estimator. On the other hand, the calibration strategies proposed in this chapter for constructing appropriate input and output data may be applicable to various other longitudinal micro data sets, which frequently contain information on sales, employment, and investment. In any case, great caution seems to be appropriate for the interpretation of cross-section results on the topic. The findings of this study indicate that a big part of such results may be due to spurious correlations that tend to dominate the real causal impacts of ICT on the productivity of businesses.

From an economic point of view, the findings of this chapter highlight the need of investigating particular firm characteristics and strategies in more detail. The results from the preferred system GMM estimation imply that a

1% increase in ICT raises output by about 0.06 %. This corresponds to a net rate of return to ICT investment of more than 50%. These apparent excess returns are likely to be due to unobserved complementary expenses such as adjustment costs, innovation efforts, training or other intangible assets, but they may also reflect differences between firms in their ability to exploit the potential benefits of ICT usage. The findings from this study, for example, indicate that the availability of skilled workers are a prerequisite for using ICT productively.

The exploration of adjustment costs and of relevant firm characteristics and strategies related to ICT use are thus important issues for deeper insights into the productivity and welfare impacts of ICT. In the following two chapters, I investigate in more detail two particular aspects that may drive firm-level differences: innovation and innovative history on the one hand, and human capital investments on the other.

3.7 Appendix

3.7.1 GMM estimation of the production function

Referring to equation (3.9), the basis of the Generalised Method of Moments (GMM) approach employed in this study follows basically the suggestions by Arellano and Bond (1991), Arellano and Bover (1995), and Blundell and Bond (1998). It consists of assuming the choice for the $k = 3$ inputs in the initial period $x_{i1} = (l_{i1}, ict_{i1}, k_{i1})$ to be uncorrelated with the residuals $u_{it} = \eta_i + \epsilon_{it}$ in the subsequent periods $E[x_{i1}\epsilon_{it}] = 0$, for $t = 2, \ldots, T$, where T denotes the number of periods.[56] This assumption entails the following moment conditions:

$$E[x'_{i,t-s}\Delta u_{it}] = 0 \quad \text{for } t = 3, \ldots, T \text{ and } t - 1 \geq s \geq 2. \tag{3.20}$$

Note that by first-differencing of u_{it}, the fixed effect η_i, which may be correlated with the inputs, is cancelled out. The system of equations (3.20) can be summarised in matrix notation in the following way:

$$E[Z'_i Du_i] = 0 \tag{3.21}$$

with:[57]

$$Z_i = Z_i^D = \begin{pmatrix} x_{i1} & 0 & 0 & \cdots & 0 & 0 & \cdots & 0 \\ 0 & x_{i1} & x_{i2} & \cdots & 0 & 0 & \cdots & 0 \\ \vdots & \vdots & \vdots & & \vdots & \vdots & & \vdots \\ 0 & 0 & 0 & \cdots & x_{i1} & x_{i2} & \cdots & x_{i,T-2} \end{pmatrix} \tag{3.22}$$

$$T{-}1 \times k(T{-}2)(T{-}1)/2$$

---

[56] Note that in (3.9), it is assumed that the ϵ_{it} are serially uncorrelated.

[57] Note that $x_{it} = (l_{it}, ict_{it}, k_{it})$ has $k = 3$ columns, such that each zero entry in the Z_i-matrix also represents a vector $(0, 0, 0)$. Similarly, the apparent number of columns of the matrix Z must be multiplied by $k = 3$.

$$D = \begin{pmatrix} -1 & 1 & 0 & \cdots & 0 & 0 & 0 \\ 0 & -1 & 1 & \cdots & 0 & 0 & 0 \\ \vdots & \vdots & \vdots & & \vdots & \vdots & \vdots \\ 0 & 0 & 0 & \cdots & -1 & 1 & 0 \\ 0 & 0 & 0 & \cdots & 0 & -1 & 1 \end{pmatrix}$$
$$T-1 \times T$$

$$u_i = (u_{i1}, u_{i2}, \ldots, u_{iT})'.$$

The dimensions of Z_i^D show that (3.21) comprises $k(T-2)(T-1)/2$ moment conditions.[58] After solving (3.9) for u_{it} and inserting in the moment conditions (3.20), the residuals depend on the data (y, x) as well as the parameters $\phi = (\gamma_1, \gamma_2, \gamma_3, \lambda_{12}, \ldots, \lambda_{JT})$, where J denotes the number of industries such that (3.21) can be written as:

$$E[Z_i'Du_i] = E[\psi(y, x, \phi)] = 0. \tag{3.23}$$

By the analogy principle, the expected value of the population is replaced by the sample mean such that we can define $b_N(\phi) = N^{-1}\sum_{i=1}^{N} \psi(y_i, x_i, \phi)$ with N denoting the number of firms in the sample. For given sample values (y_i, x_i), the GMM estimator $\hat{\phi}(A)$ associated with a matrix A is the choice of ϕ that minimises the quadratic form:

$$\hat{\phi}(A) = \arg \min_{\phi} b_N(\phi)' \, A \, b_N(\phi), \tag{3.24}$$

where any choice of the $(T-1 \times T-1)$ weighting matrix A yields a consistent (though not efficient) estimator. For a linear model of the form $y_{it} = x_{it}\beta + u_{it}$ as in (3.9), this minimisation problem is solved by:

$$\hat{\phi}(A) = \left[\left(\sum_{i=1}^{N} x_i^{*'} Z_i\right) A \left(\sum_{i=1}^{N} Z_i'x_i^{*}\right) \right]^{-1} \left[\left(\sum_{i=1}^{N} x_i^{*'} Z_i\right) A \left(\sum_{i=1}^{N} Z_i'y_i^{*}\right) \right], \tag{3.25}$$

---

[58] Note that serial correlation of the errors ϵ_{it} may be at odds with these moment conditions. To this end, suppose that $\epsilon_{it} = \rho\epsilon_{it} + e_{it}$ and insert this into the moment condition of (3.20) for $s = 2$. It then follows that $E[\Delta\epsilon_{it}X_{i,t-2}] = (\rho - 1)E[\epsilon_{i,t-1}X_{i,t-2}] = \rho(\rho - 1)E[\epsilon_{i,t-2}X_{i,t-2}] \neq 0$ unless $\rho = 1$ or $\rho = 0$. Thus, unlike in the case of OLS, serial correlation may harm not only the efficiency but also the consistency of the estimates in the case of GMM estimation since the consistency of the GMM estimates hinges on the validity of the underlying moment conditions. However, the validity of the instruments can be tested directly using the Sargan statistic which is discussed below. This test is a further measure of how strongly potential serial correlation (among other factors) impacts the moment conditions underlying the GMM estimates, and only the combination of the test for serial correlation and the Sargan statistic will give a comprehensive picture of the validity of the moment conditions.

where $x_i^* = Dx_i$. The optimal choice for A, which yields an efficient $\hat{\phi}$, is given by $A^* = Var(\psi(y_i, x_i, \phi))^{-1}$. Since this variance-covariance matrix is not known, a two-step procedure can be applied: in the first step, an arbitrary weighting matrix A is used[59] to obtain a consistent estimate of ϕ. The one-step coefficients are then used to calculate first-differenced residuals $\hat{v}_i^* = D\hat{v}_i$, where $\hat{v}_i$ are the estimated errors obtained from the level equation (3.9). A more efficient weighting matrix for the second-step estimation is then:

$$ A_N = \left(N^{-1} \sum_{i=1}^{N} Z_i' \hat{v}_i^* \hat{v}_i^{*'} Z_i \right)^{-1}. \tag{3.26} $$

A convenient feature of the GMM estimator is that for the efficient weighting matrix A_N for any given Z_i, the minimised value of the distance function $b_N(\phi)' \, A_N \, b_N(\phi)$ from (3.24) is asymptotically χ^2_{r-k}-distributed with the number of degrees of freedom being equal to the number of overidentifying restrictions, i.e. the difference between the number of columns of Z_i (r^D) and the number of columns of x_i (denoted by k). Thus, the validity of the employed instruments can be tested empirically using the Sargan test-statistic:[60]

$$ S = S^D = \left(\sum_{i=1}^{N} \hat{v}_i^{*'} Z_i \right) A_N \left(\sum_{i=1}^{N} Z_i' \hat{v}_i^* \right) \overset{asym}{\sim} \chi^2_{r-k}. \tag{3.27} $$

The SYS-GMM estimator is an extension of the GMM estimator above. The main idea is to find variables that are uncorrelated with the fixed effects η_i and that thus can be used as instruments for the equation in levels. Arellano and Bover (1995) consider the case where the covariance between the explanatory variables x_{it} and the individual effects η_i are constant over time, such that $E(x_{it}\eta_i) = E(x_{is}\eta_i) \ \forall s$.[61] Together with the moment conditions of (3.20), this gives the $(T-2)$ additional moment conditions for the equations in levels:[62]

$$ E(\Delta x_{i,t-1}' u_{it}) = 0, \quad t = 2, \ldots, T. \tag{3.28} $$

These additional moment restrictions can be implemented by letting $u_i^S =$

---

[59] The DPD98 programme used in the regressions for this monograph employs $A = DD'$ for this purpose.

[60] For the regression GMM[-2] in column (4) of Table 3.1, e.g., the number of moment conditions r (with $T = 6$) is $r = 3 \cdot (6-2)(6-1)/2 = 30$ such that the corresponding Sargan statistic has $r - k = 30 - 3 = 27$ degrees of freedom.

[61] As shown by Blundell and Bond (1998), the joint stationarity of the dependent and the independent variables is a sufficient, yet not necessary prerequisite for these restrictions to hold.

[62] Arellano and Bover (1995) show that, given the moment conditions of (3.20), further moment conditions of the type $E(\Delta x_{i,t-s}' u_{it}) = 0$ are redundant since, e.g. $E(\Delta x_{i,t-1}' u_{it}) - E(\Delta x_{i,t-1}' u_{i,t-1}) = E(x_{i,t-1}' \Delta u_{it}) - E(x_{i,t-2}' \Delta u_{it})$ such that the first term $E(\Delta x_{i,t-1}' u_{it})$ is just a combination of the last three terms which are already implied by conditions (3.20) and (3.28).

$\binom{Du_i}{u_i}$ and:

$$Z_i^S = \begin{pmatrix} Z_i^D & 0 & 0 \cdots & & 0 \\ 0 & \Delta x_{i2} & 0 \cdots & & 0 \\ \vdots & \vdots & \vdots & & \vdots \\ 0 & 0 & 0 \cdots & \Delta x_{i,T-1} \end{pmatrix}, \qquad (3.29)$$

$$T-1 \times k(T-2)(T+1)/2$$

where Z_i^D is the instrument matrix (3.22) for the equation in first differences. Thus, the moment conditions of the system GMM estimator are:

$$E[Z_i^{S'} u_i^S] = 0. \qquad (3.30)$$

The validity of the additional instruments obtained from the orthogonality conditions (3.28) can be tested using a Difference Sargan test.[63] Since the set of instruments used for the equation in first differences Z_i^D is a strict subset of the set of instruments used for the system of equations in levels and in first differences, the corresponding Difference Sargan statistic is:

$$S^\Delta = S^S - S^D \overset{asym}{\sim} \chi^2_{r^S - r^D}, \qquad (3.31)$$

where S^S and S^D are the Sargan statistics obtained for the system GMM and first difference GMM correspondingly, and r^S and r^D are the corresponding number of columns of the instrument matrices Z^S and Z^D.[64]

3.7.2 Imposing common factor restrictions by minimum distance

In order to obtain the structural parameters $\theta = (\rho, \gamma_1, \gamma_2, \gamma_3)$ of equation (3.9a), a two-step procedure is applied. In the first step, the reduced-form equation (3.10) with parameters $\pi = (\pi_1, \dots, \pi_7)$ is estimated by SYS-GMM. In the second step, the estimates of the parameters π_i are used to deduce the structural parameters as of (3.9a) by testing and imposing the corresponding common factor restrictions $\pi_1 = \rho$, $\pi_2 = \gamma_1$, $\pi_3 = \gamma_2$, $\pi_4 = \gamma_3$, $\pi_5 = -\gamma_1 \cdot \gamma_2$, $\pi_6 = -\gamma_1 \cdot \gamma_3$, and $\pi_7 = -\gamma_1 \cdot \gamma_4$ using a minimum distance (or asymptotic least squares) procedure.

Let the function $h : \mathbb{R}^4 \to \mathbb{R}^7$ relate θ to π such that $\pi = h(\theta) = (\rho, \gamma_1, \gamma_2, \gamma_3, -\rho, \gamma_1, -\rho\gamma_2, -\rho\gamma_3)'$. Using this function, the focus of interest are thus the structural parameters $\theta = (\rho, \gamma_1, \gamma_2, \gamma_3)'$ that minimise the norm $\pi - h(\theta)$.[65]

The main difficulty in deriving a suitable minimum-distance estimator for the given purpose consists in the non-linearity of the problem. In order to

---

[63] See, e.g., Arellano and Bond (1991) for further details on this test.

[64] For the exemplified case, $r^S - r^D = k(T-2)$.

[65] The following specifications and derivations follow Blundell et al. (1996), Wooldridge (2002, ch. 14) and the more general discussion of asymptotic least squares by Gouriéroux and Monfort (1995, ch. 9 and 10).

simplify calculations, I additionally specify the function $g : \mathbb{R}^7 \rightarrow \mathbb{R}^7$ such that $g(\pi) = (\pi_1, \pi_2, \pi_3, \pi_4, -\pi_5/\pi_1, -\pi_6/\pi_1, -\pi_7/\pi_1)'$ which makes $g(h(\theta)) = (\rho, \gamma_1, \gamma_2, \gamma_3, \gamma_1, \gamma_2, \gamma_3)'$ linear in the components of θ. For given reduced-form estimates $\hat{\pi}$, the structural parameter estimates $\hat{\theta}$ are then imposed to minimise the quadratic distance:

$$\hat{\theta} = \arg\min_{\theta} \, [g(\hat{\pi}) - g(h(\theta))]' \, \hat{\Omega}^{-1} \, [g(\hat{\pi}) - g(h(\theta))] \tag{3.32}$$

$$= \arg\min_{\theta} \begin{pmatrix} \hat{\pi}_1 - \rho \\ \hat{\pi}_2 - \gamma_1 \\ \hat{\pi}_3 - \gamma_2 \\ \hat{\pi}_4 - \gamma_3 \\ -\hat{\pi}_5/\hat{\pi}_1 - \gamma_1 \\ -\hat{\pi}_6/\hat{\pi}_1 - \gamma_2 \\ -\hat{\pi}_7/\hat{\pi}_1 - \gamma_3 \end{pmatrix}' \hat{\Omega}^{-1} \begin{pmatrix} \hat{\pi}_1 - \rho \\ \hat{\pi}_2 - \gamma_1 \\ \hat{\pi}_3 - \gamma_2 \\ \hat{\pi}_4 - \gamma_3 \\ -\hat{\pi}_5/\hat{\pi}_1 - \gamma_1 \\ -\hat{\pi}_6/\hat{\pi}_1 - \gamma_2 \\ -\hat{\pi}_7/\hat{\pi}_1 - \gamma_3 \end{pmatrix}, \tag{3.33}$$

with $\hat{\Omega} = [\partial g(\hat{\pi})/\partial\pi'] \, \widehat{var(\hat{\pi})} \, [\partial g(\hat{\pi})/\partial\pi']'$, where $\widehat{var(\hat{\pi})}$ denotes the estimated variance covariance matrix of the unrestricted parameters $\hat{\pi}$ and:

$$\partial g(\hat{\pi})/\partial\pi' = \begin{pmatrix} 1 & 0 & 0 & 0 & 0 & 0 & 0 \\ 0 & 1 & 0 & 0 & 0 & 0 & 0 \\ 0 & 0 & 1 & 0 & 0 & 0 & 0 \\ 0 & 0 & 0 & 1 & 0 & 0 & 0 \\ \frac{\hat{\pi}_5}{\hat{\pi}_1^2} & 0 & 0 & 0 & \frac{-1}{\hat{\pi}_1} & 0 & 0 \\ \frac{\hat{\pi}_6}{\hat{\pi}_1^2} & 0 & 0 & 0 & 0 & \frac{-1}{\hat{\pi}_1} & 0 \\ \frac{\hat{\pi}_7}{\hat{\pi}_1^2} & 0 & 0 & 0 & 0 & 0 & \frac{-1}{\hat{\pi}_1} \end{pmatrix}. \tag{3.34}$$

The asymptotic variance matrix of the estimate $\hat{\theta}$ is given by:

$$var(\hat{\theta}) = \left([\partial g(h(\theta))/\partial\theta']' \, \Omega^{-1} \, [\partial g(h(\theta))/\partial\theta']\right)^{-1}. \tag{3.35}$$

where the Jacobian $\partial g(h(\theta))/\partial\theta'$ is just a 7×4-matrix of zeros and ones by the construction of the function $g(\bullet)$:

$$\partial g(h(\theta))/\partial\theta' = \begin{pmatrix} 1 & 0 & 0 & 0 \\ 0 & 1 & 0 & 0 \\ 0 & 0 & 1 & 0 \\ 0 & 0 & 0 & 1 \\ 0 & 1 & 0 & 0 \\ 0 & 0 & 1 & 0 \\ 0 & 0 & 0 & 1 \end{pmatrix}. \tag{3.36}$$

Finally, the validity of the common factor restrictions that link the structural equation (3.9a) to the reduced-form specification (3.10) can be tested. For large cross-sections N, the minimised value of the distance function of

(3.32) has an asymptotic χ^2-distribution with three degrees of freedoms since:

$$[g(\hat{\pi}) - g(h(\hat{\theta}))]' \, \hat{\Omega}^{-1} \, [g(\hat{\pi}) - g(h(\hat{\theta}))] = S^{MD} \overset{asym}{\sim} \chi^2_{(r^{red} - r^{struct})}, \quad (3.37)$$

where $r^{red} = 7$ represents the number of the reduced-form parameters comprised by π and $r^{struc} = 4$ is the number of structural parameters contained in θ.

3.7.3 Tables

Table 3.6. Comparison of samples and population by industry

	full		samples small		extended		population*
service industry (NACE digits)	#	%	#	%	#	%	%
wholesale trade (51)	163	13.9	83	14.4	172	14.1	10.6
retail trade (50, 52)	183	15.6	87	15.1	190	15.6	31.3
transport and post (60-63, 64.1)	210	17.8	104	18.0	222	18.2	11.7
electronic processing and telecommunication (72, 62.2)	100	8.5	44	7.6	100	8.2	3.4
consultancies (74.1, 74.4)	100	8.5	48	8.3	103	8.4	12.1
technical services (73, 74.2, 74.3)	142	12.1	75	13.0	152	11.7	10.7
other business-related services (70, 71, 74.5-.8, 90)	279	23.7	137	23.7	292	23.9	20.3
total	1177	100	578	100	1222	100	100

*Population: German service firms with 5 and more employees in 1999.
Source: German Statistical Office, ZEW, and own calculations.

Table 3.7. Comparison of samples and population by size class

	full sample		small sample		ext. sample		population*	
size class (# employees)	#	%	#	%	#	%	% firms	% sales
5-9	189	16.1	88	15.2	205	16.8	57.6	9.4
10-19	189	16.1	105	18.2	206	16.9	24.0	9.9
20-49	246	20.9	137	23.7	254	20.8	11.7	9.7
50-99	156	13.3	87	15.1	156	12.8	3.5	6.9
100-199	167	14.2	76	13.2	168	13.8	1.6	6.0
200-499	102	8.7	48	8.3	102	8.3	1.0	7.0
500 and more	128	10.9	37	6.4	131	10.7	0.6	51.1
total	1,177	100	578	100	1,222	100	100	100

*Population: German service firms with 5 and more employees in 1999.
Source: German Statistical Office, ZEW, and own calculations

Table 3.8. Detailed statistics for the samples

	mean	std.	min.	max.	percentiles 10%	50%	90%	per employee mean	median
FULL SAMPLE (4,939 obs. for 1,177 firms)									
value added*	54.541	717.21	0.118	27,380	0.362	2.647	40.705	121,917	60,307
employees	614.563	9379	1	310,792	7	42	506	—	—
ICT capital*	5.058	131.25	<0.001	6,537	0.006	0.488	0.923	3,946	1,392
non-ICT capital*	102.387	1833.645	0.001	60,340	0.061	1.107	56.360	218,492	24,979
East (dummy)	0.421	0.494	0	1	0	0	1	—	—
SMALL SAMPLE (1,847 obs. for 578 firms)									
value added*	18.513	88.658	0.032	1,124	0.362	2.306	22.821	120,448	58,857
employees	183.673	613.885	1	7,200	7	36	300	—	—
ICT capital*	0.362	1.466	<0.001	30,855	0.006	0.041	0.529	3,106	1,240
non-ICT capital*	24.946	102.911	0.003	1,450	0.062	0.900	41.378	228,230	24,852
East (dummy)	0.444	0.497	0	1	0	0	1	—	—
% university	0.191	0.264	0	1	0	0.061	0.667	—	—
% vocational	0.566	0.303	0	1	0.129	0.615	0.944	—	—
EXTENDED SAMPLE (5,107 obs. for 1,222 firms)									
value added*	53.145	705.526	0.012	27,380	0.351	2.495	39.805	122,198	60,575
employees	596.7	9224	1	310,792	7	40	499	—	—
ICT capital*	4.892	129.075	<0.001	6,537	0.004	0.045	0.892	3,801	1,302
non-ICT capital*	100.300	1,803	0.001	60,340	0.060	1.060	55.375	226,947	25,574
East (dummy)	0.422	0.494	0	1	0	0	1	—	—

*measured in € million, except for values per employee

Table 3.9. One-step results for the ICT-augmented production function

inputs (logs)	dependent variable: log(value added)				
	(3) GMM[-1] 1st diff.	(4) GMM[-2] 1st diff.	(5) SYS-GMM reference	(6) SYS-GMM not interact.	(7) SYS-GMM extended
labour	0.515***	0.247	0.707***	0.737***	0.723***
	(0.174)	(0.158)	(0.073)	(0.074)	(0.075)
ICT capital	0.053	0.069	0.114**	0.081*	0.052
	(0.043)	(0.041)	(0.046)	(0.049)	(0.032)
non-ICT capital	0.191	0.366	0.148***	0.155***	0.166***
	(0.198)	(0.208)	(0.046)	(0.049)	(0.046)
East Germany	—	—	-0.340***	-0.343***	-0.375***
			(0.051)	(0.053)	(0.049)
WALD STATISTICS [DF]:					
inputs	14.7[3]	13.9[3]	446[4]	441[4]	494[4]
time & ind. dummies	108[35]	130[35]	586[41]	488[11]	583[41]
ERRORS (P-VALUES):					
AR(1)	0.010	0.000	0.002	0.003	0.002
AR(2)	0.118	0.042	0.028	0.025	0.030

***,**,* denote significance at the 1%, 5%, and 10% level. Heteroscedasticity-consistent standard errors in parentheses. Results are based on the one-step estimation corresponding to Table 3.1. See footnotes on this table for further details.

Table 3.10. Results for the dynamic specification of the production function

	dependent variable: log(value added)			
	(1) static (one-step)	(2) static (two-step)	(3) dynamic (one-step)	(4) dynamic (two-step)
log(value added$_{t-1}$)	—	—	0.638*** (0.135)	0.105*** (0.084)
log(labour$_t$)	0.768*** (0.099)	0.722*** (0.079)	0.391** (0.159)	0.352*** (0.123)
log(ICT$_t$)	0.090** (0.042)	0.057* (0.030)	0.161 (0.136)	0.136 (0.079)
log(non-ICT$_t$)	0.109 (0.069)	0.166*** (0.051)	0.294 (0.243)	0.194 (0.179)
log(labour$_{t-1}$)	—	—	-0.066 (0.165)	-0.051 (0.138)
log(ICT$_{t-1}$)	—	—	-0.097 (0.074)	-0.031 (0.045)
log(non-ICT$_{t-1}$)	—	—	-0.266 (0.224)	-0.182 (0.174)
R^2	0.829	—	0.950	—
WALD STAT.[DF]:				
inputs	193[3]	292[3]	790[7]	1428[7]
time and ind. dummies	429[41]	530[41]	59[34]	62[34]
SARGAN (P-VALUES)	—	0.021		0.128
ERRORS (P-VALUES):				
AR(1)	0.001	0.003	0.003	0.001
AR(2)	0.026	0.046	0.333	0.332

***,**,* denote significance at the 1%, 5%, and 10% level. SYS-GMM estimates include a constant, a regional dummy variable for East-German firms as well as interacted industry and year dummy variables. Heteroscedasticity-consistent standard errors reported in parentheses. The underlying sample consists of an unbalanced panel with 708 firms and 3532 observations covering the years 1994-1999.

Table 3.11. Additional results for alternative treatment of skills

inputs	dependent variable: log(value added)		
	(1)	(2)	(3)
log(labour)	0.368***	0.552***	
	(2.649)	(3.275)	
log(ICT capital)	0.018	0.057	0.053
	(-0.529)	(-0.897)	(0.061)
log(non-ICT capital)	0.187	0.076	0.125
	(1.344)	(0.982)	(1.442)
HUMAN CAPITAL[a]:			
%university		1.119***	
		(2.674)	
%vocational		0.670***	
		(3.125)	
log(university)			0.115*
			(1.695)
log(vocational)			0.240**
			(2.038)
log(no formal edu.)			0.050
			(1.379)
observations	708	708	708
number of firms	222	222	222
R^2	0.695	0.726	0.761
WALD STAT.[DF]:			
inputs	73[3]	91[5]	81[5]
time and ind. dummies	262[34]	291[34]	377[34]
SARGAN (P-VALUES)	0.423	0.661	0.649
ERRORS (P-VALUES):			
AR(1)	0.732	0.467	0.327
AR(2)	0.119	0.270	0.280

*,**, and *** denote significance at the 10%, 5%, and 1% level. Results are based on the two-step SYS-GMM estimator as detailed in Appendix 3.7.1 and contain a constant as well as interacted time and industry dummies. t-values reported in parentheses are obtained from heteroscedasticity-consistent one-step estimation results (see comments in section 3.5.1 and footnote 31, p. 76 in particular).
[a] '%' refer to shares of the workers with corresponding qualification in the number of total employees, whereas log($\bullet$) refers to the logarithm of the corresponding number of employees.

Table 3.12. One-step results for the translog production function

inputs (log)	dependent variable: value added (logs)	
	SYS-GMM full	SYS-GMM extended
labour	1.044***	1.006***
	(0.256)	(0.277)
ICT capital	0.044	0.070
	(0.156)	(0.119)
non-ICT capital	0.214**	0.224**
	(0.085)	(0.090)
labour^2	-0.041*	-0.040
	(0.024)	(0.027)
ICT capital^2	0.002	0.011**
	(0.012)	(0.005)
non-ICT capital^2	0.006*	0.004
	(0.011)	(0.011)
labour × ICT	0.047	0.042*
	(0.030)	(0.023)
labour × non-ICT	-0.020	-0.018
	(0.018)	(0.020)
ICT × non-ICT	-0.006	-0.007
	(0.015)	(0.012)
East Germany	-0.512***	-0.513***
	(0.188)	(0.189)
observations	4939	5107
firms	1177	1222
R^2	0.850	0.846
WALD-STATISTICS[DF]:		
all inputs	4,784[10]	4,039[10]
additional inputs†	4.96[6]	34.17[6]
time and ind. dummies	531.5[41]	528.5[41]
ERRORS (P-VALUES):		
AR(1)	0.002	0.004
AR(2)	0.008	0.014

*,**, and *** denote significance at the 10%, 5%, and 1% level. Heteroscedasticity-consistent standard errors reported in parentheses. The results are based on a one-step SYS-GMM estimation and contain a constant and industry dummies interacted with year dummy variables and a dummy variable for location in East Germany and complement the corresponding two-step results from columns 2 and 3 in Table 3.5. † refers to additional inputs *not* included in Cobb-Douglas specification.

4

ICT productivity
and innovations*

> *Computers are useless. They can only give you answers.*
> Pablo Picasso (1881-1973)

4.1 Introduction

Evidence from the previous chapter shows that investments in information and communication technologies (ICTs) contribute to firm productivity. However, the characteristics of ICT as a general purpose technology highlighted in chapter 2 suggest that productivity contributions may depend on specific characteristics and strategies of firms and that complementary innovations play a major role in this context. To the extent that firms differ with respect to these aspects, the productivity contributions of ICT may likewise vary substantially between different firms.

Various earlier studies have provided empirical evidence supporting this view. Reviewing a broad range of firm-level studies in both manufacturing and services, Brynjolfsson and Hitt (2000) point to the importance of management strategies and organisational changes for differing returns to ICT across firms. A study by Brynjolfsson et al. (2002) based on large U.S. firms listed at the stock markets reveals that computer-intensive firms focus strongly on innovative organisational forms. Moreover, firms that combine computer use with these organisational characteristics are valued disproportionately higher at the stock markets than firms that invest only in one of these dimensions. These findings are corroborated by Bresnahan et al. (2002) who find similar complementarities in production function estimations for a cross section of large U.S. firms. All these studies have an important message in common: in order to assess the productivity impact of ICT it is crucial to investigate the firm-specific circumstances in which ICT are used.

---

* This chapter is largely based on Hempell (2005a).

The purpose of this chapter is to shed more light on the role of complementary process and product innovations as determinants of the productivity of ICT use. Unlike most previous studies of the topic, the approach envisaged in this study explicitly stresses the importance of ICT being part of the innovation process within a firm.

Evolutionary approaches of innovation have emphasised the dynamic dimension of innovation due to learning effects. Innovation activities do not only help to create new knowledge but also to accumulate expertise that helps to exploit external knowledge (e.g., Cohen and Levinthal, 1989) and to facilitate subsequent own innovational activities either in a specific technological field (Stiglitz, 1987) or in terms of changes in organisational routines (Nelson and Winter, 1982; Dierickx and Cool, 1989). I argue that due to the enabling character of ICT applications, the success of ICT use depends on a firm's innovative history: if ICT use is productive only with complementary innovations, firms that have introduced innovations in the past will be better prepared for using ICT than firms without such innovation experience. The resulting hypothesis is that productivity effects of ICT are higher in experienced firms.

Like in the previous chapter, the empirical analysis of this chapter focuses on the dynamic service sector as a particularly intensive user of ICT. Resorting to the *MIP-S* data set, the empirical analysis draws on data from more than 1200 German firms in business-related and distribution services for the period from 1994 to 1999. The econometric estimations are based on the preferred SYS-GMM estimator derived in the previous chapter which allows to control for firm-level fixed effects, simultaneity of input and output decisions as well as measurement errors. The results indicate that experience accumulated in the course of earlier innovations raises the productivity of ICT usage. In contrast, such experience does not affect the productivity of conventional investments. The complementarities between ICT and innovative experience are robust to the inclusion of variables that control for potential complementarities between innovations and skills of the workforce. There are also some indications that firms with concurrent innovation activities (independently from earlier experience) can use ICT more productively. However, these productivity differentials fail to reach statistical significance.

The remainder of this chapter is organised as follows. Section 4.2 presents the theoretical background and is followed by an overview of the employed data in section 4.3. Section 4.4 discusses the econometric issues and presents the empirical results for both a simple ICT-extended production function framework and the more specific model that takes into account the role of innovative experience. Section 4.5 concludes with some comments on the implications of the findings.

4.2 Theoretical background

The theoretical background is based on the synthesis of two main ideas. First, evidence from recent studies indicates that the productive use of ICT is closely linked to complementary innovations within firms. This link is hypothesised to be a special feature of ICT as opposed to other, more conventional types of capital. Second, it is argued that innovative capabilities are mainly firm-specific and must be accumulated over time. In the resulting model, both effects together lead to predicting a higher productivity of ICT within 'experienced' firms.

Deriving these hypotheses, the subsequent parts briefly review the idea of innovational complementarities of ICT use, discuss the dynamic aspects of innovative capabilities, point to some specifics of innovation in services, and finally present a production function framework that allows to assess the hypotheses empirically.

4.2.1 ICT and innovational complementarities

As discussed in detail in chapter 2 of this book, ICT can be characterised as a GPT, that is noted for its broad diffusion, a great potential for technical improvements and innovational complementarities. These properties that distinguish ICT from most other capital goods have motivated researchers to compare it to other important inventions in the past such as electricity and the steam engine (David, 1990; Bresnahan and Trajtenberg, 1995; Helpman, 1998; Rosenberg and Trajtenberg, 2001). Innovational complementarities are the key to the 'enabling' character of ICTs: they necessitate innovations in their application to become fully productive. Since they form a key motivation to this chapter, the main arguments are briefly reviewed in this section.

Innovational complementarities in application sectors are particularly widespread in the case of ICT. Various industries outside the ICT sector are using ICT components for own product and process innovations. For example, cars and domestic appliances are increasingly equipped with microcomputers that operate navigation systems and control operations of components. Similarly, service industries use cash machine tellers, online banking, e-commerce, and web-based after-sales support for new services and processes. Most importantly perhaps, ICT is used for improving the quality of existing products and services, in particular customer service, timeliness and convenience (Brynjolfsson and Hitt, 1995; Licht and Moch, 1999).

Moreover, ICT applications have great impacts also on processes and the organisation of work inside firms and administrations (Bresnahan and Greenstein, 1996). Firms employ more flexible and more easily programmable manufacturing tools that embody ICT (Milgrom and Roberts, 1990); supply chain management tools increasingly link the production processes of suppliers and clients; and new tools for customer care, such as customer relationship management, help to recognise changes in demand more quickly

(Hammer, 1990; Rigby et al., 2002). In many instances, these developments involve innovations and changes in the organisation of workplaces that take time to be implemented (Brynjolfsson and Hitt, 2000; Brynjolfsson and Hitt, 2003).

The importance of complementary innovations in ICT using firms can hardly be underestimated. They are subject to high uncertainties and their costs typically exceed the direct investment costs of ICT (Bresnahan and Greenstein, 1996). Moreover, as pointed out by Brynjolfsson et al. (2002) and Bresnahan et al. (2002), successful innovation associated with ICT use is very complex, involving simultaneous changes in various business areas.[1] Similarly, Milgrom and Roberts (1990; 1995) provide a model of complementarities and examples of how new technologies must be complemented by whole systems of innovations to achieve advances in productivity whereas isolated measures may even lower firm performance.

The fact that the productive use of ICT requires complex systems or 'clusters' of complementary innovations has two important implications. First, these clusters make imitation of successful ICT applications very difficult. Second, while specific technological know-how may be important for ICT use, expertise in organising and coordinating complementary systems of innovations in firms may be even more important. Firms that are familiar with organising complex internal changes thus have strong incentives to pursue competitive advantages through ICT-based innovations in spite of their inherent risks of failure. These aspects may help explain, for example, the ongoing success of firms such as DELL and Wal-Mart, where combining strong ICT investments with far-reaching innovations of business processes is associated with impressive productivity gains and business performance (Brynjolfsson et al., 2002).

The 'enabling' character of ICT also contrasts with most other types of capital. New vintages of conventional capital, such as machines, vehicles, or other equipment, are often faster, more reliable or more energy-efficient than old vintages and directly contribute to increasing productivity by raising the speed of production or by reducing costs of materials. In contrast, computers and networks basically do nothing more than facilitate the exchange, processing and storage of information. To affect productivity, these characteristics must be exploited through innovations in products, processes, and the organisation of work. In this sense, technical progress is not fully embodied in ICT but requires complementary knowledge and innovation activities by its users. Strong complementarities with innovative experience are thus expected to be a feature that distinguishes ICT from other types of capital.

---

[1] Brynjolfsson et al. (1997) provide results from a case study of a large medical products producer, showing that investments in computer integrated manufacturing was associated with a whole list of innovations, including elimination of piece rates and a more frequent and richer interaction with customers and suppliers.

Use of new technologies and innovations are also associated with new requirements for workers. As highlighted by Autor et al. (2003) for the U.S. and Spitz (2004) for Germany, changes in job contents due to computerisation may explain a substantial part of the educational upgrading observed in recent decades. Similarly, Falk and Seim (2001) and Jacobebbinghaus and Zwick (2002) show that firms that invest in new technologies reveal higher demand for high-skilled labour while low-skilled labour is not affected. These studies highlight innovations and technology use as an important source of a skill-biased technological change. Even though these consequences are not the main topic addressed in this chapter,[2] the role of human capital for both innovation and use of new technologies in firms will be given special room in the theoretical model of section 4.2.4 and the subsequent empirical analysis.

4.2.2 Innovative capabilities and the role of experience

Individual firms may differ in their capabilities to innovate. As maintained by Cohen (1995), two sorts of capabilities are distinguished in the innovation literature. On the one hand, firms may be specialised in a particular technology or a related expertise which leads them to pursue different innovative activities. On the other hand, the ability to innovate is determined by organisational and procedural capabilities that condition the process of innovation. "In this view, firms are characterised as pursuing similar innovative activities, but some firms are more successful than others in either generating or profiting from innovation." (p. 203).[3]

Both aspects of capabilities, which I denote as *specialisation* and *organisation* capabilities for simplicity, can be interpreted either as the outcome of an exogenously given random process (e.g., Cohen and Klepper, 1992) or a dynamic process where learning from past innovations contributes to a stock of accumulated capabilities (e.g., Cohen and Levinthal, 1989). These dynamically accumulated capabilities to innovate are what I denote as 'innovative experience'. As set out in the following, both types of innovative capabilities — specialised and organisational ones — are sources of innovative experience, but have differing implications.

On the one hand, experience due to specialisation is linked to a certain technology. In their seminal paper on the theory of 'localised technological change', Atkinson and Stiglitz (1969) consider the fact that technological advances may have asymmetric effects on different technologies of production. They maintain that innovations that affect one technology, i.e. one way of

---

[2] See also the more detailed discussion in chapter 5 on these issues.

[3] Considering product innovations in the electronics and the food-processing industry, von Tunzelmann (1998) investigates the dichotomy between advantages from technical specialisation on the one hand and increasing complexity, i.e. diversity of technologies required for product innovations, on the other. Based on industry studies, he finds that multi-technology companies try to reconcile the contradiction with greater specialisation in sub-units of the firm.

producing a good, may have no or only limited effects on other technologies. In this framework, accumulation of experience in production due to learning-by-doing (Arrow, 1962) may be localised to a certain technology and give rise to specialisation benefits. As a consequence, a high localisation of learning in production implies that firms may be locked-in with a particular technology and have little incentives to switch to alternative technologies. As pointed out by Stiglitz (1987), this learning due to specialisation may not be confined to production (localised learning-by-doing) but may also extend to the process of innovation (localised learning-to-learn).

A related idea is contained in the concept of 'absorptive capabilities' put forward by Cohen and Levinthal (1989). They argue that innovation activities (and R&D in particular) do not only generate new information, but also enhance a firm's ability to identify, assimilate and exploit existing externally available knowledge. This ability is greatest in technological fields that are related to the stock of prior knowledge. Moreover, possessing related knowledge may also help to predict the nature and commercial potential of technological advances in a specific field (Cohen and Levinthal, 1990). This helps to reduce the inherent risks of innovations in the specific field, but may also facilitate imitation of successful innovations introduced by technologically leading competitors if the underlying intellectual property can be protected only imperfectly.

Dynamic spillovers due to learning-by-doing and learning-to-learn imply that optimising firms will envisage non-myopic strategies. Firms will accept initial losses in new technologies if learning spillovers are sufficiently high to provide future profits. Moreover, non-convexities in production, for example due to high fixed costs, are exacerbated by these dynamic spillovers. These dynamics may be intensified by the sequential nature of innovations, i.e. when innovations are explicitly based on successful earlier innovations in the specific technological field. Mansfield (1968) and Stoneman (1983) argue that a firm's innovative success enhances its technological opportunities and thereby makes further success more likely. This 'success breeds success' hypothesis finds empirical support in a study by Flaig and Stadler (1994). They find that firms that have introduced innovations in the past are indeed more likely to innovate in subsequent years.

These effects of localised learning apply particularly well to product innovations in R&D-intensive industries, e.g. producers of ICT such as microprocessors, memory items, and software. Scientific knowledge plays a major role in these industries and absorptive capacities as a source of experience help firms to exploit knowledge from public institutions (such as universities) and competitors. Moreover, innovations in these industries are often sequential in the sense that solutions entailed in earlier innovations facilitate problem solving in current research. In the case of ICT producers, these intertemporal spillovers may be intensified additionally by network externalities and the ability to set standards (see e.g. David, 1987).

In contrast to localised learning, innovative experience based on accumulated *organisational* capabilities reflects the more general flexibility to adapt to new economic environments. The dynamics of the organisational dimension have received major attention in evolutionary approaches of innovations. Nelson and Winter (1982) point out that apart from the skills of the individual workers, processes of organisational learning play a major role for a firm's capabilities to innovate. They argue that firms (like other organisations) act in 'routines' as patterns of regular and predictable behaviour. These patterns do not only apply to specific production techniques but also to higher-order decision rules and patterns of innovative activities. Much of an organisation's knowledge is tacit and firm-specific and must be acquired over time. Inspired by Nelson and Winter's approach, Cohen and Levinthal (1990) suggest that innovations in organisations have to resort to some degree of diversity of knowledge within firms. They highlight that even though learning of individuals is highest when the object of learning is related to what is already known, a firm's absorptive capacity it not simply the sum of the absorptive capacities of its employees but equally depends on the transfer and coordination of knowledge across and within subunits. More diverse knowledge structures will enhance the firm's capacity for making novel linkages and associations beyond what specialised individuals can achieve. This aspect of ingenuity in innovations seems particularly important in the context of clusters of innovations associated with the use of ICT as discussed above.

The organisational aspect of innovative capabilities and their dynamics have also received major attention in the management literature. Various exponents of 'resource-based' approaches to the firm have highlighted accumulated intangible assets and core competencies as explanations for sustained competitive advantages of individual firms (see, e.g., Wernerfelt, 1984). To become a source of sustained competitive advantages, these resources and capabilities must be valuable, rare, imperfectly imitable, and not substitutable (Barney, 1991). Similarly, intangible resources have been identified as main determinants for the ability of firms to conduct R&D (Galende and de la Fuente, 2003).

Complementing this resource-based view, the 'dynamic capability approach' emphasises the dynamic nature of firm-specific resources (Teece et al., 1997). Dierickx and Cool (1989) provide a model of intangible assets that are accumulated internally and that form the basis of competitive advantages due to *asset mass efficiencies* and *time compression diseconomies*. *Asset mass efficiencies* mean that the more accumulated assets a firm has, the lower are the marginal costs of increasing the stock further. *Time compression diseconomies* imply that the marginal costs of investments in intangibles in a given period increase more than proportionally, such that asset accumulation cannot be rushed.[4] Both these features prevent competitors with a smaller stock of relevant intangibles from imitating the production technology by catching

---

[4] This idea corresponds to strictly convex adjustment costs in investment theory.

up. Moreover, if there are complementarities between different types of asset stocks, combinations of these assets are even more difficult to be replicated by imitators. As exemplified by Dierickx and Cool (1989), if product and process innovations originate in customer request or suggestions, it may be particularly difficult to develop technological know-how for firms that do not dispose of an own extensive service network.[5]

These aspects of sustained differences between firms suggest that the organisational dimension of innovative experience is particularly important for innovative activities based on ICT *use*. As pointed out in the previous section, the general purpose character of ICT implies that using these technologies is most successfully complemented by clusters of innovations and that firms may vary in their capability to co-ordinate these innovations. The considerations from evolutionary and dynamic capability theories suggest that firms must acquire this capability internally over time and that experience collected in the course of earlier innovations is important for this process. Unlike the localised nature of innovative experience that is necessary for advances in the innovation of particular technologies (such as ICT production), the character of experience relevant for the manifold innovations based on ICT *use* will be confined less to a particular or 'localised' technological field but will consist in organisational experience resulting from diversity of expertise and the ability to combine and exploit this expertise. In the following section, I set out that this view may be particularly relevant in the service sector where processes, 'products' (i.e. services), and organisational aspects are more closely interrelated than in manufacturing.

4.2.3 Specifics of innovation in services

Investments in ICT are most intensive and most dynamic in services (see, e.g., OECD, 2000a). In earlier studies on innovation, the service sector was widely characterised as a mere applier of technological innovations developed in the manufacturing sector, with ICTs being the most important example. This view has been changing substantially during the last decades.[6] In the following, I limit myself to discussing those aspects that appear particularly relevant for interpreting innovative experience in the context of ICT adoption in services.[7]

---

[5] In an empirical investigation of the dynamic capability model, Knott et al. (2003) conclude that such complementarities may play a major role. Antonelli (2003) provides a theoretical framework of how *complexity* (the generation of knowledge requires the combination of diverse bits of knowledge) and *fungibility* (some specific knowledge can be applied in a variety of different contexts) can cause increasing returns in the generation of knowledge.

[6] Tether et al. (2001) and Tether (2003) provide broad discussions and classifications of these theoretical approaches.

[7] For a broader discussion of innovation in services and a survey of empirical findings from the German innovation data, see Hempell (2003a).

In his famous taxonomy of technological activities, Pavitt (1984) classifies services as 'supplier dominated' industries where technological progress is due to technologies developed in manufacturing. Among various critics, Barras (1986; 1990) challenges this view by presenting his theory about a "reverse product cycle" in services as compared to manufacturing. Based on evidence on computerisation in banking, accountancy and local government services, he suggests that technology adoption initiated its own innovation dynamics in services: initially, service firms use new technologies mainly for making production and delivery of services more efficient. Only in latter stages, new technologies serve for improving service quality and customisation and for eventually creating new services.

Other researchers point to more elementary aspects of services that make innovation dynamics in services inadequate to compare to those in manufacturing (e.g., Gallouj and Weinstein, 1997; Sundbo, 2000). Among the most prominent of these characteristics are *intangibility* and *interactive aspects* of services. *Intangibility* relates to the fact that services and the process of their production cannot be separated; Services lack an independent physical existence and are not visible. When it comes to innovation, this makes it difficult to distinguish between innovation of products and processes in services.[8] Moreover, the quality of various services (such as consulting or technical services) is closely linked to the knowledge and skills of people involved in production and the way these competencies are organised (Gallouj and Weinstein, 1997). *Interaction* between providers and consumers of services makes it difficult not only to determine the authorship of an innovation but also to differentiate between mere variations of existing services and original innovations.

Jointly, these peculiarities of services imply that quality and ingenuity of services can not, or at least not in the first place, be attributed to 'hard' (Tether, 2003), 'tangible' (Gallouj and Weinstein, 1997) or 'embodied' (Evangelista, 1999) technologies, such as equipment, ICT and structures. Instead, 'soft', 'intangible', or 'disembodied' dimensions of technologies involved in the production of services (human skills, legal or financial expertise, organisational and operating practices, etc.) play a pivotal role. Emphasising the role of interaction with clients, Gallouj and Weinstein (1997) and Gallouj (2000) further decompose intangible aspects of technology into individual *competencies* that are based on individual skills, training, experience and interactions with clients on the one hand, and *systems* of codified or formalised competencies (routines, organisational competencies) on the other.[9] They argue that the interaction with clients is not only by itself a subject and a 'laboratory' of innovations, but also a critical area for the supplier's capacity to absorb and

---

[8] Challenging this view, however, Sirilli and Evangelista (1998) and Evangelista (2000) report evidence from Italian innovation surveys indicating that firms in services are well able to distinguish between both types of innovation.

[9] Gallouj and Weinstein (1997) illustrate these notions as an analogy to Nelson and Winter's (1982) distinction between 'skills' and 'routines' that has become widely accepted in evolutionary economics.

assimilate new competencies. Gallouj (2000) suggests that innovations in services can often be classified as 'ad hoc innovation', 'recombinative innovation', and 'formalisation innovation' or a combination of the categories. These are inherently complex since they are based on knowledge and experience accumulated in the past and presume an understanding of the complex nature of the characteristics of services and the processes to generate them. These views are consistent with results from innovation surveys in Germany (Janz, 2000) as well as the Community Innovation Survey (Tether, 2003) which show that customers and internal sources dominate suppliers as sources for innovation in all services industries.

Moreover, Gallouj and Weinstein (1997) discuss various types of innovations in their framework and emphasise that intangible dimensions of technology (including individual competencies) are pivotal for innovation in services. They conclude that interactions between the various dimensions of innovations imply that innovational dynamics in services may be determined less by the characteristics and technological trajectories of tangible or hard technologies, such as ICT, but rather by intangible aspects of services technologies (organisation, routines, management methods) as well as cognitive trajectories, such as accumulation of expertise in individual and collective learning processes.

This hypothesis contrasts distinctly with more traditional approaches discussed above that interpret services as a technologically passive and dependent sector. Instead, it complements the considerations of ICT as a GPT from chapter 2: to the extent that competencies and routines are essential for innovation trajectories in services, firms must complement technological advances embodied in equipment (and ICT in particular) by accumulation of expertise and experience within the firm in order to generate own innovational advances.

A common objection towards the approaches discussed so far concerns the fact that services are too heterogeneous to treat them under a 'one-fits-all' theory.[10] Some researchers have tried to overcome this weakness by developing taxonomies and typologies that highlight differences of innovational patterns between service industries (e.g., Evangelista, 2000). However, using both data from the Community Innovation Survey, Tether et al. (2001) and Tether (2003) find that innovation behaviour varies substantially not only between but also within sectors. They suggest that firms face a variety of fields for innovation to engage in — such as introducing cost-reducing processes, offering more flexible and customised services or specialising in particular markets with bespoke services — and that strategic positioning may explain differential innovation behaviour within industries. These considerations relate to the

---

[10] While Barras' (1986) approach has been criticised as being too narrowly tailored to the peculiarities of banking and insurances, approaches that emphasise interactions with clients as a source for innovation (Gallouj and Weinstein, 1997, e.g.) may lack generality due to their focus on knowledge-intensive business services, such as consultants or technical services.

dynamic aspects of innovation and indicate that evolutionary and resource-based approaches apply not only to manufacturing but equally well to service industries. In the empirical part of this chapter, these strategic aspects will be taken into account by differentiating between experience resulting from product and process innovations.

Summarising the theoretical considerations so far, the following implications can be highlighted. First, by its general purpose properties, ICT forms a special type of investment good compared to other (non-ICT) types of capital. The productivity effects from ICT use are expected to be determined by the firm's ability to complement investments by own innovational efforts (*innovative capabilities*). Second, innovative capabilities are firm-specific and are the result from learning effects from innovations in the past (*innovative experience*). Jointly, these considerations imply that *firms that have innovated in the past can use ICT investments more productively than firms that have not*. Moreover, two overlapping types of innovative experience can be distinguished. (a) If the relevant learning process is localised in ICT, it will be mainly yesterday's ICT-based innovations that increase the productivity of ICT use today. (b) If the organisational capabilities of introducing innovations prevail, experience also from yesterday's innovations in other technological fields are likely to enhance productivity of ICT use today.

4.2.4 Empirical model

In order to investigate the hypotheses derived above, I use a production function framework that allows the productivity contributions of the inputs to vary with a firm's innovative experience. A Cobb-Douglas production technology is considered in which the coefficients of the inputs may vary between innovators and other firms:

$$Y_{it} = F(A_{it}, L_{it}, ICT_{it}, K_{it}, J_i) = A_{it} e^{\gamma J_i} L_{it}^{\xi_1(J_i)} ICT_{it}^{\xi_2(J_i)} K_{it}^{\xi_3(J_i)}, \qquad (4.1)$$

where Y_{it} denotes the output of firm i in period t, L_{it} is labour input, ICT_{it} and K_{it} represent ICT and non-ICT capital, and A_{it} represents multi-factor productivity. Innovative experience J_i is assumed to be quasi-fixed in the time span considered in the empirical analysis (which comprises six years) since innovative background cannot be changed easily in the short term.[11]

In the empirical analysis, a firm's innovative experience J_i will be proxied by a dummy variable equalling one for innovative firms. Under this premise, the functional form of $\xi_v(J_i)$ can be expressed as follows without loss of generality:

$$\xi_v(J_i) = \beta_v + \gamma_v J_i, \qquad v = 1, 2, 3, \qquad (4.2)$$

where β_v is the elasticity of input v for firms classified as non-innovators and

---

[11] The exact definition of the variable J_i for the empirical analysis is discussed in the next section.

$\beta_v + \gamma_v$ is the elasticity for innovators. Moreover, multi-factor productivity A_{it} is decomposed into a common scale parameter c, a permanent or quasi-fixed component η_i, reflecting firm-specific characteristics that do not vary considerably in the short run (like strategies, management ability, unobserved intangibles, etc.) and a time-variant part ϵ_{it} that captures short-term shocks like variations in demand, accidents, factor utilisation, etc., such that:

$$\log(A_{it}) = c + \eta_i + \epsilon_{it} . \tag{4.3}$$

Taking logs on both sides of (4.1) and inserting (4.2) and (4.3) yields:

$$y_{it} = c + \beta_1 l_{it} + \beta_2 ict_{it} + \beta_3 k_{it} \tag{4.4}$$
$$+\gamma J_i + \gamma_1 l_{it} J_i + \gamma_2 ict_{it} J_i + \gamma_3 k_{it} J_i + \eta_i + \epsilon_{it},$$

with small letters denoting the corresponding logarithmic values.

Thus, the model corresponds to an ICT-extended Cobb-Douglas framework that allows different input coefficients to vary between innovators and non-innovators. In this specification, the coefficients β_h (with $h = 1, 2, 3$) represent the elasticities of output with respect to inputs L, ICT, and K in non-innovative firms, whereas $\beta_h + \gamma_h$ are the corresponding elasticities in innovative firms. The test for the hypothesis that innovative experience enhances the productivity of input h thus amounts to testing whether γ_h is significantly positive. The direct contributions of innovation J_i to multi-factor productivity, in contrast, are captured by γ.

One implication of (4.4) is that, for any given share of ICT capital in output ICT/Y, the marginal product of ICT will be higher among innovators. In the simplest (static) case, firms invest in ICT to equate the marginal product of ICT (MPI) to its user costs r.[12] Assuming r to be equal across firms, the optimal ICT stock for all firms is given by the first-order condition $\partial Y_{it}/\partial ICT_{it} = \gamma_2(J_i) \cdot Y_{it}/ICT_{it} = r$. For any given output level Y_{it}^* the optimal level of ICT capital is thus given by $ICT_{it}^* = Y_{it}^*/r \cdot \gamma_2(J_i)$. Similarly, given equal wages w for labour input L, the first-order condition with respect to labour gives $\partial Y_{it}^*/\partial L_{it} = \gamma_1(J_i) \cdot Y_{it}^*/L_{it}^* = w$ such that the optimal endowment of workplaces with ICT capital is:

$$\frac{ICT_{it}^*}{L_{it}^*} = \frac{w\gamma_2(J_i)}{r\gamma_1(J_i)} = \frac{w(\beta_2 + \gamma_2 \cdot J_i)}{r(\beta_1 + \gamma_1 \cdot J_i)}. \tag{4.5}$$

This implies that if innovative experience complements ICT but not labour input ($\gamma_2 > 0$ and $\gamma_1 = 0$), the endowment of innovative firms with ICT per employee will be higher than in non-innovative firms. In contrast, analogue considerations for K imply that if innovations complement neither K nor L, non-ICT capital per worker will be uncorrelated to innovations.

---

[12] These user costs are typically defined to consist of depreciation, expected price changes of the capital good, taxes, and market interest rate.

A final issue concerns the role of human capital in this framework. Even though innovations may not affect labour input in general, there might be a positive effect on the productivity of high-skilled labour. This link is not the main topic of interest of this chapter, but its omission may lead to misleading results: if innovations raise the productivity of skilled labour and the share of skilled labour is positively correlated with ICT investment, a positive coefficient β_2 may rather reflect innovation-skill complementarities than higher benefits from ICT in innovative firms.

In order to account for these interferences, the model is slightly extended in the following way. Define N as the total number of workers consisting of low-skilled, medium-skilled and high-skilled employees N_l, N_m, and N_h such that $N_{it} = N_{l,it} + N_{m,it} + N_{h,it}$. With $\vartheta_m(J_i)$ and $\vartheta_h(J_i)$ denoting the productivity differentials of medium and highly skilled workers (as compared to the productivity of the low-skilled) conditional on innovation J_i, effective labour is:

$$
\begin{aligned}
L_{it} &= N_{l,it} + (1 + \vartheta_m) \cdot N_{m,it} + (1 + \vartheta_h) \cdot N_{h,it} \qquad (4.6)\\
&= N_{it} - N_{m,it} - N_{h,it} + (1 + \vartheta_m) \cdot N_{m,it} + (1 + \vartheta_h) \cdot N_{h,it}\\
&= N_{it} + \vartheta_m \cdot N_{m,it} + \vartheta_h \cdot N_{h,it}\\
&= N_{it} + \vartheta_m \cdot \frac{N_{m,it}}{N_{it}} N_{it} + \vartheta_h \cdot \frac{N_{h,it}}{N_{it}} N_{it}\\
&= N_{it} \cdot [1 + \vartheta_m s_{m,it} + \vartheta_h s_{h,it}],
\end{aligned}
$$

with $s_{m,it} = N_{m,it}/N_{it}$ and $s_{h,it} = N_{h,it}/N_{it}$ denoting the shares of medium- and high-skilled employees in total workforce. Taking logs and with small values for $\vartheta_m(J_i)$, $\vartheta_h(J_i)$, $s_{m,it}$ and $s_{h,it}$, (4.6) can be approximated by:

$$
\begin{aligned}
l_{it} = \ln L_{it} &= n_{it} + \ln[1 + \vartheta_m(J_i)s_{m,it} + \vartheta_h(J_i)s_{h,it}] \qquad (4.7)\\
&\approx n_{it} + \vartheta_m(J_i)s_{m,it} + \vartheta_h(J_i)s_{h,it},
\end{aligned}
$$

with $n_{it} = \ln N_{it}$.[13] Defining $\vartheta_j(J_i) = \theta_j + \delta_j J_i$ ($j = m, h$) without loss of generality and substituting for l_{it} in (4.4) yield:

$$
\begin{aligned}
y_{it} =\ & c + \beta_1 n_{it} + \beta_2 ict_{it} + \beta_3 k_{it} \qquad (4.8)\\
&+ \gamma J_i + \gamma_1 n_{it} J_i + \gamma_2 ict_{it} J_i + \gamma_3 k_{it} J_i\\
&+ \beta_1 \theta_m s_{m,it} + [\gamma_1 \theta_m + (\gamma_1 + \beta_1)\delta_m] J_i s_{m,it}\\
&+ \beta_1 \theta_h s_{h,it} + [\gamma_1 \theta_h + (\gamma_1 + \beta_1)\delta_h] J_i s_{h,it}\\
&+ \eta_i + \epsilon_{it},
\end{aligned}
$$

---

[13] As discussed and empirically explored in chapter 3, a more precise second-order Taylor approximation may be preferable given the relatively high values for the shares of medium- and high-skilled workers. However, this would add a variety of additional regressors in the empirical specification that would substantially reduce the precision of the estimated coefficients due to multicollinearity.

where I make use of the fact that the dummy variable $J_i = J_i^2$. This extension of model (4.4) with the additional skill variables $s_{m,it}$, $s_{h,it}$ and their interactions with innovation dummy J_i can then be used for assessing the impact of possible interferences of skills.

4.3 Data

The model discussed in the previous section is applied to data from the *Mannheim Innovation Panel in Services* (*MIP-S*), which surveys the innovation behaviour of German firms. This data set is broadly described in section 3.4 of the previous chapter. In particular, I follow the same proceedings for deriving the measures of output of firms as well as for constructing firm-specific stocks of ICT and non-ICT as tangible inputs in the production process. Moreover, in order to assess the role of skills for innovational complementarities, I proxy the varying importance of high- and medium-skilled workers by the share of employees with university degree and with vocational degree just as before in chapter 3. Due to numerous item non-responses in the skill variables,[14] the resulting 'small sample' containing this information is used mainly to explore the effects from including human capital variables based on equation (4.8).

A new issue as compared to the data description in chapter 3 concerns the criteria for distinguishing between firms with innovative experience and 'unexperienced' firms. In each wave of the *MIP-S* survey, firms are asked whether they have successfully introduced new or significantly improved services or new processes within the last three years. The employed definition of innovation, which is based on the international guidelines summarised in the so-called *OSLO manual* (OECD/Eurostat, 1997), requires an innovation to be new to the firm (not necessarily new to the market) and to be based on technologically new knowledge. It thus includes both original innovators and imitators.

For the analysis, firms that have innovated sufficiently early are regarded as experienced. More specifically, a firm is classified as an 'experienced innovator' ($J^{exp} = 1$), if it has introduced a product or process innovation in the first year in which it was observed or in one of the two preceding years. All other firms are treated as unexperienced and are assigned with the value $J^{exp} = 0$. To illustrate this definition, consider two firms A and B for which data over the period 1994-97 are available. Suppose firm A has reported a product innovation for one of the years 1992-94. It is thus classified as an 'experienced' firm ($J^{exp} = 1$). In addition, suppose that firm B, in contrast, has reported no innovation for 1992-1994 (even though it may have reported one for a later period). It is labelled as a 'not-experienced' firm ($J^{exp} = 0$). Firm A

---

[14] Only 591 of the 1,222 firms of the sample reported information on the skill structure of their employees.

Table 4.1. Alternative classification of innovators

variable	short label	definition[*]
$J_i^{exp} = 1$	experienced product or process innovator	product or process innovator (or both) in the earliest year observed
$J_i^{exp,pd} = 1$	experienced product innovator	product innovator in the earliest year observed
$J_i^{exp,pc} = 1$	experienced process innovator	process innovator in the earliest year observed
$J_i^{inn} = 1$	product or process innovator	product or process innovator (or both) in at least one of the periods observed
$J_i^{inn,pd} = 1$	product innovator	product innovator in at least one of the periods observed
$J_i^{inn,pc} = 1$	process innovator	process innovator in at least one of the periods observed
$J_i^{ict} = 1$	ICT-based innovator	use of ICT was important to facilitate innovations in period 1993-95

[*] Note: according to the question design in the underlying questionnaire, a firm is defined to be an innovator in the year Y if it has successfully introduced an innovation in the year Y or some of the two preceding years ($Y - 1$ or $Y - 2$). All firms not fulfilling the corresponding definitions are assigned the value 0.

is considered being 'experienced' since for the whole period for which we can observe its inputs and outputs it can rely on experience from earlier innovation.

An alternative definition focusses on the weaker criterion of whether a firm has innovated in *any* of the periods for which data are available. According to this definition, a firm is a — not necessarily experienced — innovator ($J^{inn} = 1$) if it has introduced an innovation during one of the periods (and $J^{inn} = 0$ otherwise).[15] This broader definition is supposed to account for the more general role of innovations, independently of whether these are introduced before or during the period for which productivities are analysed. The comparisons between results based on these two definitions thus highlight the particular role of innovative experience.

Apart from surveying innovations in general, the MIP-S survey also allows to distinguish between types of innovation, i.e. between the introduction

---

[15] Suppose the above mentioned firm B has introduced an innovation in 1996. Thus, firm B is denoted as an innovator but not as an experienced one. Firm A, in contrast, satisfies both criterion since being an 'experienced innovator' implies being an 'innovator'.

of new or significantly improved services ('product innovation', abbreviated by pd)[16] or of new or significantly improved processes ('process innovations', pc)[17]. As discussed in section 4.2.3 and corroborated by statistics in Table 4.9, both types of innovations are closely linked with each other in many cases.[18] Nevertheless, the performance of firms with only one type of innovation may shed light on the question whether strategic positioning in one field of innovation is relevant. The various definitions used in the empirical analysis are summarised in Table 4.1. The corresponding shares of 'innovators' and 'experienced innovators' by industry and type of innovation are summarised in Tables 4.9 and 4.10 in the Appendix.

Finally, firms were asked whether the use of ICT was important for innovative activities (both product and process innovations) during the period 1993-95. The dummy variable J_i^{ICT} is one if a firm answered 'yes' to this question. Interacting J_i^{ICT} with experience variables $J_i^{exp,pd}$ and $J_i^{exp,pc}$ will allow to analyse to what extent firms with innovative experience in the technological proximity of ICT are particularly effective in using ICT. This distinction will be used to assess to what extent innovational learning is localised.

The sample used for the estimation contains only firms with consistent information from at least three consequent periods in order to allow for applying suited panel estimators (see next section). The resulting unbalanced sample consists of 1,222 firms with a total of 5,107 observations, corresponding to an average of 4.2 observed periods per firm. Tables 4.11 and 4.12 show that the sample reflects industry and size structure of German business-related and distribution services fairly well.[19] The majority of firms in the reference sample are small and medium-sized firms with more than two thirds of the businesses employing less than 100 workers. Tables 4.7 and 4.8 report summary statistics and correlations for the logarithmic values of the variables that are employed in the econometric regressions.

Finally, some simple statistics may give some first insights into the challenges for measurement of ICT productivity and the role of innovations. Table 4.2 reports the (cross-sectional) means and medians of the firms' (longitudinal) averages of capital and output intensity (measured capital and output per

---

[16] Examples are the introduction of improved after sales services, 24-hour or emergency consultancies, electronic accounting systems, etc.

[17] Examples are introducing electronic ordering systems, e-commerce, new security systems, etc.

[18] For example, about 72% of the firms with experience from product innovations have also introduced process innovations (see Table 4.9).

[19] Exceptions are retail trade, which is substantially undersampled, whereas traffic and postal services as well as software and telecommunication are oversampled. As far as firm size is concerned, large firms are oversampled in their mere number and undersampled in their respective share in sales (see last two columns of Table 4.12).

Table 4.2. Capital intensity and labour productivity by innovative experience

| variables | all firms | | experienced firms | | others | |
(per worker)	mean	median	mean	median	mean	median
ICT	3,801	1,302	4,094	1,705	3,343	790
non-ICT	226,947	25,574	182,428	22,758	296,481	29,432
value added	122,198	60,575	114,497	57,870	134,225	65,632
# firms	1,222		667		555	

Values in € in prices of 1996. "Experienced firms" refers to firms that have success-fully introduced a process or a product innovation in the first observed year or one of the two preceding years (J_i^{exp}, see Table 4.1, p. 115). The figures are calculated as the means and medians of the unweighted firms' means over time, based on the full sample of 1,222 firms.

employee) for the firms in the sample.[20] The figures indicate that in the me-dian firm of the sample, a workplace is equipped with € 1,300 of ICT capital, and with about € 25,600 of non-ICT capital, thus highlighting the fact that the share of ICT capital in the total capital stock is very low. Comparing the medians of ICT per worker and conventional capital per worker in Table 4.2, ICT accounts for 4.8% of total tangible capital stock. Similarly, aggregating the firms' time averages of both types of capital yields a share of ICT capital in total capital of 5% (not reported in the tables). These values correspond very well to a share of 3% calculated by Schreyer (2000) using aggregate data for Germany (including the less ICT-intensive manufacturing sector) in 1996. As argued by Griliches (1994), such small shares of ICT input together with measurement errors may make it difficult to distinguish the output contri-butions of ICT from stochastic events. In the econometric analysis, potential biases from measurement errors will therefore be addressed explicitly.

Beyond this, the further columns from Table 4.2 also shed some light on differences between experienced and other firms with respect to the demand for ICT capital. As pointed out in the discussion of equation (4.5), the the-oretical considerations in the previous section imply that the endowment of workplaces with ICT will be higher among experienced firms. In fact, ICT intensity measured as the average ICT stock per worker in experienced firms (defined according to its narrow definition) exceeds the corresponding value of non-experienced firms by a factor of about 1.2. This difference is even more pronounced (factor 2.2) if median values are considered. In contrast, the per capita values of output and conventional capital are substantially higher among non-experienced firms. These simple statistics are consistent with the hypothesis that innovative experience is important for productive investments

---

[20] The corresponding mean values are substantially higher than the median since some firms — in particular real estate — display very high values for both inputs and for output per employee.

in ICT but not so much for the use of other types of capital. The next section will investigate to what degree these findings can also be supported by an econometric analysis based on the production function framework developed in the previous section.

4.4 Empirical results

In the first part of this section, I present results from various empirical specifications for the theoretical framework described in section 4.2.4. In the second part, I discuss the results in a broader context, including evidence from a related two-country study for Germany and the Netherlands.

4.4.1 Results for the theoretical framework

In order to estimate the empirical model of equation (4.4) consistently, I apply a system GMM (SYS-GMM) estimator which is broadly described in the previous chapter 3. This estimator helps to control for unobserved firm effects, measurement errors in the variables and simultaneity of inputs and output which may induce substantial biases in pooled or within OLS regressions. In order to control for variations in factor utilisation induced by industry-specific business cycles, dummies for 7 industries[21] interacted with years are added to the specification. Finally, a dummy variable for East German firms controls for the productivity differentials due to the transformation process after the German unification.

The corresponding results from applying OLS and the SYS-GMM estimators are reported in Table 4.3.[22] In the first two columns, the results for the simplest specification of the production function are reported. To illustrate the importance of using appropriate estimation techniques, OLS results are compared to the outcomes from SYS-GMM. Corroborating similar findings from chapter 3, the coefficient of ICT is twice as high in the OLS regression, pointing to a substantial bias from omitted fixed effects.

In the preferred SYS-GMM specification of column 2, labour and non-ICT inputs are significantly positive, but ICT is only very marginally significant

---

[21] The industry classifications with the corresponding NACE codes are summarised in Table 4.11 in the Appendix. Since there are no output data available for banking and insurance (only the balance sheet total and insurance premiums, respectively), these industries are excluded from the analysis.

[22] All estimations were computed using the DPD98 programme developed by Arellano and Bond (1998) running in GAUSS. For the point estimates, the results from the efficient two-step estimator are reported while the corresponding t-values are obtained from the one-step results. The latter are used because inference based on one-step GMM estimators appears to be much more reliable when either non-normality or heteroscedasticity are suspected (Blundell and Bond, 1998). See also chapter 3 on these issues.

Table 4.3. Factors of production and innovational complementarities

	dependent variable: log(value added)			
	(1) overall OLS	(2) overall SYS-GMM	(3) $J = J^{exp}$ SYS-GMM	(4) $J = J^{inn}$ SYS-GMM
log(labour)	0.662***	0.686***	0.601***	0.809***
	(34.779)	(9.681)	(5.112)	(4.581)
log(ICT)	0.091***	0.049	0.019	0.007
	(6.742)	(1.614)	(0.691)	(0.489)
log(non-ICT)	0.208***	0.189***	0.164***	0.182**
	(14.888)	(3.587)	(2.142)	(2.317)
innovation (J)			0.027	0.717
			(0.847)	(1.042)
INTERACTIONS WITH INNOVATION DUMMY:				
$J\times$ log(labour)			0.037	-0.164
			(-0.527)	(-0.975)
$J\times$ log(ICT)			0.076**	0.039
			(1.993)	(0.660)
$J\times$ log(non-ICT)			0.031	0.025
			(-0.292)	(-0.103)
R^2	0.840	0.836	0.838	0.834
WALD STAT.[DF]:				
inputs (w/o constants)	510[3]	111[3]	458[6]	629[6]
time and ind. dummies	672[41]	685[41]	750[41]	698[41]
Sargan (p-values)		0.193	0.465	0.566
ERRORS (P-VALUES)				
AR(1)	0.000	0.003	0.003	0.003
AR(2)	0.000	0.039	0.056	0.033

***, **, and * denote significance at the 1, 5 and 10% level. t-values reported in parentheses are obtained from heteroscedasticity-robust first-step results (see Blundell and Bond (1998) and chapter 3, in particular footnote 31, p. 76, for more details). The signs of the coefficients and the reported corresponding t-values may therefore differ in some cases.
SYS-GMM estimates are obtained from two-step estimation containing a constant, a regional dummy variable for East-German firms as well as interacted industry and year dummy variables. The definition of the variable 'innovator' and the corresponding interactions differs between columns (3) and (4) as indicated by the subscripts of J^x in the first row (see Table 4.1, p. 115, and section 4.3 for definitions). The underlying sample consists of an unbalanced panel with 1,222 firms and 5,107 observations covering the years 1994-1999.

(p-value of 0.106). The output elasticity of labour amounts to two thirds which is consistent with the share of income from labour in the aggregate statistics. The coefficients of ICT and non-ICT capital are 4.9% and 18.9%, respectively. The corresponding Sargan-statistic ($p = 0.193$) does not reject the validity of the instruments at the usual significance levels even though the null-hypothesis of no autocorrelation in the errors is rejected at the usual levels.[23]

In the third column of Table 4.3, the results are reported for the specification according to equation (4.4) in which all input elasticities are allowed to be different for experienced and non-experienced firms. In these results, the simple coefficients represent the elasticities for unexperienced firms while the estimates for the interactions (corresponding to coefficients $\gamma_1, \gamma_2, \gamma_3$ in equation (4.4)) thus denote the additional output elasticities for experienced firms compared to non-experienced ones. The hypothesis of innovative experience complementing ICT use predicts the interaction term for ICT to be positive.

The results show that the coefficient of ICT in experienced firms is indeed significantly higher than in unexperienced ones. In contrast, for labour and non-ICT capital, the null-hypothesis of equal elasticities for both types of firms cannot be rejected. These results support the conjecture that innovative experience complements the usage of ICT but not the use of the conventional inputs labour and non-ICT capital.

In column 4 of Table 4.3, the regression with interactions is replicated for the alternative classification of firms J_i^{inn} according to whether they have introduced an innovation in any (not necessarily the first) observed periods. This specification thus abstracts from the role of experience and only considers complementarities between ICT use and innovations independently of the temporal sequence. In this specification, the interaction term for both ICT and non-ICT are positive but fail to reach statistical significance. There is thus no robust evidence pointing to impacts of innovations on the productivity of any particular input of production.[24] Jointly, the results of (3) and (4) indicate that obviously it is earlier innovations in the first place that matter for productive ICT use today. This finding supports the conjecture that innovative *experience* rather than just concurrent innovations help to use ICT productively.

In a more detailed analysis considering different *types* of innovation, Table 4.4 reports the results for further regressions in which the innovation dummy is interacted only with the ICT input. The first two columns refer to the classification according to the experience (J_i^{exp}) concept while the latter two consider innovations at an unspecified point of time (J_i^{inn}). The results confirm the findings of Table 4.3 showing that also for considering process and product innovations separately, early innovations do have a significant impact on

---

[23] The tests for first-order and second-order correlation — AR(1) and AR(2) in Table 4.3 — refer to the specification in first differences. No autocorrelation in the level-equations thus implies negative first-order correlation and no second order correlation.

[24] The not-interacted innovation dummy is substantially higher than in the estimation of column 3, highlighting a more prominent role of direct productivity contributions of innovations independently of the use of particular inputs. However, in both cases the coefficient of the innovation dummy is estimated imprecisely and fails statistical significance.

Table 4.4. ICT productivity and firm-level innovations

	(1)	(2)	(3)	(4)
	dependent variable: log(value added)			
	early innovation		some innovation	
	inn.: $J^{exp,pc}$	inn.: $J^{exp,pd}$	inn.: $J^{inn,pc}$	inn.: $J^{inn,pd}$
log(labour)	0.639***	0.652***	0.668***	0.693***
	(9.201)	(9.105)	(9.056)	(9.529)
log(ICT)	0.027	0.010	0.036	0.023
	(1.099)	(0.582)	(1.375)	(1.318)
log(non-ICT)	0.186***	0.189***	0.198***	0.201***
	(3.319)	(3.105)	(3.847)	(4.114)
innovation	0.263	0.196	0.045	0.014
	(1.640)	(1.358)	(-0.212)	(-0.710)
innov.$\times$ log(ICT)	0.125**	0.089**	0.019	0.016
	(2.222)	(2.070)	(-0.053)	(-0.456)
R^2	0.837	0.835	0.836	0.836
WALD STAT.[DF]				
inputs (w/o constants)	97[3]	85[3]	81[3]	85[3]
time and ind. dummies	737[41]	722[41]	723[41]	733[41]
Sargan (p-values)	0.199	0.198	0.449	0.200
ERRORS (P-VALUES)				
AR(1)	0.003	0.003	0.003	0.003
AR(2)	0.049	0.052	0.044	0.041

***, **, and * denote significance at the 1, 5 and 10% level, respectively. All regressions are estimated by two-step SYS-GMM as detailed in Appendix 3.7.1 to chapter 3. t-values reported in parentheses are obtained from heteroscedasticity-robust first-step results (see Blundell and Bond (1998) and chapter 3, in particular footnote 31, p. 76, for more details). The signs of the coefficients and the reported corresponding t-values may therefore differ in some cases.

The definitions of the variable 'innovator' and the corresponding interactions differ between columns as indicated by the subscripts of J^x in the first row (see Table 4.1, p. 115, and section 4.3 for definitions).

ICT productivity while innovations in later periods are positive but insignificant. Interestingly, the experience from process innovations seems to matter more in quantitative terms: the elasticity of ICT among firms with experience in process innovations amounts to 0.152 (from 0.027+0.125) as against more modest 0.099 (0.010+0.89) among firms with early product innovations. This finding of a higher impact of experience from process innovations is corroborated in further unreported regressions in which the dummies for experience from product and from process innovations are interacted with ICT in one regression simultaneously.

Is localisation or technological proximity of experience important for the productivity contributions of ICT? In order to address this question, I rerun specifications (1) and (2) of Table 4.4 and include the additional interaction of ICT capital with only those experienced firms who attributed high importance of ICT for their early innovations. The coefficient of the interaction $\log(ICT) \cdot J^{exp,*} \cdot J^{ICT}$ thus measures the 'extra' elasticity (i.e. productivity contribution) of ICT in firms with early, ICT-related innovations as compared to experienced firms where ICT had no special importance for innovations. In short, this additional term informs about the relevance of experience being localised in ICT.

The results for the relevant ICT variables from this exercise are displayed in Table 4.5.[25] While for process innovations the additional term is insignificant, small and negative, it is positive (but also insignificant) in the case of product innovations. However, the additional term impairs the precision also of the other ICT coefficients. These statistically weak results do not allow to draw any strong conclusions. However, they may be interpreted as a sign consistent with theoretical conjectures that localisation is — if at all — relevant mainly for complementarities between ICT use and product innovations.

As pointed out in section 4.2.4, the above results may be induced by complementarities between ICT and skills if firms with early innovations also employ a high fraction of highly qualified personnel. In order to analyse this potential interference, Table 4.6 reports results for the skill-augmented model equation (4.8). Due to numerous item non-responses in the skills variables, however, the underlying sample is substantially smaller with the number of firms dropping from 1,222 to 591. In order to illustrate the impacts of this change in the sample, the specification for the simplest Cobb-Douglas case (analogue to the first column of Table 4.3) is replicated in the first column of Table 4.6. The most striking change is that the ICT coefficient in particular drops steeply to an insignificant value of 0.015 from 0.049 in the large sample.

The second column of Table 4.6 reports the results for the Cobb-Douglas specification augmented by the shares of employees with university degree and vocational training. Even though the coefficients of these variables are highly significant (both statistically and economically), the size of the other inputs is hardly affected by this extension of the model. This phenomenon corroborates similar findings in the previous chapter and may be due to the fact that the skill composition *within* firms changes very little over time, whereas the heterogeneity *between* firms is accounted for also in the former specification by controlling for firm-specific fixed effects.

Controlling for potential interferences of skills on the interaction between ICT and innovative experience, the results from the estimation of the full equation (4.8) are replicated in column 3 of Table 4.6. As in the preceding specifications, the interaction between ICT and innovative experience enters

---

[25] The other coefficients and statistics are very similar to the ones of specifications (1) and (2) in Table 4.4.

Table 4.5. Technological proximity of innovative experience

dependent variable: log(value added)		
innovation type J^*:	(1) process (pc)	(2) product (pd)
$\log(ICT)$	0.046 (1.504)	0.014 (0.704)
$\log(ICT) \times J^{exp,*}$	0.127 (1.152)	0.061 (1.118)
$\log(ICT) \times J^{exp,*} \times J^{ICT}$	-0.010 (0.780)	0.044 (1.512)
Sargan (p-values)	0.261	0.398
ERRORS (P-VALUES):		
AR(1)	0.004	0.004
AR(2)	0.058	0.064

All regressions are estimated by two-step SYS-GMM as detailed in Appendix 3.7.1 to chapter 3. t-values reported in parentheses are obtained from heteroscedasticity-robust first-step results (see Blundell and Bond (1998) and chapter 3, in particular footnote 31, p. 76, for more details). The signs of the coefficients and the reported corresponding t-values may therefore differ in some cases.

The dummy variable $J^{exp,*}$ denotes experienced product innovator in the first column and process innovator in the second. J^{ICT} denotes innovators for which ICT was important for innovation in early periods (see Table 4.1, p. 115, and section 4.3 for definitions).

The econometric specifications and the sample are the same as in columns (1) and (2) of Table 4.4 and include the same control variables plus a dummy variable for the interaction $J^{exp} \cdot J^{ICT}$.

significantly positive, which points to the robustness of the earlier findings concerning the role of innovative experience. A drawback of the specification underlying column 3 is, however, that — unlike in the previous specifications — the Sargan test rejects the validity of the instruments at the 5% level. Moreover, the interaction between ICT and the share of employees with university degree enters significantly negative, implying the somewhat counterintuitive result that the productivity contributions of skills are lower in experienced firms.

In order to shed some more light on these results, the estimation equation is extended beyond the regression model of equation (4.8) in column (4) by additionally including an interaction between ICT and the share of employees with university degree. This interaction term takes a positive though insignificant value which is consistent with complementarities between ICT and skills found in chapter 3 (see Table 3.4) as well as in other studies.[26] However, the

---

[26] See, e.g., Caroli and van Reenen (2001) and Bresnahan et al. (2002).

Table 4.6. Innovative experience, skills and the productivity of ICT

	dependent variable: log(value added)			
	(1)	(2)	(3)	(4)
log(labour)	0.737***	0.656***	0.723***	0.701***
	(4.379)	(6.518)	(5.518)	(5.412)
log(ICT)	0.015	0.017	0.022	-0.004
	(0.621)	(1.086)	(-0.080)	(-0.333)
log(non-ICT)	0.168	0.208	0.100	0.091
	(1.386)	(1.475)	(0.845)	(0.877)
%university	—	0.827***	0.737**	1.410***
		(3.096)	(2.327)	(2.922)
%vocational	—	0.475***	0.352*	0.688**
		(2.835)	(1.796)	(2.191)
innovation (J_i^{exp})	—	—	0.526***	0.750**
			(1.594)	(2.211)
log(ICT) $\times$ J_i^{exp}	—	—	0.177**	0.211***
			(2.062)	(2.738)
%univ. $\times$ J_i^{exp}	—	—	-0.510**	-0.794**
			(-2.108)	(-2.481)
%voc. $\times$ J_i^{exp}	—	—	-0.093	-0.227
			(-0.660)	(-0.973)
log(ICT) $\times$ %univ.	—	—	—	0.083
				(0.246)
R^2	0.825	0.836	0.834	0.830
WALD STATISTICS[df]:				
inputs (w/o constants)	199[3]	486[5]	2957[8]	3913[9]
time and ind. dummies	393[34]	449[34]	513[34]	583[34]
Sargan (p-values)	0.591	0.198	0.044	0.119
ERRORS (p-values):				
AR(1)	0.024	0.029	0.003	0.002
AR(2)	0.146	0.163	0.022	0.028

***, **, and * denote significance at the 1, 5 and 10% level, respectively. All regressions are estimated by two-step SYS-GMM as detailed in Appendix 3.7.1 to chapter 3. t-values reported in parentheses are obtained from heteroscedasticity-robust first-step results (see Blundell and Bond (1998) and chapter 3, in particular footnote 31, p. 76, for more details). The signs of the coefficients and the reported corresponding t-values may therefore differ in some cases. The underlying sample consists of an unbalanced panel with 591 firms and 1887 observations covering the years 1994-1999.

qualitative results from column (3) are broadly corroborated with the negative interaction terms being even higher in absolute values. The Sargan test does not reject the validity of the instruments used at the 10% significance level.

Summing up the results so far, there is broad evidence that innovative experience has a significant but asymmetric effect on the productivity of the various factors of production. The impacts are significant only for the use of ICT, with the impact from process innovations being particularly high. The positive effect of successful innovations in the past on ICT productivity is robust to the inclusion of variables controlling for skills and various interactions of these variables with ICT and innovative experience.[27]

4.4.2 Discussion and alternative explanations

One might object that the empirical results suffer from an estimation bias due to the fact that the employed innovation variables are endogenous. In fact, productive firms tend to be more profitable and find it easier to overcome constraints in external financing of innovations since they are able to use retained profits as internal resources.[28] Controlling for this endogeneity in the estimations would require to find instrumental variables that affect a firm's decision to innovate but not the productivity of firms. Given the available data, there is no variable that might serve as an appropriate candidate.[29] In the following, however, I discuss various economic sources that might induce the endogeneity problem and conclude that none of them seems to matter for the preferred specification.

First, it should be noted that reverse causality is very unlikely to be a problem. Since innovative experience is defined by a firm's innovation decision *prior* to observed productivity, this kind of endogeneity is precluded by the temporal sequence of both events. This characteristic of the estimation specification reduces the problem to considering variables that may affect both variables (innovation decision and productivity of ICT) simultaneously either because they are unobserved or because they may affect productivity in a form different from the employed functional form of the production function.

One candidate in this sense is technological opportunity. Businesses of some industries may be more suited than others to improve products or processes by the use of ICT. Those better suited businesses will be able to reap higher productivity gains from ICT; but they are more likely to be early adopters of ICT for restructuring their processes, too. If this were true, the higher productivity potentials found would be spurious. This argument indeed

---

[27] As set out in section 4.3, the innovation variables from the employed data include both 'genuine' innovators as well as imitators. Unfortunately, the data constraints do not allow for a further distinction with respect to these characteristics.

[28] For a review of the literature on financial constraints and innovations, see e.g. Hall (2002).

[29] In addition, the search for an instrumental variable is complicated by the fact that, due to the unbalanced panel structure of the sample, many variables are available only for certain years of the survey. Employing such variables would dramatically reduce the size of the sample.

poses a serious objection, if most of the 'experienced' firms in the sample belonged to the same industries. As can be seen from Table 4.9 in the appendix, however, the innovator shares do not vary greatly between industries. To illustrate this point in more detail, Table 4.10 in the appendix summarises the share of experienced process innovators (*epc*) by industry at the more detailed NACE 2-digit level.[30] In most of the industries, the share is quite close to the sample average of 61%.[31] This contradicts an eminent importance of technological opportunity as the driving force behind the results.

A related objection may be that the results could be dominated by a higher productivity of ICT use in larger firms. From the innovation literature, it is well known that bigger firms are more likely to innovate (Cohen, 1995). The innovation proxies might therefore rather capture size effects. To address this issue, the robustness of the results has been checked in additional regressions in a translog production function framework (not reported). Among other features, this more flexible framework explicitly controls for firm-size effects.[32] As a result in this specification as well the ICT coefficient turns out to be significantly higher in experienced firms. Moreover, if it was really firm size driving the results, the same link between firm size, innovation propensity and ICT elasticity would be expected to hold for innovators in general (including the wider definition as 'panel innovator'). However, for firms that have introduced an innovation in *some* period, the productivity effects of ICT were not found to be higher.

Moreover, it may be argued that apart from innovative experience, past innovations may reflect other firm characteristics such as management ability and flexibility. Though certainly rightly so, these underlying factors seem much more likely to impact multi-factor productivity captured by the dummy for innovative experience rather than by the *interaction* of ICT and experience. That is, management characteristics are expected (and partially found) to have a direct impact on overall firm productivity and not so much on the productivity potentials of one of the particular factor inputs.

A final objection relates to the question to what extent the obtained results are data-specific and apply to the German case only. Addressing this concern, I conducted an empirical analysis based on joint work with the CPB Netherlands to assess whether similar findings were obtained for Germany and Holland (Hempell et al., 2004). These analyses formed part of an international research cooperation initiated by the OECD.[33] Employing comparable innovation data from the *Community Innovation Survey* (CIS) (which the MIP-S data is part of) from the years 1996 (CIS 2) and 1998 (CIS 2.5), this paper

---

[30] The distribution of the innovator shares for the alternative classifications is very similar (not reported).

[31] In 8 of the 13 industries, the corresponding shares ly within the range of 51 and 71%.

[32] See extension 3 in section 3.3.3 for further details on this specification.

[33] Important results from this OECD working group on ICT and business performance are summarised in OECD (2003 and 2004).

explores for both countries whether the productivity effects from ICT were higher among firms that had reported product or process innovations in both waves of the survey. The productivity analysis is based on input and output information for the period 1994-99 (as in the empirical analysis in this book) and for 1993-99 for the Netherlands. The employed samples are each based on roughly 1,000 firms from identically defined service industries. However, the composition of the samples differ substantially in some respects. In particular, the weights of wholesale and retail trade in the Dutch sample are twice as high as in the German sample (74% versus 36%).

Despite these differences, we find that in both countries the output elasticities with respect to ICT obtained from SYS-GMM estimations were significantly higher among innovating firms (amounting to 0.107 for Germany, and 0.088 in the Netherlands) compared to non-innovative firms (0.022 and 0.041, respectively) whereas there are no significant differences in the coefficients for non-ICT capital in both cases. Even though the empirical specification of this two-country analysis is somewhat different from the analysis in this chapter, the qualitatively very similar results suggest that the complementarities between innovation activities and ICT productivity are not an artefact of the specific data set employed but may well apply to the case of other data sources and countries, too.

4.5 Conclusions

In this chapter, I argue that the success of firms in using ICT as an input in production is highest if complemented by own innovative activities in application sectors. Moreover, due to learning effects, firms that introduce innovations in early periods will accumulate innovative experience that helps them to innovate in later periods and thus to make productive use of ICT.

Based on innovation data for firms in the German business-related and distribution services with firm-level data, I explore these hypotheses in an extended production function framework with labour and two types of capital inputs, i.e. ICT capital and other 'conventional' capital. I employ a SYS-GMM estimator as described in detail in chapter 3 in order to control for a variety of potential estimation biases, like unobserved heterogeneity, simultaneity of inputs and output and measurement errors. I detect various impacts and complementarities of ICT investment.

First, for an extended Cobb-Douglas production function framework I find that firms which have introduced innovations in the past ('experienced' firms) are especially productive in ICT usage. The elasticity of output with respect to ICT capital is nearly four times as high as in non-experienced firms. An analysis that distinguishes between product and process innovations reveals that experience is particularly relevant for renewing processes. The output elasticity of ICT in firms with early process innovations amounts to about 15% and is significantly higher than for non-experienced firms (3%).

Second, experience gathered from past process innovations is quantitatively more substantial than experience from the introduction of new services. The finding is consistent with theoretical arguments as well as with evidence from case studies which stress the particular relevance of ICT for re-engineering business processes within firms. Because of this close link, experience from past process innovations may help reduce the risks of innovation projects and will improve the firm's expectation formation with regard to the costs and benefits of ICT-induced changes.

Third, unlike innovative experience, innovations at some unspecified point of time (e.g. accompanying current ICT investments) have positive but not statistically significant impacts on ICT productivity. Apparently, the successful implementation of ICT requires a knowledge base in firms which in turn depends to a large extent on firms' innovation behaviour in the past.

Finally, the positive dependence of ICT productivity on innovative experience is a feature that distinguishes ICT investments from other capital inputs. Thus, the increasing importance of innovation may well be identified as an important consequence from increased ICT diffusion. Obviously, firms have not been equally prepared for the large range of innovation possibilities induced by the rapid diffusion of ICT. As a consequence, the induced wave of innovation has contributed to a widening of productivity differentials between firms.

Taken together, these findings support the hypotheses developed in this chapter which assign ICT the role of a 'special' capital input: unlike other capital goods, the productive use of ICT is closely linked to innovations in general and the re-engineering of processes in particular. Overall, the results yield broad evidence that innovative experience is a crucial prerequisite for firms to meet the challenges of ICT as an enabling technology.

There are several implications of these findings concerning both theoretical and policy issues. At the theoretical level, the results contribute to a clarification of the role of ICT as a general purpose technology giving rise to complementary innovations. In spite of the diverse uses and the rapid diffusion of ICT throughout all industries, the productivity effects of ICT are far from self-enforcing but rather demand an active implementation strategy within firms. The role of innovative experience found in this chapter indicates that the determinants for the efficient use of ICT belong to a firm's long-term strategies rather than being characteristics that can be adapted easily in the short term. Innovative experience is likely to be acquired over years rather than within months.

Furthermore, the role of innovative history found at the micro level may also be useful for shedding more light on the differences of ICT-induced productivity effects found between countries. In fact, the competitive and innovative business environment in the U.S. may be one reason that helps explain why the productivity impact of ICT has been much higher there than in continental Europe. The higher innovation pressure in the U.S. over the last decades may have led firms to collect much more diverse innovative experience than more protected firms in Europe. This may have enabled firms in the U.S. to reap higher benefits from the use of ICT. In this respect, ICT may have led to a further widening of the productivity gap both between the U.S. and Europe and between other regional parts of the world economy.

As far as economic policy is concerned, the findings of this chapter point to the importance of an innovative business environment that is needed to lay the fundamentals for an efficient use of ICT. New technologies like ICT may be compared to the invention of a new fertiliser in farming: though its potential uses may be fairly general and its costs quite low, a sound climate, a cultivated soil and a gifted farmer will still be needed to actually increase crop yield. Unlike in the case of farming, however, the climate in the economy may be favoured to a large extent by sound policies. The results of this study suggest that enhancing innovation incentives by deregulation and increased competition may serve as an important driver of both the rapid diffusion and a productive use of ICT.

4.6 Appendix

4.6.1 Tables

Table 4.7. Summary statistics

	mean	std.	minimum	maximum
log(value added*)	1.822	1.886	-3.771	10.888
log(employees)	3.899	1.691	0.000	12.647
log(ICT capital*)	-2.446	2.701	-16.003	9.456
log(non-ICT capital*)	0.979	2.641	-6.270	11.679
East Germany (dummy)	0.422	0.494	0	1

*measured in million €; sample with 5,107 observations from 1,222 firms

Table 4.8. Correlations of variables

	log(value added*)	log(emp.)	log(ICT*)	log(non-ICT*)
log(value added*)	1.00			
log(employees)	0.85	1.00		
log(ICT capital*)	0.64	0.62	1.00	
log(non-ICT capital*)	0.67	0.65	0.46	1.00
East Germany (dummy)	-0.17	-0.08	-0.09	0.04

*measured in million €; sample with 5,107 observations from 1,222 firms

Table 4.9. Share of innovators by industry

industry	J^{exp}	J^{inn}	$J^{inn,pc}$	$J^{inn,pd}$	$J^{exp,pc}$	$J^{exp,pd}$	$J^{exp,pc}$ & $J^{exp,pd}$
wholesale trade	55.8	78.5	64.5	75.6	37.2	52.3	33.7
retail trade	53.7	74.7	63.2	70.0	37.9	47.9	32.1
transport & postal services	59.9	80.6	69.8	78.4	50.0	55.0	45.0
electronic data proc. & telecom.	81.0	97.0	90.0	97.0	60.0	78.0	57.0
consultancies	68.0	88.3	82.5	83.5	54.4	62.1	48.5
technical services	72.7	91.6	84.6	84.6	58.7	61.5	47.6
other business-related services	54.5	76.7	67.1	75.3	37.0	49.7	32.2
all industries	61.0	81.8	71.9	78.6	45.4	55.5	39.9

All values are percentages of firms that take the value one for the corresponding innovation variable J. For the underlying definitions, see section 4.3 and Table 4.1, p. 115.

Table 4.10. Share of firms with innovative experience by industry

industry*	50	51	52	60	61	63	64	70	71	72	73	74	90
share of innovative firms (%)**	46.5	55.8	58.0	54.5	66.7	63.6	66.7	47.0	42.1	81.1	70.6	66.2	60.9
# firms in sample	71	172	119	88	6	121	12	83	19	95	17	355	64

* defined at NACE 2-digit level.
** shares of firms that are experienced innovators ($J^{exp} = 1$). See definition of J^{exp} in Table 4.1, p. 115.

Table 4.11. Comparison of sample and population by industry

		sample		population[*]
industry	NACE-digit	# firms	share (%)	share (%)
wholesale trade	51	172	14.1	10.6
retail trade	50, 52	190	15.6	31.3
transport and postal services	60-63, 64.1	222	18.2	11.7
electronic processing and telecom.	72, 62.2	100	8.2	3.4
consultancies	74.1, 74.4	103	8.4	12.1
technical services	73, 74.2, 74.3	152	11.7	10.7
other business-related services	70, 71, 74.5-.8, 90	292	23.9	20.3
all industries		1,222	100	100

[*]German service firms with 5 and more employees in 1999.
Source: German Statistical Office, ZEW and own calculations

Table 4.12. Comparison of sample and population by size class

	full sample		population[*]	
size class (# employees)	# firms	firms (%)	firms (%)	sales (%)
5-9	205	16.8	57.6	9.4
10-19	206	16.9	24.0	9.9
20-49	254	20.8	11.7	9.7
50-99	156	12.8	3.5	6.9
100-199	168	13.8	1.6	6.0
200-499	102	8.3	1.0	7.0
500 and more	131	10.7	0.6	51.1
all size classes	1,222	100	100	100

[*]German service firms with 5 and more employees in 1999.
Source: German Statistical Office, ZEW and own calculations

5

ICT productivity
and human capital investments

> Computers are incredibly fast, accurate, and stupid.
> Human beings are incredibly slow, inaccurate, and
> brilliant. Together they are powerful beyond imagi-
> nation.
>
> Albert Einstein (1879-1955)

5.1 Introduction

Various studies have suggested that the rapid diffusion of computers and the Internet has contributed to transforming industrialised economies towards 'knowledge-based economies'. Falling ICT prices mean that the marginal costs of accessing, transmitting and storing information are decreasing. This implies that the ability of workers to select and analyse information increases in importance regarding firms' competitiveness and the comparative advantages of economies (Audretsch and Thurik, 2001). Moreover, as illustrated in the preceding chapters 3 and 4, falling prices of ICT broaden the scope for innovation in varied parts of the economy. These innovations need to be backed by skilled workers who are able to adjust to changing work tasks and to contribute to innovation activities in firms with own ideas and flexibility (Brynjolfsson et al., 2002; Arnal et al., 2003).

Consequently, complementarities between ICT and intangible assets (like innovation, organisational changes, or intellectual property rights) have been identified as important drivers of the increased demand for highly skilled workers (Bresnahan et al., 2002). For example, new organisational practices based on ICT help to reshape work tasks towards skill-intensive activities while other, more routinised subtasks are separated out to be handled by computers. Autor et al. (2003) and Spitz (2004) report evidence for strong impacts of computer usage on the composition of work tasks in American and German enterprises. A variety of further studies support this hypothesis pointing to empirical evidence for a substantial skill-bias in ICT-adopting firms.[1]

However, adjustment of workers' skill to computers is unlikely to be achieved by simply substituting highly educated for low-skilled workers. Empirical studies suggest that hirings and separations involve substantial adjustment costs, which are particularly high in the case of high-skilled workers (Hamermesh and Pfann, 1996). On the one hand, these costs are due to labour legislation. On the other hand, much of the knowledge related to processes and the internal organisation of businesses tends to be tacit and therefore firm-specific (Nelson and Winter, 1982). New workers must acquire this knowledge. This is often done by formal training courses or on-the-job training.

Training programmes are not only directed towards new workers. In many instances, they are also designed to update skills of current personnel to special applications and changing tasks. Various applications of ICT are designed individually to the environment of companies by linking specific databases, coordinating business processes or interconnecting workplaces, for example. Moreover, resulting re-organisations of processes and the introduction of new products and services frequently require specific training measures in order to prepare employees for specific new tasks and skills. To the extent that the corresponding training needs are mainly firm-specific, businesses may have incentives to invest in training their workers.[2]

Even though several studies have pointed to complementarities between training measures and ICT,[3] surprisingly few attempts have been made so far to investigate this link empirically. One important exception is a study by Bresnahan et al. (2002) who find strong positive impacts of ICT investments on the demand for skilled workers and firms' investments in human capital. However, the particular role of training remains only a side-aspect of their study.

A more detailed understanding of the interaction between new technologies, education and training is also growing in importance in macroeconomics and in policy-oriented research. For example, Helpman and Rangel (1999) analyse the different impacts of technology-specific experience and general knowledge on the growth effects from the adoption of new technologies. Moreover, a recent study by the OECD has pointed to the particular relevance of training for policy makers:

> "A skilled labour force is a prerequisite for success in today's economy. The education and training of current workers is likely to be the most effective means of maintaining and upgrading the skills of the current

---

[1] See Katz and Autor (1999), Chennells and van Reenen (1999) and Acemoglu (2002) for reviews of the literature on the impacts of new technologies on the demand for educated workers.

[2] This is a main message from the classical human capital theory set forth by Becker (1964). Section 5.2.1 gives a more differentiated picture of this issue.

[3] See the literature review in the next section.

labour force. Given swiftly changing technologies, work methodologies and markets, policymakers in many OECD countries are encouraging enterprises to invest more in training, and to promote more general work-related training of adults. While much is known about what governments and individuals expend to promote learning within formal education institutions, far less is known about the extent of learning at the workplace or in other settings outside formal education and after the completion of initial education." (OECD, 2002, p. 247)

The aim of this chapter is to assess the link between ICT investments and the need for training in more detail at the firm level. In a first step, I employ a framework of firm-level factor choice to explore complementarities between ICT investment, non-ICT investment and training expenditures in service firms. I then investigate to what extent differing abilities of firms in coordinating investments in ICT and training may lead to productivity advantages. Finally, I consider whether wage reactions entail disincentives for firms to invest in training. Accordingly, I run wage cost regressions in order to find out whether the productivity increases from training programmes are offset by corresponding wage increases. A special focus will be directed towards the role of ICT and formal education of workers in this context.

For the empirical assessment of these issues, I use the *MIP-S* data, a detailed set of panel data from German firms in business-related and distribution services that already formed the basis for the empirical analysis in the two preceding chapters 3 and 4. These service industries are particularly relevant for the context at hand since they play a key role in the transformation process of industrialised towards knowledge-based economies.

In the quantitative analysis, I consider various methodological issues that have been raised in the empirical literature concerning the productivity of training. First, training expenditures tend to be a long-term investment. Exploiting the longitudinal structure of the data, I construct stocks of tangible and intangible capital from accumulated investment in ICT, non-ICT and training in order to take potential lags between the time of investment and its productive effects into account. Second, by considering firm-level data both on output and wage costs, I address the question to what extent firms are able to appropriate the productivity gains from their training investments. This issue is important for considering the incentives of firms to invest in training. Third, I take advantage of the panel structure of the data by using system GMM estimators in the production function and wage cost regressions. This approach helps to address various potential biases in productivity analysis, like unobserved heterogeneity, simultaneity and measurement errors, as discussed in chapter 3. Finally, I consider the role of education for the ability of workers to adjust their skills in training programmes. The inclusion of education also helps to relate the results to existing studies that examine the conjecture of a skill-bias in labour demand resulting from the diffusion of ICT.

The chapter is organised as follows. In the next section, I review the related literature and set out some theoretical considerations that help to focus the empirical analysis on specific working hypotheses. In section 5.3, I present the empirical approaches for the analysis. Section 5.4 discusses the data and statistical descriptives, and section 5.5 reports and discusses the empirical results. Section 5.6 provides some concluding remarks.

5.2 Theoretical issues

This chapter links two economic topics that have been considered separately in the previous literature: the productivity contributions of ICT investment on the one hand, and productivity and incentives of training programmes on the other. There are, however, only very few attempts to address both issues jointly. In this section, I first survey several studies that have explored questions similar to the ones raised in this chapter. Building on these earlier contributions, I then present theoretical considerations that help to focus the empirical investigation on specific hypotheses concerning the input choices of ICT and training as well as the role of formal education.

5.2.1 Previous studies

Various previous studies that investigate the productivity contributions of ICT have pointed to the possibly important role of complementary training for a successful adoption of ICT in firms. Several of these studies have found large implicit returns to ICT investment that exceed those of other types of capital.[4] Similarly, also the results from the preferred econometric approach in chapter 3 provides evidence of excess returns to ICT (i.e. returns that exceed the user costs of ICT capital) that amount to more than 50%.

Brynjolfsson and Hitt (2000) argue that unobserved complementary costs associated with ICT investments (including training expenditures) may explain these differences. If such additional costs are particularly important for ICT but are not included in the econometric analysis, the results will suffer from an omitted variable bias that overstates the true productivity contributions of ICT. Brynjolfsson and Hitt (2003) find that measured productivity contributions associated with computerisation are up to five times greater over long periods (using 5- to 7-year differences) than for shorter time-spans (1-year differences). They explain these differences by time-consuming investments in complementary inputs, such as organisational capital. Similarly, Brynjolfsson et al. (2002) argue that training expenditures may be interpreted as investments in intangible assets that act as complements to ICT investments. Cummins (2003) interprets training programmes as part of a wider definition of

---

[4] See, e.g., Lehr and Lichtenberg (1999) and Brynjolfsson and Hitt (2003).

irreversible adjustment costs. Once these costs are dispensed, they implicitly contribute to a firm's organisational capital by causing differences in the valuation of installed and uninstalled tangible capital.

While there is a broad consensus that ICT contributes to firm-level productivity, empirical evidence from earlier studies on the productivity of training is more ambiguous.[5] An important part of this heterogeneity may be due to varying methodological approaches: the decision to invest in training is likely to be endogenous with respect to a firm's performance. Bartel (1994), Dearden et al. (2000) and Zwick (2005) find that less productive firms (*ceteris paribus*) tend to invest more in training. If this endogeneity is not controlled for in the empirical analysis, the true productivity contributions of training will be understated. This effect from endogeneity is just the reverse of those found in studies on ICT productivity where well-performing firms have been found to invest more in ICT (see chapter 3 and, e.g., Brynjolfsson and Hitt, 1996).

In addition, there may be substantial time lags between the training measures and its contributions to productivity. Participation in training programmes may even diminish productivity if reduced working hours due to training courses are not controlled for. Furthermore, even though training programmes prepare employees for new tasks, the productivity effects from training will show up with a time lag after employees have accustomed to the new tasks. The impacts of training expenditures on immediate productivity might therefore be rather small (Black and Lynch, 1996). One solution to this problem is to treat training as a form of investment in human capital formation that pays off over a longer period. Productivity then depends on a training stock from a firm's accumulated training expenditures in the past (Dearden et al., 2000; Ballot et al., 2001a).

An important issue of training programmes is the question of who will have incentives to pay for training: the firm or the worker? The content of the training seems particularly relevant in this context. According to the human capital theory by Becker (1964), firms will be willing to invest mainly in training that is firm-specific. On the contrary, this theory predicts that the costs of general training will have to be borne by the workers due to the threat of poaching. The level of general training may be suboptimally low if the access of workers to credits is constrained by market imperfections.

More recent theories, however, argue that frictions and information asymmetries in the job-market may motivate employers to even finance general training of their workers (Katz and Ziderman, 1990; Acemoglu and Pischke, 1996; Acemoglu, 1997). This argument may apply particularly well to the German job market where turnover rates are relatively low. However, productivity gains from general training are observed for countries with more flexible labour markets, too. In an empirical analysis of training measures in Irish enterprises, Barrett and O'Connell (2001, p. 658) find that general training yields higher productivity effects than firm-specific training. They

---

[5] See Dearden et al. (2000) for an extensive review.

consider efficiency wage arguments and the literature on psychological contracts as potential explanations for these findings that obviously conflict with the implications of Becker's work. Autor (2001a) points to the aspects of self-selection and screening that play a role when firms provide their workers with upfront training. He argues that offering firm-sponsored training will differentially attract workers of greater unobserved ability (self-selection), while the coupling of training with testing of skills will facilitate the screening of workers' abilities.

Dearden et al. (2000) explicitly examine the division of rents from training between firms and employees by comparing output and wage changes due to training programmes. They find that indeed only about a third of the productivity gains from training in British industries are captured by the workers through higher wages. Following a similar approach, Ballot et al. (2001b) find for French and Swedish firms that the predominant part of the productivity gains from investment in training (as well as R&D) can be appropriated by the investing firm. These results support the case for rather high incentives of firms to pay for training. However, the studies do not distinguish between general or firm-specific training programmes.

Even though the empirical literature on both issues (productivity of ICT on the one hand and benefits from training on the other) is extensive, indeed, only few empirical efforts have been made to explicitly assess the question of whether the increasing diffusion of ICT may increase training incentives for the firms. Some few studies indicate that ICT investments are often combined with increased training efforts. Brynjolfsson and Hitt (1998) report that firms which invest in ICT intensively train a higher fraction of their workers and screen new employees more intensively for education than less ICT-intensive firms do. Brynjolfsson et al. (2002) find that the share of workers that receive off-the-job training is strongly correlated to various measures of ICT investment and that this correlation is robust to controlling for firm size, worker occupation and industries. Black and Lynch (1996) find significant evidence that employer-provided computer training has a positive and significant effect on productivity in establishments in the service sector (though not in manufacturing). For other forms of training, they do not find any statistically significant productivity impacts. They interpret these findings as evidence that "it is not so much *whether* you train workers, but rather *what you train the workers* in that affects establishment productivity" (p. 266).

Workers are not equally able to learn and to update their skills for new tasks facilitated by the use of ICT. Several contributions have highlighted the importance of education for the ability of workers to adjust to new technologies. Apart from specific ICT skills, the increased computerisation of work also leads to a shift towards tasks with increased skill requirements and training needs. Autor et al. (2003) argue that computers substitute for workers in performing cognitive and manual tasks that can be accomplished by following explicit rules and complement workers in performing nonroutine problem-solving and complex communication tasks. They find that changing tasks can explain about 60% of the estimated relative demand shift favouring college labour during the years 1970 to 1998 in the U.S. Spitz (2004) obtains very similar results for task shift and educational demand in Germany. Bartel and Lichtenberg (1987) present firm-level evidence that highly educated workers are better enabled to adjust to and to implement new technologies. Taking a more aggregate view, Baily (2002) points to the importance of a continual development of skills associated with increasing investments in ICT. He argues that an important source for the growing demand for skilled labour and increasing returns to education in the U.S. economy may be the superior ability of educated workers to acquire new skills and to take advantage of training. Chun (2003) reports evidence that the education of workers facilitates both the adoption and the (continuous) use of information technologies in U.S. industries.

Other studies consider the joint occurrence of ICT usage, organisational changes and training efforts in firms. These analyses are generally embedded in the overall question of whether the combination of ICT usage and re-organisation entail a skill-bias in the demand for workers. Bresnahan et al. (2002) explore the effects of organisational changes, skills of production workers and ICT investment on human capital investment for a sample of approximately 300 large U.S. firms. They proxy human capital investment by a combination of the share of workers involved in training measures and the manager's qualitative assessments of the importance of cross-training workers and pre-employment screens for education. The determinants of worker training alone, however, are not reported in the study. They find that decentralisation and ICT investments are the predominant forces behind investments in human capital, whereas the level of worker skills predicts human capital investments only if organisational changes are omitted from their regressions. Falk (2001) investigates the reverse direction of causation and finds evidence that both investments in ICT and training efforts are the primary forces behind firms' introducing organisational changes in German service firms. These changes in turn are important factors for shifting labour demand towards workers with higher education. Caroli and van Reenen (2001) find that the productivity gains from organisational changes are declining in the firm's share of unskilled workers. They suggest that — jointly with other factors — this result may reflect that the costs of training for multitasking entailed by organisational changes decrease with the skills of workers.

Summing up, the previous empirical literature on ICT and training entails the following lessons. First, ICT is often complemented by other investments that must be taken into account for assessing the productivity effects of ICT. Second, the implementation of new technologies (including ICT) tends to be associated with training efforts and the changes in work tasks can be addressed more easily by high-skilled workers. Third, the incentives for firms to invest in training are theoretically and empirically ambiguous and obviously depend on the specific kind and the aims of the training programmes. Fourth, the omission of firm-specific effects and endogeneity issues in the analysis tends to understate the benefits from training and at the same time overstate the productivity of ICT investments. Fifth, lags between the time of investments and its effects may understate the benefits from either kind of investment if these are not explicitly considered. In the following analysis on complementarities between ICT and training, I will pay special attention to these results.

5.2.2 Theoretical hypotheses

The propensity to invest in ICTs varies substantially between firms. As shown in the graph in Appendix 5.7.2 to this chapter (page 172) and set out in some more detail in section 5.4, the share of ICT in total tangible investment varies tremendously even within industries. Given that markets in the ICT-producing sectors are rather competitive, it is very unlikely that these variations are primarily due to price differentials potentially encountered by firms in their investment decision. Instead, it is much more likely that these differences mirror differing abilities of firms to make productive use of new technologies. As set out in the previous chapter 4, the propensity of firms to introduce innovations may be causal for these differences. In this chapter, I consider differences in workers' educational attainment and differing investments in training as an additional approach for understanding varying ICT use.

If the endowments of firms with complementary assets were variable and could be adjusted easily, these assets would not be an important source of disparities in the reaction to falling prices of ICT. When computers and other ICT assets get cheaper, firms will adjust the complements correspondingly and exhibit very similar patterns of demand for new technologies embedded in capital investment. However, while ICTs tend to have a relatively short life cycle and are replaced quite frequently, several of the potential complements to ICT seem to be less variable. As shown in the previous chapter 4, the ability of firms to use ICT for own innovations is contingent on innovation strategies in the past. Similarly, other intangible assets of firms, like skills of workers, organisational practices, or intellectual property, seem to be quasi-fixed in the short term since they involve very high adjustment costs and are difficult to accumulate in the short run.[6]

As pointed out in the preceding section, replacement of workers may be a second-best strategy in order to adjust skills to the use of new technologies. Turnover costs tend to be high and firm-specific knowledge may play a crucial role for the need of updating workers' skills. Consequently, adjusting skills by training programmes may be a superior instrument in the short term whereas in the medium and longer term, firms will also change recruitment strategies and demand more high-skilled workers. This shift itself may even be a consequence of rather than an alternative to the increasing need for training efforts if well-educated workers can be trained more effectively to continuously

---

[6] See Brynjolfsson et al. (2002).

changing work tasks. Falling prices of ICT facilitate innovations of products, processes and organisations within firms. If these changes necessitate a continuous adjustment of skills, a skill-bias in the demand for new workers may arise from better learning capabilities. This argument entails the growing importance of 'lifelong learning' and of formal education as a basis for the ability to learn.

This means that ICT investment, innovations, training and a high level of education may form a cluster of complements that continues to grow in importance with falling prices of ICT. In order to point to the role of education as a necessary prerequisite for the ability to acquire new skills, I treat a firm's endowment with educational skills as a quasi-fixed asset that determines the ability to update workers' skills through training programmes. This aspect expands the scope of the analysis beyond the complementarities of ICT and training. It additionally includes the question to what extent the educational level of the workforce plays a role for the adjustment of skills to new tasks.

Summarising these ideas, the following two hypotheses form the main focus of the subsequent analysis. First, *the productivity of ICT is substantially enhanced by complementary training measures.* Second, *workers with a higher formal educational level can be trained more efficiently.*

The expectations about the incentives for firms to pay for training measures are more ambiguous. As found in various previous studies, a substantial part of the changes induced by investments in ICT refer to innovations in firms. On the one hand, training measures supporting these innovations may be directed to tasks that are firm-specific, like firm-specific software applications, administration of databases, or multi-tasking. On the other hand, training needs might be fairly general if organisational changes enhance the importance of interactive and communication skills required for the work in teams, the dealing with customers and suppliers, inspiring and coaching subordinates, etc. (Bresnahan et al., 2002). Taking additionally into account that the results in the empirical literature are ambiguous about the incentives of firms to pay for either type of training, it is difficult to assess from a theoretical point of view whether gains from ICT-related training can indeed predominantly be appropriated by the firms or their employees. This question is thus left open for the empirical investigation without any ex-ante hypothesis.

5.3 Empirical approach

The hypothesised complementarity of ICT and training has at least two important implications that can be investigated empirically at the firm level. A first implication concerns *homogeneous* patterns of factor choice. If adjustment costs associated with ICT and training are small or do not vary significantly, the choice of both inputs will depend on a similar set of determinants and will be highly correlated with each other. A further implication analysed in a second approach is that joint investments in ICT and training will yield higher productivity contributions than uncoordinated investments in either kind of asset. Empirically, this implication can be addressed only if lags, adjustment costs, uncertainties, or errors prevent managers from installing a unique optimal combination of complementary factors instantaneously. The resulting *heterogeneity* in the productivity of factor usage can be explored in a production function framework.

The third question envisaged in this chapter concerns the *incentives* for firms to invest in training that complements ICT investments. If the productivity gains from such training expenditures are offset by wage increases of a similar magnitude, resulting disincentives will slow down both firms' training efforts and investments in ICT. In the empirical application, it is therefore investigated how the benefits from training are partitioned between the investing firm and its employees.

5.3.1 Correlations in factor choice

If training and ICT use are complements, optimising firms will combine ICT investment with increased training efforts. Consequently, the choice of both inputs will be positively correlated for a cross-section of firms. This implication is a direct result from the model of complementarities summarised in chapter 1 (section 2.3.3, p. 25ff.). However, as pointed out in the discussion of this model, correlation of input choices is a necessary but not sufficient condition for complementarities. Two input choices may be correlated simply because some third variable impacts both in a similar fashion. For example, training expenditures and ICT investments may be correlated simply because both choices are complementary to innovation activities.

In order to control for the influence of other variables and firm characteristics, I consider the correlation of training and ICT choice conditional on a large set of control variables. Apart from the level of output, these include important firm characteristics like firm size, industry, corporate structure (indicating whether a firm is part of a group of companies) and a regional dummy for firms located in East Germany. Further controls are strategic choices of firms that are likely to simultaneously affect the choices for ICT and training investments. These variables include the share of high- and medium-skilled workers in the firm, the share of apprentices in the workforce (for training equation only), export activities, and information on product or process innovations in the past. Finally, I include information from a subjective assessment of whether firms face competition from foreign firms in their market. Since investment decisions are largely determined by expectations about future sales, I additionally include dummy variables that indicate whether firms expect their sales to increase or decrease in the future. In addition, investment in other type of tangible (non-ICT) capital goods serve as a further control for other unobserved determinants that affect firms' investment behaviour.[7]

---

[7] Interpreting the factor choice as a system of factor demand would require to include input prices varying across firms, which are not available however. As

For scrutinising the correlation between training and ICT investments conditional on these control variables, I regress training expenditures on ICT investment and the control variables. Moreover, I also consider the reverse direction and regress ICT investment on training and controls. Complementarities imply that in these two regressions, training and ICT investment affect significantly positive the choice of the corresponding other input even after controlling for the broad number of control variables.

Finally, in a third specification, I employ non-ICT investment as the dependent variable with ICT, training and the controls as regressors. This specification will serve as a reference result for revealing the patterns underlying conventional capital investment. The direct comparison of the results for ICT and non-ICT investment input choice will indicate whether complementarities with training are a particularity of ICT or whether new vintages of other capital goods are complemented by training expenditures, too.

The empirical model for the input choice of firm i for the inputs training (q_{1it}), ICT (q_{2it}) and non-ICT (q_{3it}) can thus be summarised by the following system of equations:

$$
\begin{pmatrix} q_{1it} \\ q_{2it} \\ q_{3it} \end{pmatrix} = \begin{pmatrix} 0 & \beta_{12} & \beta_{13} \\ \beta_{21} & 0 & \beta_{23} \\ \beta_{31} & \beta_{32} & 0 \end{pmatrix} \begin{pmatrix} q_{1it} \\ q_{2it} \\ q_{3it} \end{pmatrix} \tag{5.1}
$$
$$
+ \begin{pmatrix} \alpha_1 \\ \alpha_2 \\ \alpha_3 \end{pmatrix} y_{it} + \begin{pmatrix} \hat{\alpha}_1 \\ \hat{\alpha}_2 \\ \hat{\alpha}_3 \end{pmatrix} E(\Delta y_{i,t+1}) + \Theta C_{it} + \begin{pmatrix} \epsilon_{i1} \\ \epsilon_{i2} \\ \epsilon_{i3} \end{pmatrix},
$$

with $(q_{1it}, q_{2it}, q_{3it})'$ representing the (log) factor choice for ICT, training, and non-ICT investments in period t.[8] y_{it} denotes the (log) level of output, $E(\Delta y_{i,t+1})$ expected changes in future sales, vector C_i collects the firm characteristics and strategies discussed above, and $(\epsilon_{1it}, \epsilon_{2it}, \epsilon_{3it})'$ is a vector of normally distributed error terms. Since external shocks will affect the choice

---

discussed by Bresnahan et al. (2002) who employ a very similar approach, investment considered here can be interpreted as short-term input choices that are dependent on quasi-fixed inputs and strategies included in the explanatory variables.

[8] Bresnahan et al. (2002) employ a similar specification in logarithms to explore correlations in regression analysis. An alternative to the specification in logarithms consists in using investment intensities (calculated as the shares of investment expenditures in sales) as measures of factor choice in order to avoid the usage of logarithms and the resulting loss of observations with zero investment. Tobit regression can then be used to account for the fact that investment expenditures are restricted to positive values. However, kernel density estimates summarised in Table 5.2 in the Appendix (p. 173) provide no evidence supporting the necessary normality assumptions for Tobit regressions so that the specification in logarithms is preferred. In the discussion of the corresponding empirical findings, I explicitly discuss the robustness of the results with respect to potential selection and specification issues.

in all three factors simultaneously, I employ a seemingly unrelated regression (SUR) to estimate this system of equations.

Apart from revealing evidence on complementarities and common determinants, the analysis will possibly also point to differences in the patterns of factor choice. Some variables that strongly favour training expenditures may have a small (or even negative) impact on ICT investment, and vice versa. The educational level of workers, for example, may be more relevant for training investment than for ICT use if education is mainly a prerequisite for the ability of workers to continuously update their skills to changing tasks. In this respect, the analysis may reveal differing prerequisites that prevent firms from choosing similar combinations of ICT and training investment. This heterogeneity in combining complements forms the basis for the production function approach which is described in the subsequent subsection.

5.3.2 Productive interactions

A further approach to measuring complementarities is to assess the productive interaction more directly in a production function framework. Complementarities imply that the marginal returns to one input increase with the use of corresponding complements. As set out in more detail in section 2.3.3, complementarities can be investigated in a production function framework by including interaction terms between the relevant input variables. In an analysis for a cross-section of firms, the estimated coefficients of the interaction terms are a measure of the productivity gains that are due to complementarities.

A prerequisite for the production function approach to work is that the inputs are not perfect complements. This means that other forces like adjustment costs, uncertainties, experimentation or management errors prevent firms from adjusting to one unique optimal combination of factors instantaneously (see Caroli and van Reenen, 2001; Bresnahan et al., 2002). As suggested in the previous sections, such distorting factors are likely to play a role for ICT and training investment. In response to falling prices of ICT, some firms may be able to complement ICT investments with corresponding training programmes more readily than other firms and reap higher productivity gains due to the coordination of the inputs.

The ability to supplement ICT investments by corresponding training measures may be contingent on the educational background of the workers. If — as argued above — a particular productive advantage of educated workers consists in their ability to adjust to changing work tasks, the combination of education and training will raise the productivity of ICT investments. In this case, the complementarity is three-fold and the ability of firms to accommodate to a 'high-ICT, high training' optimum will rise with the endowment with well-educated workers.

I will analyse the productive interactions of ICT, training and education in a Cobb-Douglas production function framework that is extended by the interactions of the relevant input variables ICT, training, and educational level of workers. This proceeding is very similar to the approach envisaged in several earlier empirical studies on complementarities, such as Caroli and van Reenen (2001), Dearden et al. (2000), Bresnahan et al. (2002) or Brynjolfsson et al. (2002). The econometric specification for the logarithm of output (value added) y_{it} of firm i in period t is:

$$y_{it} = \beta_1 l_{it} + \beta_2 k_{it} + \beta_3 ict_{it} + \gamma_1 s_{h,it} + \gamma_2 s_{m,it} \qquad (5.2)$$
$$+\beta_4 t_{it} + \boldsymbol{\Psi}'(ict_{it}, t_{it}, s_{h,it}, s_{m,it})\theta + \eta_i + \epsilon_{it}$$

where l, k, ict, t represent the logarithms of the number of employees, the stocks of non-ICT capital, ICT capital and training, s_h and s_m are the shares of highly educated and medium skilled workers. η_i denotes time-invariant un-observed firm-specific effects impacting productivity and ϵ_{it} is an asymptotically normally distributed error term. The vector $\boldsymbol{\Psi}(ict_{it}, t_{it}, s_{h,it}, s_{m,it})$ contains various interactions between the variables for ICT, training and shares of skilled labour that extend the basic Cobb-Douglas specification to account for complementarities (with θ being the vector of its coefficients).

The first line of (5.2) corresponds to the production function setup augmented by heterogeneous labour quality in chapter 3 where heterogeneity of labour input is controlled for. As discussed in section 3.5.1 (extension 2), the coefficients of the skill shares s_h and s_m are proportional to the productivity differential between these groups of workers as compared to workers with no formal education.

The second line contains the training stock as an additional input in the production function. Analogous to ICT and non-ICT capital, firm-sponsored training is thus considered as an intangible asset that contributes to firm productivity. Additional interaction terms between ICT, training, and educational level are used to empirically explore to what extent productivity of one input is contingent upon the use of the corresponding other variables.

One key aspect of this study is to assess to what extent the combination of training and ICT usage increase productivity. The interaction of these two variables may be interpreted as the additional productivity gains that can be obtained from specific training measures that supplement ICT investments.[9] Moreover, the interaction of training and skill-shares indicate to what extent training of educated employees yields higher benefits than training unskilled workers, or to what degree training of educated workers is more 'productive'. A threefold interaction of education, training and ICT may then be interpreted as the specific benefits from ICT-related training of highly educated workers. If, first, ICT investment enhances training needs and, second, training educated workers is more productive than training workers with low formal education, and third, education is particularly important for adjusting to ICT, the interaction of all three inputs will be positive.

---

[9] Due to symmetry, the interaction equally reflects the additional productivity gains from ICT investments that are complemented by investments in training.

5.3.3 Training incentives from ICT investment?

Even though training may raise productivity, incentives of firms to invest in training may be small. If the predominant part of productivity gains from training investments are appropriated by workers through higher wages and if market failures (e.g., credit constraints) prevent firms from imposing the financial burden on their workers, firms' training efforts will be suboptimal. If complementarities between ICT use and training exist, disincentives with respect to training will also lead to underinvestment in ICT. It thus seems worthwhile to ask whether computerisation may not only foster training needs but also training incentives for firms.

In order to assess how productivity gains from training are shared by the firm and its employees, I apply a similar approach as developed in Dearden et al. (2000). I run additional wage regressions in which the log of the total payroll w_{it} of firm i in period t is explained by exactly the same inputs that enter the production function:

$$w_{it} = \tilde{\beta}_1 l_{it} + \tilde{\beta}_2 k_{it} + \tilde{\beta}_3 ict_{it} + \tilde{\gamma}_1 s_{h,it} + \tilde{\gamma}_2 s_{m,it} \tag{5.3}$$
$$+ \tilde{\beta}_4 t_{it} + \mathbf{\Psi}'(ict_{it}, t_{it}, s_{h,it}, s_{m,it})\tilde{\theta} + \eta_i + \epsilon_{it}.$$

By comparing the elasticities of the inputs in the production function and the wage regressions, I examine the share of the productivity increases from the various types of investments that are appropriated by the workers through higher wages. For example, abstracting from the interactions, $\rho_{4w} = \tilde{\beta}_4/\beta_4$ corresponds to the share of productivity gains from training appropriated by the workers and the residual $\rho_f = 1 - \tilde{\beta}_4/\beta_4$ represents the corresponding share accruing to the firm.

The decision of firms to invest in worker training will be determined mainly by the expected *net returns* from training investments. These will result from the gross return $r_t^{gr} = \beta_4 Y/T$ minus the return appropriated by workers $r_t^w = \tilde{\beta}_4 Y/T$, where Y/T denotes the inverse of the share of the training stock T in output Y. The net returns of training to the firm are thus $r_t^f = (\beta_4 - \tilde{\beta}_4)Y/T$. Assuming the 'capital costs' of the training stock to be determined by the market interest rate r and the depreciation of the training stock (δ_t) — consisting in turnover of employees, obsolescence and other factors —, the optimal stock of training T^* will result from equating capital costs and expected returns ($\delta_t + r = r_t$): $T^* = \frac{\beta_4 - \tilde{\beta}_4}{r + \delta_t} \cdot Y$. The demand for training stock T will thus increase in the 'net' elasticity ($\beta_4 - \tilde{\beta}_4$) and the desired output level Y, and will decrease in the market interest rate r and depreciation δ_t.

The *incentives* of firms to raise the training stock due to rising ICT investment will thus not only depend on possibly higher gross returns (reflecting the overall *need* to complement ICT by training) but rather on potentially higher net returns mirrored by the differential $\beta_4 - \tilde{\beta}_4$.[10] Assessing the ques-

---

[10] A part of this increase in the optimal training stock due to ICT may be offset by an increase in the rate of depreciation of trained knowledge. If computer related

tion whether computerisation of firms leads to increasing training incentives, I will therefore compare the differentials in the coefficients of the interaction terms in the output and the wage regression. If positive incentives prevail, these differentials will be positive.

5.4 Data

The empirical approaches outlined in the previous section are applied to data from the *Mannheim Innovation Panel in Services* (*MIP-S*) which surveys the innovation behaviour of German service firms. This set of unbalanced panel data covering the time period from 1994 to 1999 is described in section 3.4. In particular, I follow the same proceedings for deriving value added as a measure of output of firms. Moreover, I proxy the shares of high- and medium-skilled workers by the share of employees with a university degree and with vocational degree just like in the two preceding chapters 3 and 4.

Expenditure on ICT and non-ICT investments and training expenditures will be used to proxy the firm's corresponding factor choices. However, for the productivity regressions this is a very noisy measure if time lags (between the time of investment and its productivity effects) as well as cyclical fluctuations (that may strongly impact investment decisions) are important. In order to attenuate this problem, I make use of the longitudinal structure of the data and use an approach proposed by Hall and Mairesse (1995) to construct separate stocks for the tangible assets non-ICT and ICT capital as well as the intangible training stock. For the cases of ICT and non-ICT capital, this approach is described in detail in section 3.4 (see in particular equation (3.19) on page 70). In addition, I use the same method for training expenditures which are treated as contributing to an intangible training stock that depreciates over time. In the parametrisation for constructing this intangible stock, I follow the suggestions by Dearden et al. (2000) who propose a depreciation rate of $\delta =15\%$ of the training stock and an average growth rate of $g =2\%$.

Training investments as surveyed by the *MIP-S* include all kinds of training expenditures by firms. Apart from ICT-related training, it comprises varied other training measures that may be indirectly related to ICT use, like training related to new services or improvement of communication skills. On the one hand, this comprehensiveness is an advantage since — as shown in the previous chapter — implementing ICT requires innovations which necessitate adjustments of skills. On the other hand, some forms of training may

---

knowledge (like software skills) becomes obsolete more rapidly than training directed towards other purposes, higher training expenditures will be necessary to maintain (rather than increase) the level of the knowledge stock as 'replacement investment'. However, also in this case the use of computers will enhance the need for continuous training of the employees, and the quantitative assessment of those much more specific aspects is therefore left for future research.

be independent of ICT use, e.g. instruction courses in new vintages of non-ICT capital. Unfortunately, there is no further information available which would allow to classify different sorts of training expenditures. To the extent that the unobserved relatedness of training to ICT use varies between firms, this broad measure will be subject to a measurement error when it comes to investigating complementarities between ICT and training.

For the empirical approaches I resort to varying samples of the survey. This choice results from the trade-off between the aim of including a larger variety of variables in the factor choice approach on the one hand and the exploitation of the longitudinal structure of the data in the productivity and the wage regressions on the other hand. After dropping observations with item non-responses in the variables of interest, I am left with 1,630 observations from 1,241 firms for the factor choice approach. The variables included in the factor choice regressions are the (lagged) shares of employees with a university degree, completed vocational training as well as the share of apprentices in the workforce. Moreover, various dummy variables control for further firm strategies: the variables 'exporter' and 'foreign competition' control for whether the firm has reported exports or competition from abroad in one of the observed periods (not necessarily the preceding), and the variables for continuous innovation of products and processes, respectively, refer to the innovation strategies of firms. These innovation dummy variables equal one if a firm has been reporting a product/process innovation in all the preceding periods (including the current one) that have been surveyed by the *MIP-S*.

For the regressions analysing investment, firms' expectation about the development of sales in the corresponding future three-year period are included. Firms were asked to assess on a five-point Likert scale whether they expected sales to grow or fall. Taking the mid-range (no change) as the reference, I constructed four dummy variables that take the value one if sales are expected to grow strongly, grow, fall, or fall strongly. Investment choice is expected to be positively correlated to these expected changes in sales. Further controls include the corporate structure ('part of group of companies'), a regional dummy for East German firms as well as time and industry dummies. The classification of industries is analogue to the one used in the previous two chapters and is summarised in Table 5.8 in the Appendix 5.7.2 to this chapter.

For the productivity and wage regressions, panel estimators will be applied that require excluding firms with less than three subsequent observations. Moreover, banks and insurances are dropped from these regressions since the output measures available for these industries (balance sheet totals for banks and total insurance revenues for insurances) are an unreliable measure for productivity calculations. To ensure the consistency of the panel data, I exclude several outliers.[11] The resulting panel sample consists of 1,249 observations

---

[11] In the longitudinal dimension, outliers with unreasonable jumps in sales or employment are excluded from the analysis. This is done on a case-by-case basis, taking into account the size of the firm and the comparison with changes in other

from 393 firms. In those regressions that focus on the various interactions in the production function, a slightly greater sample with 1,275 observations from 401 firms is used. The additional observations are obtained from the eight additional firms which did not report information on wages but on the other relevant variables. However, as will be shown, the empirical results are hardly affected by this small sample variation.

The means and standard deviations of the variables of the two samples are summarised in Table 5.7 in the Appendix 5.7.2 to this chapter. Moreover, Table 5.8 compares the composition of the samples with each other and with the population of businesses in Germany. The comparison shows that the industry weights in the two samples are very similar and reflect the structure of the population of firms overall fairly well.[12]

Table 5.1. Training expenditures and investment in ICT and non-ICT

training expenditures per employee (in €)	ICT investment		non-ICT investment		overall
	low	high	low	high	
mean	787	1,262	1,135	915	1,025
median	108	556	250	278	261

Results are based on time averages of investment expenditures from an unbalanced panel 1994-98 of 4,053 firms in business-related and distribution services. Firms are classified as 'high' if the corresponding investment expenditures per worker exceed the median value and as 'low' otherwise.

Since one aspect of the analysis of this chapter concerns the correlation of investments in ICT, non-ICT, and training, some simple statistics are summarised in Table 5.1. These statistics are based on the maximum of observations available for these three variables in the period 1994-98. It contains the undeflated time averages of investment expenditures per worker for 4,053 firms. Unlike the samples that are used for the regressions and that contain logarithmic values, this maximum sample includes observations for which investments in one or several of the assets are zero.[13] I divide the sample into groups with 'high' and 'low' investment expenditures using the medians of

---

periods. In the cross-section, firms with labour productivities (value added per employee) exceeding € 500,000 are dropped.

[12] Banking and insurances are oversampled in the first sample (used for the factor choice regressions) and — as stated above — omitted in the second sample. In both samples, retail trade businesses are undersampled whereas electronic processing and telecommunication as well as transport and postal services are slightly oversampled.

[13] The shares of firms with zero expenditures in all the periods observed are 14.0% for non-ICT investments, 10.9% for ICT investments, and 17.3% for training programmes. These firms are dropped from the samples that are used for the subsequent regressions presented in the next section 5.5 since the specification

ICT and non-ICT investments per full-time worker as the classification criterion. The classification 'low' means that the firm's average expenditures on the corresponding investments are below the median and 'high' for the rest of the firms.

The statistics indicate that the mean expenditures on training per worker are about 50% higher in the high-ICT group than in the low-ICT group. The differences are even more pronounced if one considers the corresponding medians of training expenditures. In contrast, this positive correlation cannot be found for conventional (non-ICT) investment and training. Average training efforts are even slightly lower in the 'high-conventional' group. Table 5.2 supports these results with corresponding correlation coefficients. While ICT and training investments are significantly positively correlated (as well as ICT and non-ICT investments are), there is even a negative (though insignificant) correlation between non-ICT investment and training.

Table 5.2. Correlations of time averages of investments per worker

	non-ICT	ICT	training
non-ICT	1.000		
ICT	0.107***	1.000	
training	-0.013	0.087***	1.000

Correlations are based on time averages of investment expenditures from an unbalanced panel of 4,053 firms in business-related and distribution services covering the years 1994-98.
*** denotes significance at the 1% level.

These simple comparisons yield first support for the conjecture that computers and training might indeed act as complements in the production process. Moreover, the contrasting insignificant correlation between conventional investments and training indicate that the particular need for training is a feature that distinguishes ICT from other kinds of investments in tangible capital.

5.5 Empirical results

This section presents the empirical results from applying the three approaches set out in section 5.3 to the *MIP-S* data. Its first part presents evidence on correlations in factor choice of ICT and training based on regression analysis controlling for a large variety of effects. The subsequent parts then use the SYS-GMM techniques discussed in chapter 3 to explore the causal effects of

_____
is in logs. As part of the discussion, however, I will also address the question to what extent the resulting sample selection may bias the econometric results.

joint ICT use and training efforts on productivity and to address the question to what extent ICT investments affect the incentives for firms to invest in training.

5.5.1 Correlated factor choice

Table 5.3 shows the results for the interrelated investment choice of worker training, ICT capital and non-ICT capital. Since unobserved external shocks may affect the choice in all three inputs simultaneously, I use seemingly unrelated regressions (SUR).

In a first parsimonious specification that omits fixed and quasi-fixed firm choices and strategies, the chosen quantities of training, ICT and non-ICT are explained only by the choice with respect to the corresponding two other inputs, by the level of output and by industry and time dummies as well as a regional dummy for East Germany (see first three columns of Table 5.3). This corresponds to assessing the correlation of factor choice within industries and years in East and West Germany. The signs and significance levels of the results broadly resemble the simple correlation coefficients as in Table 5.2. Columns (1) and (2) show that training expenditures increase in ICT investment and vice versa, whereas there is no statistically significant direct link between training expenditures and non-ICT investments. Moreover, the usage of ICT and non-ICT is strongly correlated. One reason for this finding might be that ICT goods and software — like computers or networks — are complementary to investments in non-ICT goods since they need a 'context' of other types of tangible capital like workplaces, buildings, machines, etc. to be installed in. Moreover, financing constraints are likely to be very similar for ICT and non-ICT investments as two kinds of tangible assets.

In order to explore which underlying factors drive the strong correlation between ICT and training, I additionally include firm-specific characteristics and choices in a further specification (see last three columns of of Table 5.3). The corresponding results show that the interrelation coefficients of ICT and training remain statistically significant but are lower than in the first specification. The training coefficient in the ICT equation drops from 0.58 to 0.41 and the ICT coefficient in the training equation from 0.70 to 0.43. This finding indicates that a considerable part of the overall correlation between training and ICT investment is not due to direct complementarities but to other variables that affect the choice in both inputs in a similar way. Nevertheless, the fact that the correlation between ICT and training remains present even after controlling for a broad set of control variables points to the presence of complementarities even though, as discussed in the previous section, a very broad measure of training investments is employed. In contrast, there is no indication of any correlation between non-ICT investment and training.

Strikingly, there is a particularly strong link between some of the considered variables and the quantity of both ICT and training investment. Most

Table 5.3. Investment in non-ICT, ICT and training

| | dependent variable: log(investment) | | | | | |
	(1) training	(2) ICT	(3) non-ICT	(4) training	(5) ICT	(6) non-ICT
log(training expenditures)		0.583***	0.022		0.412***	0.020
		(0.019)	(0.032)		(0.023)	(0.035)
log(ICT investment)	0.705***		0.684***	0.434***		0.707***
	(0.023)		(0.032)	(0.024)		(0.034)
log(non-ICT investment)	0.013	0.336***		0.010	0.326***	
	(0.019)	(0.016)		(0.017)	(0.016)	
log(value added)	0.123***	0.058***	0.354***	-0.021	0.096***	0.362***
	(0.025)	(0.022)	(0.032)	(0.029)	(0.027)	(0.039)
East Germany	-0.041	-0.269***	0.691***	-0.112**	-0.268***	0.679***
	(0.065)	(0.059)	(0.083)	(0.063)	(0.061)	(0.089)
log(labour)				0.317***	0.018	-0.197*
				(0.075)	(0.074)	(0.108)
log(labour)^2				0.020***	0.007	0.020**
				(0.007)	(0.007)	(0.010)
%apprentices				1.648***		
				(0.447)		
%university$_{t-1}$				1.059***	0.537***	-0.747***
				(0.172)	(0.168)	(0.249)
%vocational$_{t-1}$				0.191	0.055	0.157
				(0.120)	(0.117)	(0.173)
exporter				0.069	-0.031	0.050
				(0.072)	(0.070)	(0.103)
product innovator				0.169**	-0.048	0.005
				(0.070)	(0.068)	(0.101)
process innovator				0.063	0.231***	-0.050
				(0.070)	(0.069)	(0.102)
foreign competition				0.133**	-0.045	-0.164*
				(0.062)	(0.061)	(0.090)
group of companies				-0.103	0.263***	-0.206**
				(0.066)	(0.064)	(0.095)

(continued on next page)

importantly, the share of workers with university degree correlates significantly positively with both assets but negatively with conventional capital
input. In quantitative terms, the link between skills and training is particularly strong with the coefficient in the regression (1.059) being about twice as

Table 5.3. Investment in non-ICT, ICT and training (continued)

	dependent variable: log(investment)					
	(1)	(2)	(3)	(4)	(5)	(6)
	training	ICT	non-ICT	training	ICT	non-ICT
INDUSTRY DUMMIES (ref. group: wholesale):						
retail trade	0.433***	-0.370***	0.413***	0.262**	-0.245**	0.322**
	(0.122)	(0.112)	(0.159)	(0.112)	(0.109)	(0.160)
transport & post	0.274**	-0.700***	2.155***	-0.095	-0.627***	2.125***
	(0.128)	(0.116)	(0.157)	(0.119)	(0.116)	(0.163)
electr. proc. & telecom	0.229	0.859***	-1.055***	0.079	0.874***	-0.849***
	(0.151)	(0.135)	(0.197)	(0.143)	(0.138)	(0.205)
consultancies	0.505***	0.456***	-0.684***	0.357***	0.561***	-0.577***
	(0.146)	(0.132)	(0.191)	(0.135)	(0.131)	(0.194)
technical services	0.276**	0.603***	-0.762***	-0.045	0.537***	-0.433**
	(0.131)	(0.118)	(0.172)	(0.133)	(0.129)	(0.191)
banking and insurances	0.120	0.525***	-1.237***	0.547***	0.622***	-1.242***
	(0.124)	(0.113)	(0.160)	(0.117)	(0.114)	(0.168)
other	0.254**	-0.477***	1.275***	0.084	-0.418***	1.261***
	(0.113)	(0.103)	(0.143)	(0.105)	(0.102)	(0.147)
EXPECTED DEVELOPMENT OF FUTURE SALES:						
decreasing strongly				-0.244*	0.063	0.062
				(0.142)	(0.139)	(0.205)
decreasing				0.152*	-0.121	-0.049
				(0.083)	(0.081)	(0.119)
increasing				0.112*	0.056	-0.158
				(0.068)	(0.066)	(0.097)
increasing strongly				0.424***	0.004	0.209
				(0.118)	(0.116)	(0.171)
R^2	0.562	0.654	0.590	0.664	0.694	0.596

***, **, and * denote significance at the 1%, 5%, and 10% level. Heteroscedasticity-consistent standard errors reported in parentheses. The results are obtained from a SUR estimation for a pooled sample of 1,241 firms with 1,630 observations for the years 1995-1999. All estimations contain industry and year dummies.

large as the one in the ICT equation (0.537). Similarly, innovation strategies play an important role for the chosen quantity of ICT and training but not for non-ICT.

However, a substantial part of training and ICT investment is related to very different factors. While ICT is increasing with the level of output, training efforts are closely related to the number of employees instead. In the training equation (3), both the coefficient of the log of employees and its square are significantly positive. This implies that training efforts are rising more than proportionally in the number of employees. This finding may reflect spill-over effects of human capital formation in the firms. Moreover, the share of apprentices in the workforce is highly significant for the case of training.[14] This correlation may reflect a firm's general strategy for human capital formation. Employing and instructing apprentices often forms part of a more general recruitment strategy and may be an indicator of a firm's ability to appropriate a large part of the rents from training. A high share of apprentices may thus reflect a firm's more general propensity to build up a firm-specific human capital stock.

Even though past innovation efforts are important for both ICT and training investment, there are striking differences with respect to the types of innovation that are important in both cases. ICT investment is obviously closely related to process innovations but less affected by product innovations. This finding corroborates findings from the previous chapter where past process innovations are found to be important for ICT productivity. Various processes in service firms can be improved and simplified through the usage of ICT, like real-time ordering in trade, the introduction of net-based ICT-systems or computer-based consultant systems in banking or insurances.

In contrast, training is positively affected by past product innovations. This is not surprising given that product innovations in services (incorporating new or significantly improved services introduced by the firms) are frequently closely related to the knowledge of the employees. Examples of new services are the inclusion of a completely new class of products (in wholesale of retail trade), new derivatives offered by banks, new insurance portfolios, or extended support services for telecommunication and software services. Such innovations typically involve the adjustment of employees' knowledge and tasks, and they are likely to be complemented by corresponding training measures. These characteristics of the innovations in services may help explain the unequal role of product and process innovations for the chosen quantities of ICT and training.

A further noteworthy result concerns corporate structure. Firms that are part of a group of companies invest much more heavily in ICT than other firms, but exhibit lower investment in non-ICT and training (with the coefficient for training being statistically insignificant, however). The positive impact on ICT is consistent with the existence of network effects that help to make coordination of activities in groups of companies easier, like the sharing of common databases or the establishment of an intranet.

---

[14] Additional (not reported) regressions show that the share of apprentices is completely irrelevant for ICT and non-ICT and has hardly any impact on the other coefficients. Since there is neither a theoretically founded reason why this share would impact these choices, it is included only in the equation explaining training investment.

In contrast, there is no evidence of a systematic link between export activities and either of the three inputs considered here. The negative (but insignificant) association between exports and ICT investment is particularly striking since the use of ICT lowers communication and transaction costs and could thus be expected to complement export activities of firms. The exposure to foreign competition reduces investment in non-ICT capital but leaves the ICT and training investment unaffected. East German firms tend to invest substantially more in conventional capital. This may be a result from the various policy measures aimed at promoting capital spending in the former socialist part of Germany. However, these higher investment activities neither comprise new technologies nor training efforts: ICT and training investment is significantly higher among firms in West Germany. This result is striking insofar as several investment subsidies granted to firms in East Germany (in particular small and medium-sized firms) have been focussed on the promotion of the use of new technologies as well as training programmes for employees.

Further regressions show that these results are very robust with respect to several changes in the specification. In order to control more effectively for cyclical effects, I employed stocks of ICT, non-ICT and training as proxies for input choice. As documented in Table 5.9 in Appendix 5.7.2 (p. 169), the results are not affected qualitatively and are hardly affected in quantitative terms when stocks instead of investment are employed.[15] Moreover, the results discussed in Appendix 5.7.1 yield no evidence of any substantial selection bias resulting from the fact that various firms with no reported training expenses were excluded from the regressions (since the specification employs logarithmic values).

Finally, Table 5.10 in the Appendix (p. 171) displays the results for estimates using investment intensities (measured as the shares of investment expenditures in sales) in Tobit regressions. This specification has the advantage of including also firms with zero investments in the specification. However, as already indicated in section 5.3.1, Tobit estimations have to rely on the assumption that the corresponding dependent variable is normally distributed (and is censored at some value, i.e. zero in the context here). Figure 5.2 in the Appendix (p. 173) illustrates on the basis of kernel density estimates that the assumption of normality is very unlikely to be satisfied in this context and that investment intensities are instead log-normally distributed over the considered sample of firms. Nevertheless, with these reservations in mind, the corresponding Tobit estimates summarised in Table 5.10 yield qualitatively very similar results to the ones in Table 5.3, substantiating further the robustness of the results.

Summarising the findings from this part, there is strong empirical evidence that firms complement the ICT investment by increased training efforts. Moreover, the correlation with training is a special feature of ICT investments as

---

[15] One exception is that using stocks, the coefficients capturing the link between training and non-ICT investments become significantly negative.

compared to other tangible investment. A high share of workers with high formal education favours training and ICT investment, though the correlation between training and ICT persists even after controlling for this aspect.

5.5.2 Complementarities in the production function

In order to investigate the relationship between ICT, training and education of workers in more detail, I employ a production function framework as set out in section 5.3.2. I apply a SYS-GMM estimator which is described in chapter 3. This estimator helps to control for unobserved firm effects, measurement errors in the variables and simultaneity of inputs and output which may induce substantial biases in pooled or within OLS regressions. I thus use the second sample described in the previous section consisting of an unbalanced panel of 401 firms with a total of 1,275 observations. In order to control for variations in factor utilisation induced by industry-specific business cycles, dummies for seven industries[16] interacted with years are added to the specification. Finally, a dummy variable for East German firms controls for the productivity differentials due to the transformation process after German unification.

Table 5.4 reports the results for the production function specified in equation (5.2). All estimations are computed using the DPD98 programme developed by Arellano and Bond (1998) running in GAUSS. For all specifications, I report the coefficients from the two-step estimation results with t-values from heteroscedasticity-consistent one-step results in parentheses.[17] In all columns, the point estimates for the (not-interacted) inputs labour, non-ICT, and ICT fit the relative shares of the factors in aggregate income statistics fairly well (only the labour coefficient is smaller than the two-thirds expected). In the sequence of the columns (1) to (6) additional variables and interactions are subsequently included in the specification.

In column 1, the shares of employees with a university degree (%university) and vocational training (%vocational) have a positive though not significant impact on output. As exposed in chapter 3, the ratio of the coefficients of labour input L and the shares of skilled labour may be interpreted as the productivity differential between the skilled employees as opposed to unskilled workers (reference group). The results obtained here imply that employees with university degree are 91% and workers with vocational training 44% more

---

[16] The industry classifications with the corresponding NACE codes are summarised in Table 5.8 in Appendix 5.7.2 to this chapter. Since there are no output data available for banking and insurance (only the balance sheet total and insurance premiums, respectively), these industries are excluded from the analysis.

[17] For the point estimates, the results from the efficient two-step estimator are reported while the corresponding t-values are obtained from the one-step results. The latter are used because inference based on one-step GMM estimators appears to be much more reliable when either non-normality or heteroscedasticity are suspected (Arellano and Bover, 1995; Blundell and Bond, 1998). See also chapter 3 on these issues.

Table 5.4. Complementarities between ICT, skills, and training

inputs (logs)	dependent variable: log(value added)					
	(1)	(2)	(3)	(4)	(5)	(6)
labour	0.453***	0.576 ***	0.582***	0.574 ***	0.567 ***	0.575***
	(3.531)	(4.423)	(5.323)	(5.999)	(5.981)	(5.570)
ICT capital	0.063 *	0.072	0.096	0.115	0.075	0.096
	(1.841)	(1.332)	(1.375)	(1.347)	(1.479)	(1.531)
non-ICT capital	0.230	0.187***	0.187***	0.198***	0.190***	0.142***
	(2.301)	(2.803)	(2.926)	(3.311)	(3.067)	(2.661)
%university	0.412	0.438	0.369	0.322	0.215	0.322
	(0.700)	(0.897)	(1.256)	(1.136)	(0.776)	(1.113)
%vocational	0.198	0.354	0.329**	0.332**	0.299**	0.441**
	(0.827)	(1.537)	(2.114)	(2.239)	(2.294)	(2.338)
training		0.116	0.087	0.057	0.117	0.062
		(0.962)	(0.782)	(0.774)	(1.078)	(0.006)
ICT × training			0.006	0.005	-0.002	
			(0.342)	(0.317)	(-0.402)	
ICT × %univ.				-0.042	0.035	
				(0.178)	(0.130)	
training × %univ.				0.046	-0.103	-0.029
				(-0.041)	(-0.434)	(0.204)
training × %univ. × ICT					0.040*	0.049**
					(1.853)	(2.186)
training × %voc.						0.107*
						(1.862)
training × %voc. × ICT						-0.004
						(-0.433)
R^2	0.870	0.878	0.880	0.880	0.881	0.882
Sargan (p-values)	0.425	0.174	0.227	0.884	0.960	0.890
errors (p-values):						
AR(1)	0.053	0.011	0.007	0.005	0.006	0.004
AR(2)	0.820	0.535	0.426	0.439	0.465	0.316

***, **, and * denote significance at the 1, 5 and 10% level.
Results are based on the two-step SYS-GMM estimator as detailed in Appendix 3.7.1
to chapter 3. t-values reported in parentheses are obtained from heteroscedasticity-
robust first-step results (see Blundell and Bond (1998) and chapter 3, in particular
footnote 31, p. 76, for more details). The signs of the coefficients and the reported
corresponding t-values may therefore differ in some cases. All specifications contain
a constant as well as interacted time and industry dummies. The underlying sample
consists of 401 service firms with a total of 1,275 observations covering the years
1994-98.

productive than workers without formal education. These values are slightly
lower than those obtained in chapter 3 for a substantially bigger sample of
firms from the *MIP-S* data.[18]

---

[18] For comparisons, see the results in Table 3.4, p. 83, and the calculations from
footnote 48, p. 82.

In the specification underlying column 2, the accumulated training efforts by the firms in terms of the calculated training stocks ("training") are added to the model. The elasticity of training is quantitatively substantial (0.115) but falls short of statistical significance at the usual levels.[19] This may be partly due to the relatively small number of observations. The point estimate of ICT is only slightly affected by the inclusion of the training variable. However, the standard error of the coefficient is enlarged such that the impact of ICT is not significantly different from zero anymore. This loss of precision may indeed arise from the complementary relation between ICT and training and the resulting collinearity between both variables.

In further (unreported) regressions, I also explored potential biases that may be induced by endogeneity of training and of ICT capital. For this purpose, I re-ran specification (2) with treating training and ICT capital as exogenous instead of using lagged values as instruments. In this specification, the two-step coefficient for ICT increases to 0.138 while the coefficient for training decreases to 0.079. This finding is consistent with the results from chapter 3 and observation from other studies that the failure to account for endogeneity *over*states the estimated productivity of ICT but *under*states the contributions of training (see section 5.2.1).

Moreover, I also explored the importance of considering productivity effects from lagged training expenditures. For this purpose, I estimated specification (2) using current training expenditures rather than the training stock. In this specification, the coefficient of training is substantially lower than in column (2) of Table 5.4 and becomes even negative. This sensitivity check shows that the productivity effects from training investments manifest themselves indeed with a time lag which must be taken into account.

In column 3, an additional interaction term between ICT capital and training is added to the specification. I employ the interacted values' deviations from the overall mean of logarithmic values. The interaction terms thus show whether combining above-average (below-average) training and ICT inputs yield supernormal (less-than-normal) productivity gains from these inputs. However, the interaction results turn out to be very small and insignificant. This may mean that there are no additional productivity gains from a joint usage of ICT and training. Alternatively, the relation may be more complex, involving more factors. As discussed in the theoretical part, the education of the workforce may affect both the productivity of ICT and of training investment. In order to explore this conjecture in more detail, specification 4 includes further bilateral interactions between education and training and ed-

---

[19] This value implies returns to training of 147% (resulting from 0.1156/0.07825, where the latter value is the average share of the training stock in value added). These are very high returns that point to further expenses that are related to training but are not accounted for in this study. However, the returns are substantially smaller than those found by Ballot et al. (2001a) for France (288%) and Sweden (441%) in a comparable analysis.

ucation and ICT. However, also in this more comprehensive specification, the interactions terms are insignificant.

In order to assess whether the *joint* adaption of ICT, high skills and training measures is the key to a productive use of ICT, an interaction of all three variables is added in a further specification (column 5 of Table 5.4). The most striking result from this regression is that this joint interaction term of *training*, *%university*, and *ICT* is both statistically and economically significant whereas the individual contributions of these three inputs as well as their pair-wise interactions are insignificant. This finding suggests that the productivity of ICT usage is indeed linked to the joint availability of a high-skilled workforce and the conducting complementary training measures.

Further exploring the joint interaction of education, training and ICT usage in more detail, column 6 reports the result for the regression including also interactions between firm training, ICT usage and medium skilled workers. The bilateral interactions between ICT and training on the one hand and ICT and education on the other (which were insignificant in specifications 4 and 5) are excluded from this regression to keep the specification tractable.[20] The most striking result is that also in this specification the threefold interaction of high-skilled labour, training and ICT is highly significant whereas the two-fold interaction of high skills and training is not. The reverse is true for the interactions that include medium-skilled workers. These findings further support the conjecture that ICT investment affects the training needs of well educated employees but not of other skill groups.[21]

Jointly, the results for the production function approach yield support for the conjecture that the productive use of ICT requires both high-skilled workers and substantial training efforts by firms. Moreover, the findings indicate that also independently of their role as complement to ICT use, training investments by firms are most productive if combined with a high share of employees with a strong educational background. These findings indicate that one important source of the overall higher productivity of high-skilled labour consists in their ability to be trained easily, in particular in combination with the use of new technologies such as ICT.

---

[20] In unreported regressions (analogue to specification 6) that include also these bilateral interactions, the point estimate of the interaction between ICT, high-skilled labour and training remains unchanged but exhibits much higher standard errors of the interaction terms. This finding points to problems of multicollinearity resulting from the inclusion of too many interaction terms and motivates the more parsimonious specification 6 in Table 5.4.

[21] Exploring the robustness of the results, I additionally ran specification (6) employing ICT and training values per employee for the interaction terms. The point estimates of the interaction between ICT, training and high-skilled labour (0.0537) are slightly higher than in the reported specification. However, all coefficients are estimated much less precisely and the corresponding t-values — except the one for non-ICT capital — do not reach statistical significance.

5.5.3 Wage cost effects and training incentives

In a third approach, I explore the question whether the incentives for firms to invest in training their employees are enhanced by the continuing diffusion of ICT. As set out in section 5.3.3, I address this question by comparing the productivity gains with the changes in wage costs.

Table 5.5 replicates two particular productivity regressions from Table 5.4 (columns 2 and 6) and compares the results to the coefficients of analogue wage regressions. The production function estimates differ slightly from those of Table 5.4 since item non-responses in the total payroll reduce the new sample to 393 considered firms. As the direct comparison of the two tables show, the point estimates and significance levels of the coefficients are quite robust to this change in the sample.

The first two columns of Table 5.5 are based on the Cobb-Douglas function (including the skill shares and the training stock) without the interaction terms.[22] The results suggest that about half of the productivity gains assigned to ICT capital are offset by corresponding wage increases.[23] This share is even higher for non-ICT capital. These positive impacts of investments on wage costs may reflect that capital deepening is associated with higher skill requirements that are not captured by formal education. The payroll increases from a higher share of highly skilled workers (with university degree) even exceed the corresponding output gains. On the contrary, the productivity gains from training exceed the wage increases assigned to training. Only about one third of the productivity gains are offset by higher wage costs. This ratio is practically the same as the one reported by Dearden et al. (2000) for British industries. Note, however, that the corresponding coefficients of skills and training are estimated very imprecisely.

In specifications (3) and (4) in Table 5.5, the same interactions of ICT, training, and education as in the last column of Table 5.4 are added. In this specification, both the productivity and the wage cost effects from training alone are virtually zero and the impacts of ICT are similar to the previous estimates. Regarding the interaction terms, there are both similarities and differences between the impacts on productivity and on wage costs. The interaction of training and the university share mainly increases wage costs while the output increases only if also ICT capital is high (positive three-fold interaction between *training*, *%univ.* and *ICT*). A more intensive usage

---

[22] Some readers may find it easier to interpret the results for the corresponding values of output, wages, and inputs per worker. However, as long as the logarithm of employees is kept as an explanatory variable to allow for deviations from constant returns to scale, the coefficients and significance levels of all variables (except the log of labour) are identical in such a transformed regression. Therefore, the results for the coefficients can be equally interpreted as the impacts of the various investments on labour productivity and average wages.

[23] This share is calculated from the ratio of the ICT coefficient in the wage regression and the corresponding coefficient in the production function regression.

Table 5.5. Productivity and wage cost effects

	(1) log(Y)	(2) log(W)	(3) log(Y)	(4) log(W)	(5) log(Y/W)
log(labour)	0.478***	0.763***	0.492***	0.855***	-0.316***
	(3.930)	(8.982)	(5.210)	(14.526)	(-3.318)
log(ICT)	0.103	0.049	0.080	0.037	0.058
	(1.344)	(0.601)	(1.579)	(0.751)	(1.049)
log(non-ICT)	0.235***	0.168***	0.187***	0.094***	0.137
	(2.674)	(3.119)	(2.650)	(3.098)	(1.349)
%university	0.219	0.402*	-0.003	0.492***	-0.348
	(0.447)	(1.727)	(0.705)	(3.233)	(-1.345)
%vocational	0.283	0.047	0.315**	0.186	0.106
	(1.427)	(-0.261)	(2.282)	(1.504)	(1.544)
log(train.)	0.125	0.040	0.076	0.017	0.039
	(1.243)	(1.151)	(0.137)	(-0.271)	(0.306)
log(training) × %univ.			-0.036	0.056*	-0.099
			(0.244)	(1.759)	(-1.239)
log(train.) × %univ. × log(ICT)			0.060**	0.017	0.023**
			(2.526)	(0.755)	(2.086)
log(train.) × %voc.			0.129*	0.031	-0.001
			(1.953)	(1.566)	(0.985)
log(train.) × %voc. × log(ICT)			0.003	-0.007	-0.015
			(-0.188)	(-0.747)	(-0.217)
R^2	0.876	0.939	0.883	0.953	0.571
time and ind. dummies	yes	yes	yes	yes	yes
Sargan stat. (p-values)	0.158	0.489	0.980	0.983	0.947
errors (p-values):					
AR(1)	0.031	0.164	0.026	0.084	0.239
AR(2)	0.398	0.483	0.252	0.563	0.401

***, **, and * denote significance at the 1, 5 and 10% level. Y denotes value added, and W total wage costs of firms as explanatory variables.

Results are based on the two-step SYS-GMM estimator as detailed in Appendix 3.7.1 to chapter 3. t-values reported in parentheses are obtained from heteroscedasticity-robust first-step results (see Blundell and Bond (1998) and chapter 3, in particular footnote 31, p. 76, for more details). The signs of the coefficients and the reported corresponding t-values may therefore differ in some cases. All specifications contain a constant as well as interacted time and industry dummies. The underlying sample consists of 393 service firms with a total of 1,249 observations.

of ICT thus increases the net returns from training for firms with a high share of highly skilled employees. As far as the interaction between training and medium skilled workers (%voc.) is concerned, the productivity effects exceed the wage impacts. Moreover, the impact of the three-fold interaction on productivity and wages is practically equal to zero for this skill group. This indicates that for medium-skilled workers, training incentives are not affected by the intensity of ICT use.

These qualitative results from specifications (3) and (4) are corroborated also by specification (5) where the logarithm of the output/wage-cost ratio is employed as the dependent variable. This specification thus estimates directly the net returns $\beta_i - \tilde{\beta}_i$ that a firm derives from inputs i. Most strikingly, the threefold interaction of *training*, *%univ.*, and *ICT* enters significantly positive in this specification, pointing to synergies between ICT use, skills of workers, and training investments by firms.

These findings indicate that ICT usage not only increases the need for training but also fosters the incentives for firms to pay for training workers with a high educational background. Moreover, the complementarity between ICT, training and high-skilled labour implies that continuously falling prices of ICT equipment may not enhance the training efforts but may also shift labour demand to more highly skilled employees.

The underlying reasons for the ability of firms to appropriate the gains from ICT-related training of highly skilled employees are difficult to identify from the empirical results since additional information would be required for this purpose. However, the factor choice regressions in the previous subsection revealed that innovations in firms play an important role for the demand of ICT. To the extent that new processes require the updating of firm-specific knowledge of the employees, this might explain the increased training incentives for firms.

5.6 Conclusions

Over the last decades, the continuously falling prices of ICT have been spurring ICT investments dramatically and this development is likely to continue (e.g., Manasian, 2003). The analysis from the previous chapter 4 as well as earlier studies (e.g., Bresnahan and Greenstein, 1996; Bresnahan et al., 2002) provide evidence that the increasing investments in ICT are accompanied by a variety of complementary innovational efforts, like organisational changes as well as product and process innovations. Such changes and innovations have been found to be skill-biased, enhancing the needs for investments in human capital and leading to a demand shift towards skilled labour (e.g., Caroli and van Reenen, 2001; Bresnahan et al., 2002; Falk, 2001).

In this chapter, I explore whether the adoption of ICT enhances the incentives of German service firms to invest in training their employees. Applying three complementary approaches to data from German business-related and distribution service firms, I obtain results that broadly support this conjecture. First, the investment in ICT — unlike non-ICT — is strongly correlated with firms' training expenditures. Second, the productivity gains from training are highest in firms that both employ a high fraction of employees with university degree and have been investing strongly in ICT. Third, the share of the productivity gains from training appropriated by the firm is increasing with the stock of ICT.

The results from this study are consistent with earlier empirical work on the productivity gains from ICT and training as well as studies on the skill bias of new technologies. By combining approaches from various strands of the literature, however, I present some new evidence as well. First, ICT investments do not only entail a higher need for human capital investments but also foster the *incentives* for firms to pay for training programmes. Second, the ability of firms to reap productivity gains from ICT and training is crucially determined by the availability of suitably educated workers. These findings suggest that in the context of new technologies, the primary contribution of education in the production process may be the inherent ability of workers to learn and to adapt to changing work tasks more easily. This implies that the skill-bias resulting from ICT investments may thus be rather indirect: ICT requires complementary training, but the productivity of training workers depends strongly on formal education.

Jointly, these findings point to a dynamic role of education in knowledge-based societies. The rapid technological advances in particular in the ICT sector favour continuous changes in work tasks in broad parts of the economy. These changes call for a continuous adjustment of skills and the readiness for a 'life-long learning' by workers. Training programmes by firms are substantially contributing to these adjustments. A key prerequisite, however, is the provision of good education systems which form the basis for successful training facilities in firms.

5.7 Appendix

5.7.1 Sample selection in logarithmic specifications

Expenditures on investments and training are restricted to positive values. Moreover, they tend to be highly skewed and clustered around zero and follow a lognormal (rather than a normal) distribution. As illustrated in Figure 5.2, this holds also for the expenditure variables employed in this study. Consequently, I employ the logarithms of the corresponding expenditures in the estimation equation. This specification, however, excludes observations with zero expenditures from the analysis. If the decision whether to invest is impacted by a different set of determinants, this may induce a selectivity bias in the analysis.

The problem of selectivity due to zeros in logarithmic specifications is well-known in the literature.[24] The probably most popular approach to correct for this selectivity in the microeconometric literature is the two-step procedure

---

[24] See Manning et al. (1987), e.g.

Table 5.6. Investment expenditures with Heckman non-selection hazard

	non-ICT		ICT		training	
	(1)	(2)	(3)	(4)	(5)	(6)
	invest.	selection	invest.	selection	invest.	selection
log(non-ICT investment)			0.185***	0.053	0.027	0.007
			(0.016)	(0.035)	(0.018)	(0.025)
log(ICT investment)	0.387***	-0.063*			0.253***	0.068*
	(0.036)	(0.038)			(0.025)	(0.038)
log(training expenditures)	0.044	-0.051	0.236***	0.104*		
	(0.037)	(0.036)	(0.024)	(0.055)		
log(labour)	0.002	0.556***	0.099	0.328	0.463***	0.442***
	(0.125)	(0.098)	(0.077)	(0.223)	(0.083)	(0.133)
log(labour)^2	0.019*	-0.036***	0.017**	-0.023	0.017**	-0.029*
	(0.011)	(0.009)	(0.007)	(0.027)	(0.008)	(0.016)
log(value added)	0.483***	0.094**	0.215***	0.089	0.048	0.076
	(0.041)	(0.043)	(0.028)	(0.073)	(0.030)	(0.047)
%apprentices					2.363***	2.471***
					(0.497)	(0.652)
%university	-0.518**	-0.185	0.856***	0.913**	1.448***	0.880***
	(0.257)	(0.219)	(0.170)	(0.450)	(0.183)	(0.256)
%vocational	0.249	0.058	0.166	-0.027	0.330***	0.453***
	(0.178)	(0.191)	(0.118)	(0.249)	(0.125)	(0.162)
exporter	0.031	-0.133	0.006	0.451**	0.047	-0.137
	(0.106)	(0.101)	(0.071)	(0.226)	(0.074)	(0.108)
cont. product innovation	0.054	0.136	-0.012	-0.108	0.216***	0.238**
	(0.104)	(0.100)	(0.069)	(0.156)	(0.072)	(0.106)
cont. process innovation	0.069	-0.020	0.324***	0.300*	0.171**	0.253**
	(0.104)	(0.102)	(0.069)	(0.174)	(0.073)	(0.117)
foreign competition	-0.195**	-0.034	-0.065	-0.077	0.112*	-0.046
	(0.092)	(0.093)	(0.062)	(0.152)	(0.064)	(0.093)
part of group of companies	-0.140	-0.040	0.238***	-0.317**	0.004	0.339***
	(0.098)	(0.100)	(0.065)	(0.156)	(0.071)	(0.117)
East Germany	0.673***	0.186	-0.220***	-0.118	-0.102	0.205
	(0.093)	(0.093)	(0.062)	(0.137)	(0.066)	(0.097)

(continued on next page)

proposed by Heckman (1976, 1979) and its variants. This model estimates the selection hazard rate by a probit model and includes this rate as an additional explanatory in the OLS estimation of the equation of interest (outcome

Table 5.6. Investment expenditures with Heckman non-selection hazard (cont.)

| | dependent variable: log(investment) | | | | | |
| | (1) | (2) | (3) | (4) | (5) | (6) |
	non-ICT	ICT	training	non-ICT	ICT	training
EXPECTED DEVELOPMENT OF FUTURE SALES:						
decreasing strongly	-0.052	-0.389**	-0.013	-0.541**	-0.325**	-0.360**
	(0.213)	(0.172)	(0.142)	(0.235)	(0.146)	(0.166)
decreasing	-0.114	-0.089	-0.127	0.004	0.138	0.091
	(0.123)	(0.121)	(0.081)	(0.178)	(0.085)	(0.115)
increasing	-0.141	-0.017	0.069	0.011	0.185**	0.329***
	(0.100)	(0.101)	(0.067)	(0.154)	(0.071)	(0.102)
increasing strongly	0.276	-0.103	0.189	0.033	0.463***	0.220
	(0.176)	(0.170)	(0.117)	(0.361)	(0.122)	(0.174)
LR test of independent equations (p-values)	0.031			0.437		0.117
# OBSERVATIONS:						
uncensored	1,630			1,630		1,630
censored	252			73		262
total	1882			1703		1892

***, **, and * denote significance at the 1%, 5%, and 10% level. Heteroscedasticity-consistent standard errors reported in parentheses.

The results are obtained from full-information likelihood estimation of the Heckman (1976) selection model. All equations contain industry and year dummies as in the regressions reported in Table 5.3.

LR test refers to the hypothesis that the correlation of the errors in the outcome and selection equations is zero.

equation) for the subsample with non-zero observations. Alternatively, the so-called 'two-part model' estimates the model of interest without any control for sample selection and corrects only the predicted outcome by the probability of the observation satisfying the selectivity criterion (which is obtained from a suited probit estimation).[25] If one is mainly interested in the coefficients of the determinants and not so much in the predicted outcome, the two-parts model is reduced to a simple subsample estimation (of non-zero observations). The main difference to the selection model is that "[t]he two-part model maintains that the level of use, given any, is conditionally independent of the decision to use" (Leung and Yu, 1996, p. 202).

There has been an extensive discussion in the econometric literature — based both on theoretical properties and Monte-Carlo simulation — about which of the approaches is the more appropriate one. In a comprehensive

---

[25] See Leung and Yu (1996) for a detailed comparison of the two alternative approaches.

evaluation of this literature, Puhani (2000) points to the need for finding appropriate exclusion restrictions (i.e. variables that are relevant in the selection equation but not for the outcome equation). Without imposing any exclusion restrictions, the distinction between the selection and the outcome effect is due only to the differing functional form of the linear outcome function and the non-linearity of the selection hazard rate. This may cause substantial problems of collinearity for small values of the hazard rate.[26] In contrast, a misspecified exclusion restriction may be very harmful to the performance of the selection model (Rendtel, 1992).

Applied to the specific context of this study, there are few variables that may serve as candidates for exclusion restrictions. In order to explore the robustness of the results found in the main part, I investigate to what extent the qualitative results obtained for investment (as in the first three columns of Table 5.3) may be biased due to selectivity. For this purpose, I rerun all three equations individually by applying a full-information maximum likelihood estimation of the Heckman selection model. Since there are no variables that might serve as exclusion restrictions, the selection equation and the output equation contain the same set of regressors.[27] The comparison of the corresponding results for the factor choice equation reported in Table 5.6 show that the qualitative results (both in sign and significance of the main variables of interest) are the same as the findings obtained for the regressions reported in Table 5.3. Moreover, the likelihood-ratio test of independence of the two equations[28] is rejected only in the case of non-ICT investment but not for the ICT and training equations. These explorations do not provide any evidence pointing to a selection bias in the results of Table 5.3.

---

[26] Similarly, a small variability among the regressors, a large error variance in the choice equation as well as high degrees of censoring may further intensify the problem of multicollinearity (Leung and Yu, 1996).

[27] In an alternative specification, I employed expectations of diminishing sales as an exclusion restriction for the model. Given that gross investments cannot be negative, this approach is based on the hypothesis that falling sales will mainly increase the probability that the firm does not invest at all. The results of this alternative specification, however, are broadly the same as in the specification without any exclusion restriction.

[28] This test explores whether the correlation coefficient between the errors of the output and the selection equation is equal to zero.

5.7.2 Tables and graphs

Table 5.7. Descriptive statistics for regression samples

variables*	1st sample:** factor choice		2nd sample:** prod. and wage reg.	
	mean	standard dev.	mean	standard dev.
log(non-ICT investment)	-0.965	2.532		
log(ICT investment)	-2.487	2.020		
log(training expenditures)	-3.160	1.919	-3.383	1.713
log(non-ICT stock)	1.398	2.532	1.188	2.612
log(ICT stock)	-1.585	2.002	-1.980	1.775
log(training stock)	-1.270	1.880	-1.375	1.617
log(labour)	4.186	1.590	4.064	1.559
log(value added)	2.491	2.137	1.898	1.619
%university	0.195	0.253	0.221	0.279
%vocational	0.600	0.287	0.550	0.294
%apprentices	0.046	0.064		
DUMMY VARIABLES:				
exporter	0.239	0.427		
cont. product innovation	0.526	0.499		
cont. process innovation	0.423	0.494		
foreign competition	0.366	0.467		
part of group of companies	0.347	0.476		
East Germany	0.413	0.493	0.472	0.499
Expected development of future sales:				
decreasing strongly	0.043	0.203		
decreasing	0.175	0.380		
increasing	0.417	0.493		
increasing strongly	0.071	0.257		
# obs.		1,630		1,249
# firms		1,241		393

* all monetary values measured in million €; % denotes the shares of the corresponding group of employees in the total workforce.
** "1st" denotes the sample used for the analysis of the interrelated factor choice, "2nd" denotes the sample used for the productivity and wage cost regressions.

Table 5.8. Number of firms in samples and population by industry

industry	NACE-digits	1st** #	1st** %	2nd** #	2nd** %	population* %
wholesale trade	51	155	12.5	50	12.7	10.4
retail trade	50, 52	149	12.0	54	13.7	30.8
transport and postal services	60-63, 64.1	174	14.0	66	16.8	11.5
electr. processing and telecom	72, 62.2	90	7.3	33	8.4	3.4
consultancies	74.1, 74.4	95	7.7	40	10.2	11.8
technical services	73, 74.2, 74.3	144	11.6	60	15.3	10.5
banking and insurances	65, 66, 67	167	13.5	—	—	1.7
other business-rel. services	70, 71, 74.5-.8, 90	267	21.5	90	22.9	19.9
total		1,241	100	393	100	100

*German service firms with 5 and more employees in 1999 (source: German Statistical Office, ZEW and own calculations).

** "1st" denotes the sample used for the analysis of the interrelated factor choice, "2nd" denotes the sample used for the productivity and wage cost regressions.

denote number of firms, % percentages of total.

Table 5.9. Factor choice of non-ICT, ICT and training

	SUR estimation (A)			SUR estimation (B)		
	dependent variable: log(capital stock of ...)					
	(1) training	(2) ICT	(3) non-ICT	(4) training	(5) ICT	(6) non-ICT
log(non-ICT stock)	-0.070*** (0.019)	0.346*** (0.016)		-0.050*** (0.017)	0.348*** (0.016)	
log(ICT stock)	0.770*** (0.023)		0.702*** (0.032)	0.498*** (0.023)		0.744*** (0.033)
log(training stock)		0.625*** (0.019)	-0.116*** (0.032)		0.480*** (0.022)	-0.103*** (0.035)
log(value added)	0.139*** (0.025)	0.032 (0.022)	0.441*** (0.031)	-0.025 (0.028)	0.097*** (0.027)	0.421*** (0.037)
log(labour)				0.317*** (0.071)	0.013 (0.069)	-0.183* (0.102)
log(labour)^2				0.023*** (0.007)	-0.001 (0.006)	0.020** (0.009)
%apprentices$_{(t-1)}$				1.029** (0.416)		
%university$_{(t-1)}$				0.864*** (0.162)	0.630*** (0.158)	-0.649*** (0.234)
%vocational$_{(t-1)}$				0.186* (0.113)	0.049 (0.111)	0.255 (0.162)
DUMMY VARIABLES:						
exporter				0.061 (0.067)	0.008 (0.066)	-0.015 (0.096)
cont. product innovation$_{(t-s)}$				0.205*** (0.065)	-0.059 (0.064)	0.014 (0.094)
cont. process innovation$_{(t-s)}$				0.005 (0.066)	0.210*** (0.064)	-0.071 (0.095)
foreign competition				0.094 (0.059)	0.012 (0.057)	-0.230*** (0.084)
part of group of companies				-0.131** (0.062)	0.264*** (0.060)	-0.244*** (0.088)
East Germany	0.035 (0.062)	-0.295*** (0.056)	0.771*** (0.078)	-0.065 (0.059)	-0.294*** (0.057)	0.726*** (0.083)

(continued on next page)

Table 5.9. Factor choice of non-ICT, ICT and training (continued)

	SUR estimation (A)			SUR estimation (B)		
	dependent variable: log(capital stock of ...)					
	(1)	(2)	(3)	(4)	(5)	(6)
	training	ICT	non-ICT	training	ICT	non-ICT
INDUSTRY DUMMIES						
(ref. group: wholesale):						
retail trade	0.407***	-0.287***	0.355**	0.254**	-0.157	0.255*
	(0.116)	(0.105)	(0.149)	(0.105)	(0.102)	(0.149)
transport & post	0.263**	-0.603***	2.201***	-0.166	-0.499***	2.147***
	(0.123)	(0.110)	(0.147)	(0.113)	(0.111)	(0.153)
electr. proc. & telecom	0.168	0.945***	-1.531***	0.116	0.942***	-1.363***
	(0.144)	(0.127)	(0.185)	(0.135)	(0.130)	(0.192)
consultancies	0.528***	0.226*	-0.255	0.399***	0.332***	-0.232
	(0.137)	(0.124)	(0.179)	(0.126)	(0.123)	(0.181)
technical services	0.177	0.560***	-0.459***	-0.073	0.461***	-0.157
	(0.125)	(0.111)	(0.163)	(0.124)	(0.121)	(0.177)
banking and insurances	0.006	0.451***	-0.960***	0.489***	0.505***	-1.003***
	(0.117)	(0.105)	(0.149)	(0.109)	(0.107)	(0.157)
other	0.344***	-0.616***	1.688***	0.100	-0.532***	1.659***
	(0.109)	(0.098)	(0.134)	(0.101)	(0.098)	(0.138)
year dummies 1996-98	yes	yes	yes	yes	yes	yes
R^2	0.587	0.686	0.640	0.688	0.719	0.645

***, **, and * denote significance at the 1%, 5%, and 10% level. Heteroscedasticity-consistent standard errors reported in parentheses.

The results are obtained from two seemingly unrelated regressions (SUR) for a pooled sample of 1,241 firms with 1,630 observations for the period 1995 to 1998.

Table 5.10. Tobit estimates of factor choice

| | dependent variables:[†] | | |
	(1) training intensity	(2) ICT intensity	(3) non-ICT intensity
training intensity	—	0.311*** (0.044)	0.001 (0.228)
ICT intensity	0.074*** (0.011)	—	0.617*** (0.108)
non-ICT intensity	0.001 (0.002)	0.030*** (0.004)	—
log(value added)	-0.359*** (0.050)	-0.595*** (0.092)	1.227*** (0.479)
East Germany	-0.018 (0.117)	-0.669 (0.217)	6.405*** (1.105)
log(labour)	0.696*** (0.133)	0.732*** (0.243)	0.607 (1.248)
log(labour)^2	-0.024* (0.013)	-0.016 (0.024)	-0.083 (0.124)
%apprentices	4.432*** (0.753)	1.095 (1.413)	10.960 (7.368)
%university$_{t-1}$	1.741*** (0.301)	2.186*** (0.559)	2.828 (2.915)
%vocational$_{t-1}$	0.400* (0.216)	0.363 (0.397)	3.635* (2.003)
exporter	0.094 (0.136)	-0.160 (0.253)	-0.898 (1.305)
product innovator	0.417*** (0.132)	-0.435* (0.247)	3.339*** (1.266)
process innovator	0.038 (0.135)	0.616** (0.253)	-0.120 (1.303)
foreign competition	0.117 (0.119)	-0.038 (0.221)	-0.898*** (1.125)
group of companies	-0.260 (0.129)	0.412* (0.243)	-2.519** (1.246)
EXPECTED DEVELOPMENT OF FUTURE SALES:			
decreasing strongly	-0.379 (0.232)	-0.516 (0.417)	-1.629 (2.134)
decreasing	0.189 (0.154)	-0.430 (0.234)	-0.115 (1.452)
increasing	0.493*** (0.129)	0.050 (0.24)	1.318 (1.230)
increasing strongly	0.559** (0.225)	1.756*** (0.416)	1.290 (2.163)
Pseudo-R^2	0.038	0.033	0.021
# obs.	2413	2413	2413
# left-censored obs. ($y = 0$)	462	165	359

***, **, and * denote significance at the 1%, 5%, and 10% level. Standard errors reported in parentheses. [†] Intensities are measured as the share of corresponding investment expenditures in sales (in percentage points). The results are obtained from a Tobit estimation with censoring at zero. Industry and year dummies are included as further control variables.

Fig. 5.1. Histograms of shares of ICT investments in total investment

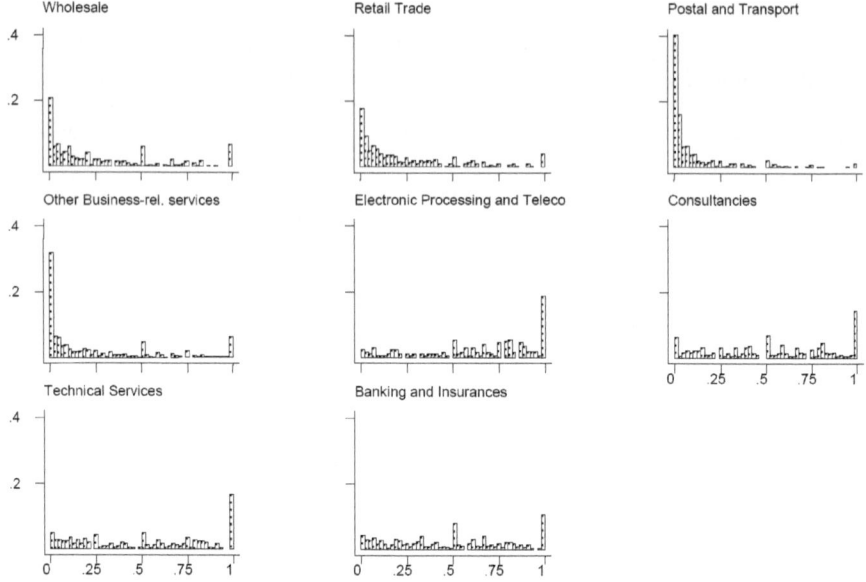

Source: ZEW Mannheim, own calculations
Observations are based on the time averages of nominal investments in tangible assets for an unbalanced panel of 4,053 firms for the period 1994-98.

Fig. 5.2. Kernel density estimates for investment intensities

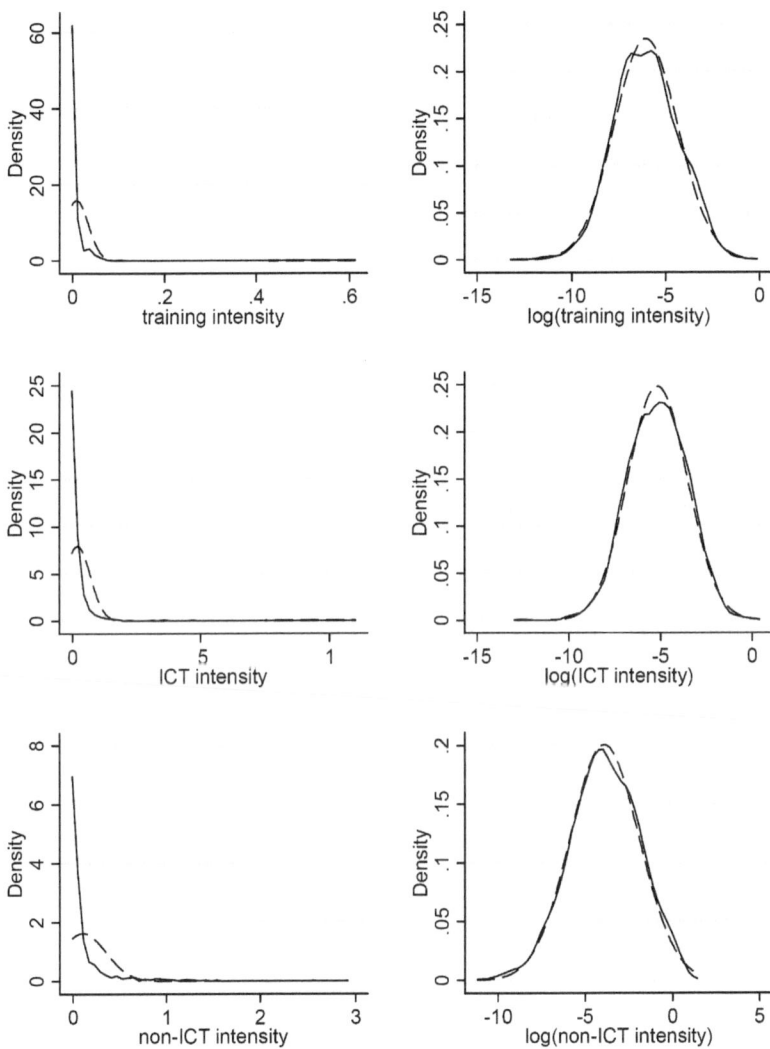

Intensities are measured as the share of corresponding investment expenditures in total sales.

Solid lines display the kernel density estimates, dashed lines show fitted normal density for comparison. The database corresponds to observations with non-zero intensities employed in the Tobit regressions in Table 5.10, p. 171 (n=1,951 for training; 2,248 for ICT; and 2,054 for non-ICT).

6

Conclusions

I do not fear computers.
I fear the lack of them.
Isaac Asimov (1920-1992)
science-fiction writer

Despite widespread disillusions about the prospects of a *New Economy*, information and communication technologies (ICTs) continue to play a key role for technological progress and growth potentials of industrialised economies. ICTs are used in broad parts of the economy, they carry a large potential for further technical improvements, and they foster innovations also in non-ICT sectors of the economy. These properties characterise ICT as a *general purpose technology* (GPT) that is shaping economic activities and that can be compared to other great inventions in the past such as the steam engine, the railway or electricity. Similar to these historical innovations, ICT is creating a potential for considerable productivity gains and thus for higher economic growth. However, ICT is also posing varied challenges to firms in order to benefit from these potentials.

This monograph analyses why and to what extent firms differ in their capabilities to make ICT work productively. In this regard, the study highlights the importance of corporate strategies — in particular innovations, firm-sponsored training, and recruitment of high-skilled workers — as important prerequisites for successful ICT usage in firms. The monograph not only entails a detailed discussion of economic theory concerning ICT use and complementary firm strategies; it also provides a comprehensive treatment of a variety of methodological issues that are relevant for measuring productivity in econometric analyses based on firm-level data.

The data sets employed for the empirical analyses of this monograph overcome several limitations of other data sources used in related empirical studies of the topic: they originate from large-scale representative surveys; include detailed information of firm characteristics and strategies; consider an economy outside the already broadly investigated U.S.; include small and medium-sized firms; and focus on service industries as main users of ICT and important drivers of economic growth.

The results from the empirical investigations add to the existing literature on the topic both by investigating the validity of earlier (predominantly U.S.-based) empirical results and by addressing a variety of economic and econometric issues on the productivity effects of ICT which have remained broadly unexplored so far. Overall, this study highlights that the diffusion of ICT has a large-scale impact on firm productivity and corporate strategies in an industrialised economy, but not in the way some apologists of a *New Economy* have suggested. Conventional economics still apply, and ICT is no panacea for productivity gains. Instead, ICT raises productivity primarily by acting as a catalyst of innovation and upgrading of skills. This can be viewed as the essence of the findings from this monograph, whose more specific results are outlined in the following seven statements.

1. *ICT use contributes to firm productivity.* The results from chapter 3 indicate that ICT use has a significantly positive impact on labour productivity in German service firms. A 10% increase in ICT capital increases firm productivity by about 0.6% on average.

   Against the background of average factor endowments in firms, these results imply that annual returns to ICT investment exceed its user costs by more than 50 percentage points. In contrast, there are no indications of excess returns to non-ICT investments. These findings are consistent with the general purpose characteristics of ICT: the apparent supernormal returns may be due to the fact that firms need to combine ICT use with additional expenditures on complementary efforts, like innovation or training of employees, the exact costs of which are very difficult to account for as separate inputs in production.

2. *Measured ICT productivity is sensitive to employed empirical methodology.* This is shown in the empirical analysis in chapter 3, where I explore a broad variety of econometric issues concerning the measurement of ICT productivity at the firm level.

   First, and most prominently, well-managed firms tend to invest particularly strongly in ICT. The productivity impacts of ICT will be drastically overstated, if these unobservable firm effects are not taken into account by using a within estimator or first-differences estimator in the econometric specification. Second, counteracting this effect, measurement errors in the explanatory variables (e.g. due to imprecise reporting of the value of investments) may lead to understating ICT productivity. This problem is exacerbated by specifications using estimation in first differences and it is particularly important for the case of ICT capital. Third and in contrast, simultaneity of firms' input and output decisions may induce an upward bias in productivity estimates since both productivity and investment expenditures tend to rise during boom periods. Employing panel data, I address these issues jointly by applying a so-called system GMM estimator which exploits the longitudinal structure of the data by using information from previous periods as instrumental variables for inputs. This estimator is used also in chapters 4 and 5 for assessing complementarities between ICT use and innovative activities on the one hand and human capital investments on the other.

3. *An important part of ICT productivity results from improved quality of output.* Survey results discussed in chapter 2 show that firms use ICT to improve various dimensions of output quality; direct cost savings in other inputs, in contrast, are by far less important motives.

   Studies based on aggregate data may not capture an important part of the productivity gains due to ICT if employed price deflators for output fail to account for corresponding quality improvements. This problem seems particularly severe in services where quality enhancements due to faster delivery, broader availability or improved convenience are particularly difficult to measure and are frequently not reflected in official price deflators. In contrast, as illustrated in a partial-equilibrium model in chapter 3, firm level studies are more likely to capture these effects in cases where consumers appreciate improved quality and therefore have a higher propensity to pay for the corresponding output. Consequently, firms are able to increase revenues.

4. *Productive ICT use is complemented by innovative activities.* Successful use of computers and Internet requires firms to introduce own innovations. Results from correlation and multivariate analyses provide varied indications that firms complement ICT use by innovations of products, processes and new management methods.

   The empirical results from chapter 2 based on the *ZEW survey on ICT* in 2002 show that ICT use is highest among firms that introduce new products or services and engage in e-commerce, supply-chain management, as well as customer relationship management and that outsource business activities to other firms. This positive relationship between ICT use and innovation activities is observable for different measures of ICT intensity and holds even if a variety of further firm characteristics, such as firm size, investment in other capital goods or the skill structure of the work force, are controlled for.

   Organisation of workplaces is associated to ICT use, too, but this correlation becomes statistically weak once the innovation activities mentioned above are taken into account. These results indicate that organisational changes may reflect more indirect consequences of ICT use related to increased innovation activities.

5. *Innovative history matters.* Service firms that have introduced innovations in the past are found to be more successful in using ICT productively than

firms that have not. As argued in chapter 4, this is because innovations based on ICT are not trivial and often require coordinated changes in varied business areas of a firm. Experience collected in the course of earlier innovations helps to establish routines that facilitate innovations in the future and to strengthen the awareness of employees with respect to the potentials accruing from new and improved ICT applications.

More specifically, the results point to a major role of process innovation as a relevant source of experience for ICT use. The productivity contributions of ICT in firms with earlier process innovations are about five times as high as among other firms. These productivity differentials are statistically significant and further robustness checks show that they cannot be attributed to a generally higher share of high-skilled workers in innovative firms. Moreover, ICT productivity differentials are smaller and statistically insignificant when contemporaneous innovations are considered. This finding highlights that accumulation of innovation expertise over time is important. Finally, productivity differentials are likewise reflected in firm behaviour. The endowment of workplaces with ICT equipment and software is higher among firms that have introduced innovations in earlier periods.

Jointly, these findings indicate that innovative trajectories are relevant for the success of ICT applications in firms. The arrival of ICT as an increasingly better and cheaper GPT seems to favour firms that have pursued innovation strategies already in the past.

6. *ICT productivity is contingent on workers' skills.* The productivity contributions of ICT are increasing with the share of high-skilled workers in firms. This finding highlights a skill bias of ICT use that is consistent with findings from a variety of other studies. Obviously, ICT investments favour tasks and activities that can be accomplished most productively by workers with a high educational level.

Results from chapter 3 reveal a positive and significant interaction term of ICT capital and the share of high-skilled workers in production function estimations. This indicates that, other things being equal, firms with a high share of high-skilled workers exhibit higher output contributions of ICT capital. This finding is backed by further results obtained both from the *ZEW survey on ICT* and the *MIP-S* data. These results, which are presented in chapters 2 and 5, show that the intensity of ICT use in firms is strongly increasing with the share of workers with university degree or comparable qualification. This result is highly robust and applies to various measures of ICT intensity (including ICT expenses, ICT capital, share of workers predominantly working with PCs, and share of workers having access to the Internet) and remains highly significant when the effects from a large variety of further firm characteristics and strategies are controlled for.

The overall importance of worker skills is also reflected by the main obstacles to increased ICT use as perceived by firms. As discussed in chapter 2, every third firm in Germany regards insufficient knowledge of workers as a factor hampering more intensive ICT use. Worker skills thus rank above costs and financing difficulties as bottlenecks to ICT uptake by firms.

7. *ICT use enhances training needs.* Increased computerisation requires workers to learn to deal with computers and to adjust to changing processes, work organisation and new tasks. Firms promote these adjustments by raising training expenditures jointly with ICT investments. However, the empirical results likewise show that a high level of formal education of workers is a prerequisite for firm-sponsored training to pay off for the firm.

Results based on the *ZEW survey on ICT use* provided in chapter 2 show that firms combine ICT expenditures with increased efforts of training workers in ICT-specific skills. Similarly, based on the *MIP-S* data, the empirical results from chapter 5 show that ICT investment and total training expenditures (which include several other forms of training) are highly correlated across firms. This correlation remains positive and significant even when a large variety of other factors, such as the skill level of workers, are controlled for. Moreover, the close link to training efforts is a special feature of ICT. Investments in other capital goods are uncorrelated to training activities.

Complementarities between ICT use and training investments are also revealed in production function regressions. Firms with high training expenditures exhibit significantly higher productivity contributions from ICT than firms with low training efforts. An important prerequisite for these complementarities, however, is a high share of employees with a strong educational background. This result adds to the findings summarised in item 6. It suggests that a considerable part of the skill bias due to ICT use may be ascribed to the fact that computerisation changes processes and work tasks in firms and that high-skilled workers can acquire the qualifications needed for these changes in training courses more readily than low-skilled workers.

The firm level evidence presented in this monograph broadly coincides with results from existing aggregate and industry-level studies in the qualitative finding that ICT has not only become a widely used input in production but has also boosted productivity in industrialised economies. However, the quantitative productivity effects of ICT found in firm level studies cannot simply be extrapolated to aggregate productivity contributions for at least two reasons.

On the one hand, the overall productivity contributions of ICT use may exceed the (direct) productivity gains as measured in firm-level regressions since at the aggregate further indirect effects may be involved. Apart from raising productivity, ICT-intensive firms may seek to exploit their productivity advantage for extending market shares at the cost of competitors. This 'business-stealing effect' increases the relative weight of successful firms in the overall economy at the cost of less productive ones and amplifies their overall productivity contribution. Moreover, by the same mechanism, highly productive firms also increase competitive pressure; in the longer term, lagging competitors are forced to increase productivity, too, or to exit the market. The impact of the retail giant *Wal-Mart* on the U.S. retail industry is a frequently cited example for both effects. Since these indirect effects are extremely difficult to account for in firm-level studies, the corresponding results may be interpreted as a lower bound of the contributions of ICT use to aggregate productivity in quantitative terms.

On the other hand, as highlighted in the third result above, firm-level productivity estimates account for productivity increases due to improvements of output quality achieved by ICT usage. In contrast, aggregate studies tend to understate these effects. This difference implies that firm-level results on ICT productivity tend to be higher than those derived in aggregate studies. Owing to these methodological differences, quantitative results from aggregate and firm-level studies are probably viewed most appropriately as two distinct but complementary approaches to the productivity contributions of ICT under differing premises.

Apart from providing complementary results on ICT productivity, the maybe most prominent advantage of firm-level studies over aggregate investigations consists in the fact that they help to identify economic factors that are crucial for success and failure of ICT uptake in terms of productivity gains. In aggregate studies, important differences between firms are wiped out in the process of aggregation. Firm-level data, in contrast, allow for distinguishing between firm characteristics and strategies associated with ICT use. These differences are also important for macroeconomics and economic policy since they highlight fields of economic activity which are relevant for the diffusion of ICT to become a driver of productivity and economic growth.

In this context, the results from this monograph highlight two important aspects of how firms make computers and the Internet contribute to productivity. First, ICT use does not substitute for but serves as a complement to firms' own innovation activities. Using ICT for innovations is not trivial and its success is contingent upon a long-term innovative strategy and the existence of an innovation 'culture' in corporations. Metaphorically speaking, ICT is a catalyst that raises the speed limit for innovations. However, firms that have been slow in the past will face more difficulties in adjusting to this higher speed than firms that are already on the fast track.

Even though these findings are obtained mainly from firm-level analyses for Germany (and are corroborated by similar findings for the Netherlands in Hempell et al., 2004), the relevance of innovative experience may also be useful for understanding varying productivity effects of ICT in different countries. The more competitive business environment in the U.S. may be one reason that helps explain why the productivity impact of ICT has been much higher there than in continental Europe. The higher innovation pressure in the U.S. over the last decades may have led firms to collect more diverse innovative experience than more protected firms in Europe. This may have enabled firms in the U.S. to reap higher benefits from the availability of cheaper and more powerful ICT and the invention of the Internet. In this respect, ICTs may have contributed to a further widening of the productivity gap both between the U.S. and Europe and between other regional parts of the world economy.

Second, increased ICT use and innovations call for higher skills of the workforce. This does not necessarily mean that people will be working "with their brain instead of their hands", as suggested by the Encyclopedia of the New Economy cited in the introduction to this book. However, skills and the ability of workers to adjust to changing routines and tasks are gaining in importance. This is reflected by the observation that firms' training investment increases with the intensity of ICT use. However, the returns to training efforts are contingent upon the basic skills of workers reflected by their formal education. Apparently, formal education is a prerequisite for workers' ability to engage in a process of 'lifelong learning'. The ability of firms (and an economy as a whole) to exploit the productivity potentials from ICT thus depends on the quality of educational policy and institutions.

Recent evidence from other studies has pointed to important challenges for Germany with respect to these issues. Most prominently, the disappointing and partly disastrous results from the PISA survey conducted by the OECD have revealed serious deficits in the German schooling system. In all three test subjects, Germany ranked below OECD average. The situation with respect to the prerequisites for acquiring computer skills at German schools is alarming, too. On average, there were only seven computers available to every 100 pupils in German secondary schools in 2001 (Hempell, 2003b). In this respect, Germany ranks lowest among industrialised countries, followed only by Portugal and Greece. The overall importance of ICT skills for the productive uptake of ICT thus strongly confirms the insight that Germany faces substantial backlogs in its educational system.

Both aspects, innovations and skills, have received much attention in recent contributions to the theory of economic growth. 'Endogenous' theories of growth suggest that due to knowledge spillovers to the overall economy, innovation and skills are important sources of overall economic growth in industrialised economies. By increasing the returns to skills and innovation, the diffusion and continuous improvement of ICT fosters investments in skills and innovation also in numerous sectors outside the ICT-producing industry. Due to these secondary effects as a catalyst of innovation and upgrading of skills, computers and the Internet do not only contribute to productivity as an increasingly cheaper and more powerful factor of production, but may induce knowledge spillovers that accelerate the growth rate of the aggregate economy.

Apart from these macroeconomic effects, the increased importance of innovations, accumulated experience, and skills of workers due to the proceeding of

ICT may also contribute to understanding recent changes in corporate strategies and firm behaviour. In particular, there has been a considerable surge in demand for consulting services over the last decade. In Germany, consulting expenditures have more than doubled from € 5.9 billion in 1992 to € 12.3 in 2002 (BDU, 2002). ICT consulting and services account for nearly 30% of this market; and some further 35% accrue to organisational consulting, which is frequently closely related to ICT investment. These figures illustrate that firms increasingly resort to external expertise to keep pace with the rapid technical advances and to improve their own production processes. Consultants may help firms to compensate for the lack of own experience in introducing the innovations and organisational changes facilitated by ICT.

For the next decade at least, two partially opposed developments concerning ICT use are likely to prevail: simplified and ubiquitous ICT access and increasingly complex and expensive innovation possibilities from ICT use. On the one hand, technical progress in ICT-producing sectors will continue to proceed at high rates. Prices for computing power and storage will keep on falling, and software will become increasingly standardised and user-friendly and thus an ubiquitous and easily applicable input. The strategic importance of ICT for the sustained competitive advantage of firms due to specialised technological knowledge may therefore become less important.

On the other hand, it would be precipitate to argue that these developments imply that 'IT doesn't matter' (Carr, 2003). This is because the technological advances of ICT hardware and software continue to facilitate a growing spectrum of ever more complex innovations that would have been impossible some years ago. Recent inventions allow firms to explore new types of knowledge management, such as data-intensive information sharing between engineering and design departments. Similarly, new ICT-based tools and broadband Internet access increasingly facilitate virtual collaboration of R&D teams located at distant places around the world (Fraunhofer-Gesellschaft, 2004). And most medium-sized and large firms still face large potentials from integrating various existing ICT applications into a single system (Sigele, 2002). Firms that leave the broadening scope of ICT applications and innovation options unattended run the risk of falling behind in productivity and competitiveness. Eventually, they will be driven out of the market by competitors that are more vigorous and purposeful with respect to these innovation potentials.

In the course ahead, computers will continue to become cheaper and easier to operate. Simultaneously, the innovation potentials facilitated by ICT use will become increasingly complex and more expensive. Innovative capabilities of firms and the skills of their workers seem thus very likely to remain pivotal for the ability of industrialised economies to exploit the productivity potentials from ICT use.

References

Acemoglu, D. (1997). Training and Innovation in an Imperfect Labour Market, *Review of Economic Studies* **64**(3): 445–464.

Acemoglu, D. (2002). Technical Change, Inequality, and the Labor Market, *Journal of Economic Literature* **40**(1): 7–72.

Acemoglu, D. and Pischke, J.-S. (1996). *Why Do Firms Train? Theory and Evidence*, NBER Working Paper 5605, National Bureau of Economic Research.

Aghion, P. and Howitt, P. (1998). On the Macroeconomic Effects of Major Technological Change, *in* E. Helpman (ed.), *General Purpose Technologies and Economic Growth*, The MIT Press, chapter 5, pp. 121–144.

Aizcorbe, A. (2002). *Why Are Semiconductor Prices Falling So Fast? Industry Estimates and Implications for Productivity Measurement*, Finance and Economics Discussion Paper Series 2002-20, Federal Reserve Board, Washington D.C.

Antonelli, C. (2003). Knowledge Complementarity and Fungeability: Implications for Regional Strategy, *Regional Studies* **39**(6/7): 595–606.

Arellano, M. and Bond, S. (1991). Some Tests of Specification for Panel Data: Monte Carlo Evidence and an Application to Employment Equations, *Review of Economic Studies* **58**(2): 277–297.

Arellano, M. and Bond, S. (1998). *Dynamic Panel Data Estimation Using DPD98 for GAUSS: A Guide for Users*. ftp://ftp.cemfi.es/pdf/papers/ma/dpd98.pdf.

Arellano, M. and Bover, O. (1995). Another Look at the Instrumental Variable Estimation of Error-Components Models, *Journal of Econometrics* **68**(1): 29–51.

Arnal, E., Ok, W., and Torres, R. (2003). Knowledge, Work Organisation and Economic Growth, *in* C. E. Barfield, G. Heiduk, and P. J. J. Welfens (eds.), *Internet, Economic Growth and Globalization*, Springer, Heidelberg, pp. 327–376.

Arora, A. (1996). Testing for Complementarities in Reduced-Form Regressions: A Note, *Economics Letters* **50**(1): 51–55.

Arora, A. and Gambardella, A. (1990). Complementarity and External Linkages: The Strategies of the Large Firms in Biotechnology, *Journal of Industrial Economics* **38**(4): 361–379.

Arrow, K. J. (1962). The Economic Implications of Learning by Doing, *Review of Economic Studies* **29**(3): 155–173.

Athey, S. and Stern, S. (1998). *An Empirical Framework for Testing Theories About Complementarity in Organizational Design*, NBER Working Paper 6600, National Bureau of Economic Research.

Atkeson, A. and Kehoe, P. J. (2002). *Measuring Organizational Capital*, NBER Working Paper No. 8722, National Bureau of Economic Research.

Atkinson, A. B. and Stiglitz, J. E. (1969). A New View of Technological Change, *The Economic Journal* **79**(315): 573–578.

Audretsch, D. B. and Thurik, A. R. (2001). What's New About the New Economy? Sources of Growth in the Managed and Entrepreneurial Economies, *Industrial and Corporate Change* **10**(1): 267–315.

Autor, D. H. (2001a). Why Do Temporary Help Firms Provide Free General Skills Training?, *Quarterly Journal of Economics* **116**(4): 1409–1448.

Autor, D. H. (2001b). Wiring the Labor Market, *Journal of Economic Perspectives* **15**(1): 25–40.

Autor, D. H., Levy, F., and Murnane, R. J. (2003). The Skill Content of Recent Technological Change: An Empirical Exploration, *Quarterly Journal of Economics* **118**(4): 1279–1333.

Baily, M. N. (2002). Distinguished Lecture on Economics in Government — The New Economy: Post Mortem or Second Wind?, *Journal of Economic Perspectives* **16**(2): 3–22.

Baily, M. N. and Gordon, R. J. (1988). The Productivity Slowdown, Measurement Issues, and the Explosion of Computing Power, *Brookings Papers on Economic Activity* (2): 347–431.

Ballot, G., Fakhfakh, F., and Taymaz, E. (2001a). Firms' Human Capital, R&D and Performance: A Study on French and Swedish Firms, *Labour Economics* **8**(4): 443–462.

Ballot, G., Fakhfakh, F., and Taymaz, E. (2001b). Who Benefits from Training and R&D? The Firm or the Workers? A Study on Panels of French and Swedish Firms, ERMES, Paris, mimeo.

Barnett, M. L., Starbuck, W. H., and Pant, P. N. (2003). Which Dreams Come True? Endogeneity, Industry Structure and Forecasting Accuracy, *Industrial and Corporate Change* **12**(4): 653–672.

Barney, J. (1991). Special Theory Forum: The Resource-Based Model of the Firm: Origins, Implications, and Prospects, *Journal of Management* **17**(1): 97–98.

Barney, J. B. (1989). Asset Stocks and Sustained Competitive Advantage: A Comment, *Management Science* **35**(12): 1511–1513.

Barras, R. (1986). Towards a Theory of Innovation in Services, *Research Policy* **15**(4): 161–173.

Barras, R. (1990). Interactive Innovation in Financial and Business Services: The Vanguard of the Service Revolution, *Research Policy* **19**(3): 215–237.

Barrett, A. and O'Connell, P. J. (2001). Does Training Generally Work? The Returns to In-Company Training, *Industrial and Labor Relations Review* **54**(3): 647–662.

Bartel, A. P. (1994). Productivity Gains from the Implementation of Employee Training Programs, *Industrial Relations* **33**(4): 411–425.

Bartel, A. P. and Lichtenberg, F. R. (1987). The Comparative Advantage of Educated Workers in Implementing New Technology, *Review of Economics and Statistics* **59**(1): 1–11.

BDU (2002). *Facts & Figures zum Beratermarkt 2002*, Bundesverband Deutscher Unternehmensberater e.V., Bonn.

Becker, G. S. (1964). *Human Capital*, Columbia University Press, Chicago.

Bensaou, B. M. (1997). Inter-Organizational Cooperation: The Role for Information Technology. An Empirical Comparison of US and Japanese Supplier Relations, *Information Systems Research* **8**(2): 107–124.

Berndt, E. R. (1991). *The Practice of Econometrics: Classic and Contemporary*, Addison-Wesley Publishing Company, Reading/Mass.

Berndt, E. R. and Malone, T. W. (1995). Information Technology and the Productivity Paradox: Getting the Questions Right, *Economics of Innovation and New Technology* **3**(3-4): 177–182.

Berndt, E. R. and Rappaport, N. J. (2001). Price and Quality of Desktop and Mobile Personal Computers: A Quarter-Century Historical Overview, *American Economic Review* **91**(2): 268–273.

Bertschek, I. and Fryges, H. (2002). *The Adoption of Business-to-Business E-Commerce: Empirical Evidence for German Companies*, ZEW Discussion Paper No. 02–05, Centre for European Economic Research, Mannheim.

Bertschek, I. and Kaiser, U. (2004). Productivity Effects of Organizational Change: Microeconometric Evidence, *Management Science* **50**(3): 394–404.

Biscourp, P., Crepon, B., Heckel, T., and Riedinger, N. (2002). How Do Firms Respond to Cheaper Computers?, CREST-INSEE, mimeo.

Black, S. E. and Lynch, L. M. (1996). Human Capital Investment and Productivity, *American Economic Review* **86**(2): 263–267.

Black, S. E. and Lynch, L. M. (2001). How to Compete: The Impact of Workplace Practices and Information Technology on Productivity, *Review of Economics and Statistics* **83**(3): 435–445.

Black, S. E. and Lynch, L. M. (2002). Measuring Organizational Capital in the New Economy, paper presented at the NBER conference 'Measuring Capital in the New Economy', April 26–27.

Blundell, R. and Bond, S. (1998). Initial Conditions and Moment Restrictions in Dynamic Panel Data Models, *Journal of Econometrics* **87**(1): 115–143.

Blundell, R. and Bond, S. (2000). GMM Estimation with Persistent Panal Data: An Application to Production Functions, *Econometric Reviews* **19**(3): 321–340.

Blundell, R., Bond, S., and Meghir, C. (1996). Econometric Models of Company Investment, *in* L. Mátyás and P. Sevestre (eds.), *The Econometrics of Panel Data: A Handbook of the Theory with Applications*, Kluwer Academic Publishers, Dordrecht, pp. 685–710.

Bresnahan, T. and Greenstein, S. (1996). Technical Progress and Co-Invention in Computing and in the Uses of Computers, *Brookings Papers on Economic Activity, Microeconomics* pp. 1–77.

Bresnahan, T. F. and Trajtenberg, M. (1995). General Purpose Technologies: Engines of Growth?, *Journal of Econometrics* **65**(1): 83–108.

Bresnahan, T. F., Brynjolfsson, E., and Hitt, L. M. (2002). Information Technology, Workplace Organization, and the Demand for Skilled Labor: Firm-Level Evidence, *Quarterly Journal of Economics* **117**(1): 339–376.

Brynjolfsson, E. (1994). Technology's True Payoff, *Informationweek*, October 10th pp. 34–36.

Brynjolfsson, E. and Hitt, L. (1995). Information Technology as a Factor of Production: The Role of Differences Among Firms, *Economics of Innovation and New Technology* **3**(3-4): 183–199.

Brynjolfsson, E. and Hitt, L. (1996). Paradox Lost? Firm-Level Evidence on the Returns to Information Systems Spending, *Management Science* **42**(4): 541–558.

Brynjolfsson, E. and Hitt, L. M. (1998). Information Technology and Organizational Design, *mimeo*, MIT Sloan School of Management. http://ebusiness.mit.edu/erik/ITOD.pdf.

Brynjolfsson, E. and Hitt, L. M. (2000). Beyond Computation: Information Technology, Organizational Transformation and Business Performance, *Journal of Economic Perspectives* **14**(4): 23–48.

Brynjolfsson, E. and Hitt, L. M. (2003). Computing Productivity: Firm-Level Evidence, *Review of Economics and Statistics* **85**(4): 793–808.

Brynjolfsson, E. and Kemerer, C. F. (1996). Network Externalities in Microcomputer Software: An Econometric Analysis of the Spreadsheet Market, *Management Science* **42**(12): 1627–1647.

Brynjolfsson, E. and Yang, S. (1996). Information Technology and Productivity: A Review of the Literature, *Advances in Computers* **43**: 179–214.

Brynjolfsson, E. and Yang, S. (1999). The Intangible Costs and Benefits of Computer Investments: Evidence from the Financial Markets, *Proceedings of the International Conference on Information Systems, Atlanta, Georgia*, MIT Sloan School.

Brynjolfsson, E., Hitt, L. M., and Yang, S. (2002). Intangible Assets: Computers and Organizational Capital, *Brookings Papers on Economic Activity* (1): 137–198.

Brynjolfsson, E., Renshaw, A. A., and van Alstyne, M. (1997). The Matrix of Change, *Sloan Management Review* **38**(2): 37–54.

Caroli, E. and van Reenen, J. (2001). Skill-Biased Organizational Change? Evidence from a Panel of British and French Establishments, *Quarterly Journal of Economics* **116**(4): 1449–1492.

Carr, N. G. (2003). IT Doesn't Matter, *Harvard Business Review* **81**(5): 41–49.

Cassiman, B. and Veugelers, R. (2002). Complementarity in the Innovation Strategy: Internal R&D, External Technology Acquisition, and Cooperation in R&D, mimeo.

Chennells, L. and van Reenen, J. (1999). *Has Technology Hurt Less Skilled Workers?*, Working Paper No. 99/27, Institute for Fiscal Studies.

Chesbrough, H. W. and Teece, D. J. (1996). When Is Virtual Virtuous? Organizing for Innovation, *Harvard Business Review* **74**(1): 65–73.

Christensen, L. R. and Jorgenson, D. W. (1969). The Measurement of U.S. Real Capital Input, 1929–1967, *Review of Income and Wealth* **15**(4): 293–320.

Chun, H. (2003). Information Technology and the Demand for Educated Workers: Disentangling the Impacts of Adoption Versus Use, *The Review of Economics and Statistics* **85**(1): 1–8.

Cohen, W. (1995). Empirical Studies of Innovative Activity, *in* P. Stoneman (ed.), *Handbook of Innovation and Technological Change*, Blackwell, Oxford, pp. 182–264.

Cohen, W. M. and Klepper, S. (1992). The Anatomy of Industry R&D Intensity Distributions, *American Economic Review* **82**(4): 773–88.

Cohen, W. M. and Klepper, S. (1996a). A Reprise of Size and R&D, *The Economic Journal* **106**(437): 925–951.

Cohen, W. M. and Klepper, S. (1996b). Firm Size and the Nature of Innovation Within Industries: The Case of Process and Product R&D, *Review of Economics and Statistics* **78**(2): 232–243.

Cohen, W. M. and Levin, R. C. (1989). Empirical Studies of Innovation and Market Structure, *in* R. Schmalensee and R. D. Willig (eds.), *Handbook of Industrial Organization, Volume II*, Elsevier Science Publishers B.V., pp. 1059–1107.

Cohen, W. M. and Levinthal, D. A. (1989). Innovation and Learning: The Two Faces of R&D, *The Economic Journal* **99**(397): 569–596.

Cohen, W. M. and Levinthal, D. A. (1990). Absorptive Capacity: A New Perspective on Learning and Innovation, *Administrative Science Quartely* **35**(1): 128–152.

Cummins, J. G. (2003). A New Approach to the Valuation of Intangible Capital, *NBER Working Paper 9924*, National Bureau of Economic Research.

David, P. A. (1987). Some New Standards for the Economics of Standardization in the Information Age, *in* P. Dasgupta and P. Stoneman (eds.), *Economic Policy and Technological Performance*, Cambridge University Press, Cambridge, chapter 8, pp. 206–239.

David, P. A. (1990). The Dynamo and the Computer: An Historical Perspective on the Modern Productivity Paradox, *American Economic Review* **80**(2): 355–361.

David, P. A. and Wright, G. (1999). General Purpose Technologies and Surges in Productivity: Historical Reflections on the Future of the ICT Revolution, *Discussion Papers in Economics and Social History No. 31*, University of Oxford.

Dearden, L., Reed, H., and van Reenen, J. (2000). *Who Gains When Workers Train? Training and Corporate Productivity in a Panel of British Industries*, IFS Working Paper No. 00/04, Institute for Fiscal Studies.

Destatis (2003a). Informationstechnologie in Haushalten — Ergebnisse einer Pilotstudie für das Jahr 2002, *Technical report*, German Statistical Office.

Destatis (2003b). Informationstechnologie in Unternehmen — Ergebnisse einer Pilotstudie für das Jahr 2002, *Technical report*, German Statistical Office.

Deutsche Bundesbank (2004). The Significance of Information and Communication Technology, *Monthly Report April* pp. 45–55.

Dierickx, I. and Cool, K. (1989). Asset Stock Accumulation and Sustainability of Competitive Advantage, *Management Science* **35**(12): 1504–1511.

Dunne, T. (1994). Plant Age and Technology Use in U.S. Manufacturing, *RAND Journal of Economics* **25**(3): 488–499.

Ebling, G. and Janz, N. (1999). *Export and Innovation Activities in the German Service Sector — Empirical Evidence at the Firm Level*, ZEW Discussion Paper No. 99–53, Centre for European Economic Research, Mannheim.

EITO (2001). *European Information Technology Observatory 2001*, EITO, Frankfurt/Main.

Evangelista, R. (1999). *Knowledge and Investment: The Sources of Innovation in Industry*, Edward Elgar, Cheltenham, UK.

Evangelista, R. (2000). Sectoral Patterns of Technological Change in Services, *Economics of Innovation and New Technology* **9**(3): 183–221.

Falk, M. (2001). Organizational Change, New Information and Communication Technologies and the Demand for Labor in Services, *ZEW Discussion Paper No. 01-25*, Centre for European Economic Research (ZEW), Mannheim.

Falk, M. and Seim, K. (2001). Workers' Skill Level and Information Technology: A Censored Regression Model, *International Journal of Manpower* **22**(1-2): 99–120.

Flaig, G. and Stadler, M. (1994). Success Breeds Success — The Dynamics of the Innovation Process, *Empirical Economics* **19**(1): 55–68.

Fraumeni, B. M. (1997). The Measurement of Depreciation in the U.S. National Income and Product Accounts, *Survey of Current Business* **77**(7): 7–23.

Fraunhofer-Gesellschaft (2004). Innovationstreiber Informations- und Kommunikationstechnik, *Fraunhofer Magazin* (2): 8–37.

Galende, J. and de la Fuente, J. M. (2003). Internal Factors Determining a Firm's Innovative Behaviour, *Research Policy* **32**(5): 715–736.

Gallouj, F. (2000). Beyond Technological Innovation: Trajectories and Varieties of Services Innovation, *in* M. Boden and I. Miles (eds.), *Services and the Knowledge-Based Economy*, Science, Technology and the International Political Economy, Continuum, London and New York, chapter 7, pp. 129–145.

Gallouj, F. and Weinstein, O. (1997). Innovation in Services, *Research Policy* **26**(4-5): 537–556.

German Council of Economic Experts (2001). *Chancen auf einen höheren Wachstumspfad — Jahresgutachten 2000/01*, Metzler-Poeschel, Stuttgart.

Gordon, R. J. (2000). Does the 'New Economy' Measure up to the Great Inventions of the Past?, *Journal of Economic Perspective* **14**(4): 49–74.

Gordon, R. J. (2003). Five Puzzles in the Behavior of Productivity, Investment, and Innovation, mimeo, Northwestern University, NBER, and CEPR — draft of chapter for World Economic Forum, Global Competitiveness Report, 2003–2004.

Gouriéroux, C. and Monfort, A. (1995). *Statistics and Econometric Models*, Vol. 1, Cambridge University Press, Cambridge.

Greenan, N. and Mairesse, J. (1996). *Computers and Productivity in France: Some Evidence*, Working Paper No. 5836, National Bureau of Economic Research.

Greenan, N., Mairesse, J., and Topiol-Bensaid, A. (2001). *Information Technology and Research and Development Impacts on Productivity and Skills: Looking for Correlations on French Firm Level Data*, NBER Working Paper No. 8075, National Bureau of Economic Research.

Griliches, Z. (1992). The Search for R&D Spillovers, *Scandinavian Journal of Economics* **94**(supplement): S29–S47.

Griliches, Z. (1994). Productivity, R&D, and the Data Constraint, *American Economic Review* **84**(1): 1–23.

Griliches, Z. and Hausman, J. A. (1986). Errors in Variables in Panel Data, *Journal of Econometrics* **31**(1): 93–118.

Griliches, Z. and Mairesse, J. (1998). Production Functions: The Search for Identification, *in* S. Strøm (ed.), *Econometrics and Economic Theory in the 20th Century — The Ragnar Frisch Centennial Symposium*, Cambridge University Press, pp. 169–203.

Hall, B. H. (2002). The Financing of Research and Development, *Oxford Review of Economic Policy* **18**(1): 35–51.

Hall, B. H. and Mairesse, J. (1995). Exploring the Relationship Between R&D and Productivity in French Manufacturing Firms, *Journal of Econometrics* **65**(1): 263–293.

Hamermesh, D. S. and Pfann, G. A. (1996). Adjustment Costs in Factor Demand, *Journal of Economic Literature* **34**(3): 1264–1292.

Hammer, M. (1990). Reengineering Work: Don't Automate, Obliterate, *Harvard Business Review* **68**(4): 104–112.

Heckman, J. J. (1976). The Common Structure of Statistical Models of Truncation, Sample Selection, and Limited Dependent Variables and a Simple Estimator for Such Models, *Annals of Economic and Social Measurement* **5**(4): 475–492.

Heckman, J. J. (1979). Sample Selection Bias as a Specification Error, *Econometrica* **47**(1): 153–161.

Helpman, E. (1998). *General Purpose Technologies and Economic Growth*, MIT Press, Cambridge and London.

Helpman, E. and Rangel, A. (1999). Adjusting to a New Technology: Experience and Training, *Journal of Economic Growth* **4**(4): 359–383.

Hempell, T. (2003a). Innovation im Dienstleistungssektor, *in* N. Janz and G. Licht (eds.), *Innovationsforschung heute*, ZEW Wirtschaftsanalysen Vol. 63, Nomos, Baden-Baden, pp. 149–183.

Hempell, T. (2003b). Verbreitung von Informations- und Kommunikationstechnologien in Deutschland, *Studien zum Innovationssystem 16-2004*, Zentrum für Europäische Wirtschaftsforschung (ZEW), Mannheim.

Hempell, T. (2005a). Does Experience Matter? Innovation and the Productivity of ICT in German Services, *Economics of Innovation and New Technology* **14**(4): (277–303).

Hempell, T. (2005b). What's Spurious, What's Real? Measuring the Productivity of ICT at the Firm-Level, *Empirical Economics*. (forthcoming).

Hempell, T., van Leeuwen, G., and van der Wiel, H. (2004). ICT, Innovation and Business Performance in Services: Evidence for Germany and the Netherlands, *in* OECD (ed.), *The Economic Impact of ICT — Measurement, Evidence, and Implications*, OECD, Paris, pp. 131–152.

Hoffmann, J. (1998). Problems of Inflation Measurement in Germany, *Discussion Paper No. 01-98*, Economic Research Centre of the Deutsche Bundesbank.

Hollenstein, H. (2004). The Decision to Adopt Information and Communication Technologies (ICT): Firm-Level Evidence for Switzerland, *in* OECD (ed.), *The Economic Impact of ICT — Measurement, Evidence, and Implications*, OECD, Paris, pp. 37–60.

Innocenti, A. and Labory, S. (2002). The Advantages of Outsourcing in Terms of Information Management, *Quaderni no. 370*, University of Siena.

Jacobebbinghaus, P. and Zwick, T. (2002). New Technologies and the Demand for Medium Qualified Labour in Germany, *Schmollers Jahrbuch* **122**(2): 179–206.

Janz, N., Ebling, G., Gottschalk, S., and Niggemann, H. (2001). The Mannheim Innovation Panels (MIP and MIP-S) of the Centre for European Economic Research (ZEW), *Schmollers Jahrbuch* **121**(1): 123–129.

Janz, N. (ed.) (2000). *Quellen für Innovationen: Analyse der ZEW-Innovationserhebungen 1999 im Verarbeitenden Gewerbe und im Dienstleistungssektor*, ZEW-Dokumentation 00–10, Centre for European Economic Research, Mannheim.

Jorgenson, D. W. (2003). Information Technology and the G7 Countries, mimeo, Harvard University, http://post.economics.harvard.edu/faculty/jorgenson/papers/papers.html.

Jorgenson, D. W. and Stiroh, K. (1995). Computers and Growth, *Economics of Innovation and New Technology* **3**(3-4): 295–316.

Jorgenson, D. W. and Stiroh, K. J. (2000). Raising the Speed Limit: U.S. Economic Growth in the Information Age, *Brookings Papers on Economic Activity* (1): 124–234.

Jovanovic, B. and Rousseau, P. L. (2002). Moore's Law and Learning by Doing, *Review of Economic Dynamics* **5**(2): 346–375.

Jovanovic, B. and Stolyarov, D. (2000). Optimal Adoption of Complementary Technologies, *American Economic Review* **90**(1): 15–29.

Kaiser, U. (2000). *A Note on the Calculation of Firm-Specific and Skill-Specific Labor Costs from Firm-Level Data*, ZEW Discussion Paper 00–08, Centre for European Economic Research, Mannheim.

Kaiser, U. (2003). *Strategic Complementarities Between Different Types of ICT-Expenditures*, ZEW Discussion Paper No. 03-46, Centre for European Economic Research, Mannheim.

Katz, E. and Ziderman, A. (1990). Investment in General Training: The Role of Information and Labour Mobility, *Economic Journal* **100**(403): 1147–1158.

Katz, L. and Autor, D. (1999). Changes in the Wage Structure and Earnings Inequality, *in* O. Ashenfelter and D. Card (eds.), *Handbook of Labor Economics*, Elsevier Science, Amsterdam, pp. 1463–1555.

Klette, T. J. and Griliches, Z. (1996). The Inconsistency of Common Scale Estimators When Output Prices Are Unobserved and Endogenous, *Journal of Applied Econometrics* **11**(4): 343–361.

Knott, A. M., Bryce, D. J., and Posen, H. E. (2003). On the Strategic Accumulation of Intangible Assets, *Organization Science* **14**(2): 192–207.

Lehr, B. and Lichtenberg, F. (1999). Information Technology and Its Impact on Productivity: Firm-Level Evidence from Government and Private Data Sources, *Canadian Journal of Economics* **32**(2): 335–362.

Leung, S. F. and Yu, S. (1996). On the Choice Between Sample Selection and Two-Part Models, *Journal of Econometrics* **72**(1-2): 197–229.

Licht, G. and Moch, D. (1999). Innovation and Information Technology in Services, *Canadian Journal of Economics* **32**(2): 363–383.

Licht, G., Steiner, V., Bertschek, I., Falk, M., and Fryges, H. (2002). *IKT-Fachkräftemangel und Qualifikationsbedarf*, ZEW Wirtschaftsanalysen Vol. 61, Nomos, Baden-Baden.

Lichtenberg, F. R. (1995). The Output Contributions of Computer Equipment and Personnel: A Firm-Level Analysis, *Economics of Innovation and New Technology* **3**(3-4): 201–217.

Lindbeck, A. and Snower, D. J. (1996). Reorganization of Firms and Labor-Market Inequality, *AEA Papers and Proceedings* **86**(2): 315–321.

Linz, S. and Eckert, G. (2002). Zur Einführung hedonischer Methoden in die Preisstatistik, *Wirtschaft und Statistik* **10**: 857–863.

Lipsey, R. G., Bekar, C., and Carlaw, K. (1998a). The Consequences of Changes in GPTs, *in* E. Helpman (ed.), *General Purpose Technologies and Economic Growth*, The MIT Press, chapter 8, pp. 193–218.

Lipsey, R. G., Bekar, C., and Carlaw, K. (1998b). What Requires Explanation?, *in* E. Helpman (ed.), *General Purpose Technologies and Economic Growth*, The MIT Press, chapter 2, pp. 15–54.

Loveman, G. W. (1994). An Assessment of the Productivity Impact of Information Technologies, *in* T. J. Allen and M. S. Scott Morton (eds.), *Information Technology and the Corporation of the 1990s*, Oxford University Press, Oxford, pp. 84–110.

Lucas, R. E. (1988). On the Mechanics of Economic Development, *Journal of Monetary Economics* **22**(1): 3–42.

Malone, T. W. (1987). Modelling Coordination in Organizations and Markets, *Management Science* **33**(10): 1317–1332.

Manasian, D. (2003). A Survey of the Internet Society, *The Economist*. January 25th.

Manning, W. G., Duan, N., and Rogers, W. H. (1987). Monte Carlo Evidence on the Choice Between Sample Selection and Two-Part Models, *Journal of Econometrics* **35**(1): 59–82.

Mansfield, E. (1968). *Industrial Research and Technological Innovation: An Econometric Analysis*, Norton, New York.

McKinsey Global Institute (2001). US Productivity Growth 1995–2000 — Understandig the Contribution of Information Technology Relative to Other Factors, report.

Milgrom, P. and Roberts, J. (1990). The Economics of Modern Manufacturing: Technology, Strategy, and Organization, *American Economic Review* **80**(3): 511–528.

Milgrom, P. and Roberts, J. (1995). Complementarities and Fit Strategy, Structure, and Organizational Change in Manufacturing, *Journal of Accounting and Economics* **19**(2-3): 179–208.

Milgrom, P., Quian, Y., and Roberts, J. (1991). Complementarities, Momentum, and the Evolution of Modern Manufacturing, *American Economic Review* **81**(2): 84–88.

Moch, D., Almus, M., Eckert, T., Harhoff, D., Hempell, T., and Licht, G. (2002). Einsatzmöglichkeiten hedonischer Techniken in der amtlichen Verbraucherpreisstatistik Deutschlands, *Research Report for the Federal Statistical Office Germany*, Centre for European Economic Research (ZEW).

Morrison, C. J. and Berndt, E. R. (1991). *Assessing the Productivity of Information Technology Equipment in the US Manufacturing Industries*, NBER Working Paper 3582, National Bureau of Economic Research.

Motohashi, K. (2001). Economic Analysis of Information Network Use: Organizational and Productivity Impacts on Japanese Firms, mimeo.

Moulton, B. R., Parker, R. P., and Seskin, E. P. (1999). A Preview of the 1999 Comprehensive Revision of the National Income and Product Accounts — Definitional and Classificational Changes, *Survey of Current Business* **79**(8): 7–20.

Müller, A. A. (1998). *Kapitalstock und Produktionspotential im privaten und öffentlichen Sektor Deutschlands*, Nomos, Baden-Baden.

Neil Gandal (1994). Hedonic Price Indexes for Spreadsheets and an Empirical Test for Network Externalities, *RAND Journal of Economics* **225**(1): 160–170.

Nelson, R. R. and Winter, S. (1982). *An Evolutionary Theory of Economic Change*, Harvard University Press, Cambridge MA.

Nestler, K. and Kailis, E. (2003). Working Time Spent on Continuing Vocational Training in Enterprises in Europe, *Statistics in Focus — Theme 3, 1–2003*, Eurostat.

Nordhaus, W. (1997). Do Real-Output and Real-Wage Measures Capture Reality? The History of Lighting Suggests Not, *in* T. F. Bresnahan and R. J. Gordon (eds.), *The Economics of New Goods*, University of Chicago Press for NBER, Chicago, pp. 29–66.

OECD (2000a). *A New Economy? The Changing Role of Innovation and Information Technology in Growth*, Paris.

OECD (2000b). The Service Economy, *Business and Industry Policy Forum Series*, Paris.

OECD (2002). *Education at a Glance — OECD Indicators 2002*, Paris.

OECD (2003). *ICT and Economic Growth — Evidence from OECD Countries, Industries and Firms*, Paris.

OECD (2004). *The Economic Impact of ICT — Measurement, Evidence, and Implications*, Paris.

OECD/Eurostat (1997). Proposed Guidelines for Collecting and Interpreting Technological Innovation Data, *Technical Report*, Paris.

Oliner, S. D. and Sichel, D. E. (1994). Computers and Output Growth Revisited: How Big Is the Puzzle?, *Brookings Papers on Economic Activity* (2): 318–324.

Oliner, S. D. and Sichel, D. E. (2000). The Resurgence of Growth in the Late 1990s: Is Information Technology the Story?, *Journal of Economic Perspectives* **14**(4): 3–22.

Osterman, P. (1986). The Impact of Computers on the Employment of Clerks and Managers, *Industrial and Labor Relations Review* **39**(2): 175–187.

Pavitt, K. (1984). Sectoral Patterns of Technical Change: Towards a Taxonomy and a Theory, *Research Policy* **13**(6): 343–373.

Pilat, D., Lee, F., and van Ark, B. (2002). Production and Use of ICT: A Sectoral Perspective on Productivity Growth in the OECD Area, *in* OECD (ed.), *OECD Economic Studies No. 35*, Paris, pp. 47–78.

Prantl, S. (2001). *Financial Distress, Liquidations and Subsidization of Young Firms*, PhD thesis, University of Mannheim, Germany.

Puhani, P. A. (2000). The Heckman Correction for Sample Selection and Its Critique, *Journal of Economic Surveys* **14**(1): 53–68.

Radner, R. (1993). The Organization of Decentralized Information Processing, *Econometrica* **61**(5): 1109–1146.

Rendtel, U. (1992). *On the Choice of a Selection-Model When Estimating Regression Models with Selectivity*, DIW-Discussion Paper No. 53, German Institute for Economic Research, Berlin.

Rigby, D. K., Reichheld, F. F., and Schefter, P. (2002). Avoid the Four Perils of CRM, *Technology Review* **80**(2): 101–109.

Roach, S. S. (1991). Services Under Siege — The Restructuring Imperative, *Harvard Business Review* **69**(5): 82–91.

Romer, D. (1996). *Advanced Macroeconomics*, McGraw-Hill, New York.

Romer, P. M. (1990a). Endogenous Technological Change, *Journal of Political Economy* **98**(5, part II): S71–S102.

Romer, P. M. (1990b). Increasing Returns and Long-Run Growth, *Journal of Political Economy* **94**(5): 1002–1037.

Rosenberg, N. and Trajtenberg, M. (2001). *A General Purpose Technology at Work: The Corliss Steam Engine in the Late 19th Century*, CEPR Discussion Paper No. 3008, Centre for Economic Policy Research.

Schrage, M. (2002). Wal-Mart Trumps Moore's Law, *Technology Review* **105**(2): 21.

Schreyer, P. (2000). *The Contribution of Information and Communication Technology to Output Growth: A Study of the G7 Countries*, STI Working Paper 2000/2, OECD.

Schreyer, P. (2002). Computer Price Indices and International Growth and Productivity Comparisons, *Review of Income and Wealth* **48**(1): 15–31.

Sigele, L. (2002). How About Now? A Survey of the Real-Time Economy, *The Economist*.

Sirilli, G. and Evangelista, R. (1998). Technological Innovation in Services and Manufacturing: Results from Italian Surveys, *Research Policy* **27**(9): 881–899.

Smolny, W. (1998). Innovations, Prices and Employment, *Journal of Industrial Economics* **46**(3): 359–381.

Smolny, W. (2000). *Endogenous Innovations and Knowledge Spillovers — A Theoretical and Empirical Analysis*, ZEW Economic Studies, Vol. 12, Physica, Heidelberg.

Smolny, W. (2003). Produktivitätsanpassung in Ostdeutschland — Bestandsaufnahme und Ansatzpunkte einer Erklärung, *Jahrbücher für Nationalökonomie und Statistik* **223**(2): 239–254.

Solow, R. M. (1957). Technical Change and the Aggregate Production Function, *Review of Economic and Statistics* **39**: 312–320.

Spitz, A. (2003). *IT Capital, Job Content, and Educational Attainment*, ZEW Discussion Paper 03–04, Centre for European Economic Research, Mannheim.

Spitz, A. (2004). *Are Skill Requirements in the Workplace Rising? Stylized Facts and Evidence on Skill-Biased Technological Change*, ZEW Discussion Paper 04-33, Centre for European Economic Research, Mannheim.

Statistisches Bundesamt (2001). *Statistical Yearbook for the Federal Republic of Germany*, Metzler-Poeschel, Stuttgart.

Stiglitz, J. E. (1987). Learning to Learn, Localized Learning and Technological Progress, *in* P. Dasgupta and P. Stoneman (eds.), *Economic Policy and Technological Performance*, Cambridge University Press, Cambridge, chapter 5, pp. 125–153.

Stiroh, K. (2002a). Are ICT Spillovers Driving the New Economy?, *Review of Income and Wealth* **48**(1): 33–57.

Stiroh, K. J. (2001). Investing in Information Technology: Productivity Payoffs for U.S. Industries, *Current Issues in Economics and Finance 6*, Federal Reserve Bank of New York.

Stiroh, K. J. (2002b). Information Technology and the U.S. Productivity Revival: What Do the Industry Data Say?, *American Economic Review* **92**(5): 1559–1576.

Stiroh, K. J. (2002c). Reassessing the Impact of IT in the Production Function: A Meta-Analysis, *mimeo*, Federal Reserve Bank of New York.

Stoneman, P. (1983). *The Economic Analysis of Technological Change*, Oxford University Press, Oxford.

Sundbo, J. (2000). Organization and Innovation Strategy in Services, *in* M. Boden and I. Miles (eds.), *Services and the Knowledge-Based Economy*, Science, Technology and the International Political Economy, Continuum, London and New York, chapter 6, pp. 109–128.

Teece, D. J., Pisano, G., and Shuen, A. (1997). Dynamic Capabilities and Strategic Management, *Strategic Management Journal* **18**(7): 509–533.

Tether, B. S. (2003). The Sources and Aims of Innovation in Services: Variety Between and Within Sectors, *Economics of Innovation and New Technology* **12**(6): 481–505.

Tether, B. S., Hipp, C., and Miles, I. (2001). Standardisation and Particularisation in Services: Evidence from Germany, *Research Policy* **29**: 1115–1138.

The Economist (2001). Wal Around the World. December 6th.

Triplett, J. (1990). Hedonic Methods in Statistical Agency Environments: An Intellectual Biopsy, *in* E. Berndt and J. Triplett (eds.), *Fifty Years of Economic Measurement: The Jubilee of the Conference on Research in Income and Wealth*, National Bureau of Economic Research, Chicago and London, pp. 207–33.

Uchitelle, L. (2000). Economic View: Productivity Finally Shows the Impacts of Computers, *New York Times* p. 23. 12th of March, section 3.

Vijselaar, F. and Albers, R. (2002). *New Technologies and Productivity Growth in the Euro Area*, Working Paper No. 122, European Central Bank.

von Tunzelmann, G. N. (1998).   Localized Technological Search and Multi-Technology Companies, *Economics of Innovation and New Technology* **6**(2-3): 231–255.

Wernerfelt, B. (1984). A Resource-Based View of the Firm, *Strategic Management Journal* **29**(2): 171–180.

Woodall, P. (2000). Untangling E-conomics — Survey of the New Economy, *The Economist*. September 21.

Wooldridge, J. M. (2002). *Econometric Analysis of Cross Section and Panel Data*, MIT Press, Cambridge/Mass.

Yang, S. and Brynjolfsson, E. (2001). Intangible Assets and Growth Accounting: Evidence from Computer Investments, *mimeo*, New York University.

Zwick, T. (2005). Continuing Vocational Training Forms and Establishment Productivity in Germany, *German Economic Review* **6**(2): 155–184.